LITERATURE AND MUSIC

Rodopi Perspectives on Modern Literature

25

Edited by
David Bevan

LITERATURE AND MUSIC

Edited by
Michael J. Meyer

AMSTERDAM - NEW YORK, NY 2002

PN
56
.M83
L44
2002

ISBN: 90-420-1191-2 (bound)
©Editions Rodopi B.V., Amsterdam - New York, NY 2002
Printed in The Netherlands

TABLE OF CONTENTS

Introduction

> There is sweet music here that softer falls
> Than petals from blown roses on the grass,
> Or night-dews on still waters between walls
> Of shadowy granite, in a gleaming pass;
> Music that gentler on the spirit lies,
> Than tired eyelids upon tired eyes;
> Music that brings sweet sleep down from the blissful skies.
> Here are cool mosses deep,
> And thro' the moss the ivies creep,
> And in the stream the long-leaved flowers weep,
> And from the craggy ledge the poppy hangs in sleep.

The poetic lines above reflect the subtle, yet powerful impact music can have upon the human psyche. Fiction no doubt is able to invoke similar emotional reactions, and, used together, the two forms of human expression create the potential for a truly significant influence on society.

Surely many critics have noted the interrelationship between the written word and musical annotation. Just recently, for example, Chicago arts critic, Howard Reich, in an interview with Barry Manilow, attributes the success of the pop musician to the fact that Manilow "thinks in pitches, rhythms and chords the way the rest of us do in words and sentences and paragraphs (*Chicago Tribune*, 6/24/01, Arts and Entertainment Section, 1); in the same article Reich quotes Frank Sinatra's comment that a great song is "a perfect marriage of a lyric and a melody." What he does not note is the fact that most great authors are aware of the corollary to Sinatra's observation: the fact that the melodic quality of word choice and pacing can often go a long way to enhance a work of fiction.

It should not be surprising then that this collections of essays centers on musical elements that authors have employed in their work, thus joining heard sounds to a visual perception of their stories. The spectrum of authors represented is a wide one, from Pound to Durrell, from Steinbeck to Cather, from Beckett to Gaines, but even more unusual is the variety of musical type represented. Classical music (the quartet, the fugue, the symphony), Jazz (the jazz riff and jazz improv) and the spiritual all appear along with folk song and random "noise."

There seems to be no limit to the multiple allusions made to musical styles and techniques employed by great writers. Indeed, each author seems to realize that it is not the type of music that s/he chooses to employ that is important. Rather it is the realization that such musical elements as harmony, dissonance, tonal repetition and beat are just as important in prose composition as they are in poetry and song. The essayists have selected some works that may be considered obscure and some that are modern classics. Each one however has captured one of the varied ways in which words and music complement and enhance each other.

It is my hope that as you sample this musical feast of analyses, you will become more aware of how many literary artists are simultaneously "word musicians." Perhaps you will be motivated to listen with "new ears" to Beethoven's 5th Symphony, to Bach's Cantata and Fugue in G Minor or to a Negro spiritual. Perhaps jazz and folk music will suddenly make sense as they appear in literary contexts. My hope is that you recognize with George Gershwin that "'true' music must repeat the thoughts and inspirations of the people and the time," and that this is also an accurate assessment of "true" literature. In fact, we might paraphrase T.S. Eliot's comments about music in *The Four Quartets*, replacing the word Music with the word Literature. Then the narrator of Dry Salvages V would value "[Literature] heard so deeply/That it is not heard at all/But you are the [Literature] while the [Literature] lasts."

By recognizing how truly diverse the music of our world can be, how the melodies and harmonies change from land to land, readers may be tempted to assert there are no connections between different cultures and the music they produce. On the other, one may discover a gift of recognition that all music mirrors the same universalities: love, loneliness, rejection, joy and sorrow, human experiences to which all societies can relate. Combining musical techniques into literature can only help us discover that the Otherness we fear is really only a veiled sameness we have not perfectly understood.

As Wordsworth says in "The Prelude," Bk. I, ll. 340 ff:

> Dust as we are, the immortal spirit grows
> Like harmony in music; there is a dark
> Inscrutable workmanship that reconciles
> Discordant elements, make them cling together
> In one society.

The genius required to mold two arts into one is revealed here. May you enjoy the journey.

Michael J. Meyer
DePaul University
August 2001

1

Music, Desire, and Death in *The Magic Mountain*

Although the most obvious choice of a novel by Thomas Mann treating the subject of music would be *Doctor Faustus*, music also plays a crucial role in *The Magic Mountain*, where it is present at every turn of the narrative. In this earlier novel primarily devoted to an exploration of illness and death, music entwines itself within the narrative so as to become an important site of discourse, progressing and intensifying throughout the novel along with its parallel discourses of desire and death. Beginning with the position articulated early in the novel by the humanist Ludovico Settembrini, this essay will trace the way music functions in *The Magic Mountain*. In Hans Castorp, the novel's main character, the reader sees the awakening not only of desire but also of attention to music, in a simultaneous and complementary, and not merely coincidental, development. It will then return to Settembrini's position, which will be read in conjunction with Mann's nonfictional writings on music up through the years of the composition of *The Magic Mountain*.

From the outset of the narrator's depiction of life at the Hotel Berghof, music is present. In a first moment of entanglement of sexuality and musicality, the first sounds Hans hears upon settling into his room are those of a couple making love as a band plays a waltz:

> An apparent chase around the furniture, the crash of an upturned chair, a grab, an embrace, slaps and kisses—and then, of all things to accompany the invisible scene, a waltz was struck up in the distance, the tired melody of a popular ballad. Hans Castorp stood, towel in hand, and listened against his best intentions.[1]

The waltz comes from one of the biweekly concerts held near the Berghof for the patients' benefit. There is a mundane regularity about the music, according to its depictions by the narrator. The next concert is described thus: "There was a concert down at the hotel again. An insipid, symmetrically fashioned operetta melody echoed through the darkness."[2] As the novel continues, Hans makes gradual progress toward participation in the life of the sanatorium. While he begins as a guest, he becomes a patient fully involved in the sanatorium's community and culture. This shift in status from guest to patient is highlighted in Hans' reaction to the music. This time, he does not merely stand listening: "Hans Castorp whistled along in a whisper (a whistle can be whispered, you know), while his chilled feet kept time under his feather comforter."[3]

It is within the context of these fortnightly concerts that the characters first discuss music explicitly. In one of his first conversations with Settembrini, Hans broaches the subject:

> "Don't you enjoy listening to music?"
> "Not when I'm ordered to do so," Settembrini replied. "Not if it's decreed by the day of the week. Not when it has a pharmaceutical odor and is prescribed from on high for reasons of health." [...]
> "Music...There is something only semi-articulate about it, something dubious, irresponsible, indifferent [...] Let music assume its most high-minded pose. Fine! And then our emotions are inflamed. And yet the real point should be to inflame our reason. Music, it would appear, is movement for its own sake—although I suspect it of quietism. Let me overstate my case: my distaste for music is political."[4]

All the rest of Mann's novel could be seen as a sort of dialogue with this position, which resonates in part with Mann's own recorded opinions about music at the time. Within the novelistic universe of *The Magic Mountain*, the reader would most certainly agree with Settembrini that music is made available for the good of one's health. Although the Platz concerts are described as among the "deviations from the normal schedule" occurring "regularly," the very regularity of the biweekly concerts makes them blend with the other aspects of the cure at the sanatorium.[5] Theodor Adorno, whose impact on *Doctor Faustus* is documented by Thomas Mann himself in a paratextual note, has described popular music thus: "What is incessantly boosted as exceptional grows dull, and the festivities to which light music permanently summons its adherents, under the name of feasts for the ears, are dismal everyday fare."[6] The world of the sanatorium with its fortnightly concerts of waltzes and popular tunes seems to be part of this musical universe where novelty gradually slips into monotony, all in the name of the cure. Hans' initial reaction to the music confirms its role as part of the treatment:

"Hans Castorp loved music with all his heart, its effect being much like that of the porter [*sic* port] he drank with his morning snack—profoundly calming, numbing, and 'doze'-inducing—and he listened now with pleasure, his head tilted to one side, mouth open, eyes slightly bloodshot."[7]

A more difficult position to evaluate in the context of the novel is Settembrini's second and main point, that music is politically suspect because it is "semi-articulate." By expounding this position, Settembrini has articulated one of the fundamental questions of the novel. By comparing music to language, Settembrini sets up a comparison across various discourses. Additional discourses, those of desire and illness, have not by this point made their most prominent entrance within the universe of *The Magic Mountain*, but will soon do so. When that happens, music allies itself with both desire and illness, all of which stand in opposition to music. Desire finds its expression not in words but in language. The ultra-rationalist Settembrini must be opposed to both music and desire as cogs in his system of reason. An additional problem is the distinction between everyday language and literary language, a question Mann entertains in his writings on music. Ultimately, all of these discourses are at play not in anything that might be called a real world but rather within the universe of fiction.

As the novel progresses, Hans gradually dissociates himself from the world of the Berghof sanatorium and its variegated musical monotony. At first, Hans is at ease with the popular melodies that surround the sanatorium. He is able to fall asleep to their accompaniment, as we have seen, and is able to affirm the value of the popular music as he says: "An unpretentious concert piece lasts perhaps seven minutes, am I correct? And each piece is something all to itself, has a beginning and an end, stands out in contrast to the rest, and that is what keeps them, in a sense, from being swallowed up in the general routine."[8] There is, however, a gradual dissociation from this music as his responses to it change. First, he feels his heart beating out of rhythm with the tunes: "He dimly noticed the disconcerting effect of his heart's pounding out of time to the music. And feeling confused and at odds with himself, he was just dozing off when Joachim suggested they needed to start back."[9]

Soon after, Hans sings for the first time in the novel. This time he doesn't merely whistle along to music already being provided for him; he spontaneously sings a tune he has stored in his mind. The music he is able to call to mind includes "sentimental folk melodies, the ones you find in the handbooks of sport and business clubs."[10] While this musical experience at first inspires him, his reaction soon changes: "After such exaltation, his sudden reward was radical gloom, a hangover that bordered on despair."[11] It is at this point that Hans' relations to music and to desire reach a breaking point. Again it is useful to consider Adorno's view of popular music. In this view, popular tunes "reckon with the immature, with those who cannot express their emotions and experiences, who either never had the power of expression or were crippled by cultural taboos."[12] What Adorno seems to imply here is that popular music provides an alternative discourse, albeit an alienating one, whereby repressed emotions can have some sort of expression for those who have no other recourse. It is through a process of identification with a "musical I" that the subject feels him or herself "integrated into the community of 'fans.' In whistling such a song, he bows to a ritual of socialization, although beyond this unarticulated subjective stirring of the moment his isolation continues unchanged."[13] As Hans feels progressively more frustrated with the popular music that comprises the musical world at the sanatorium, he begins to feel an intensification that both allows him to differentiate himself from the world of the sanatorium as he awakens to desire and restrains him within this bowing to a ritual of socialization, the same force which drives him to his death on a battlefield.

Mann himself speaks of intensification or heightening of experience in his essay "The Making of *The Magic Mountain*," calling it a "fundamental theme" of the work. Mann writes that Hans' story is "the story of a heightening process, but also as a narrative it is the heightening process itself."[14] The motive I am in the midst of tracing through the novel is one of simultaneous heightening of illness, desire, and musical experience. All three discourses develop in a parallel fashion and complement each other.

Shortly after the moment where Hans feels sudden despair after humming a popular melody, there is another, more expanded moment of a similar nature:

> Indeed, he was getting to be very particular about how he did express himself—a characteristic well worth noting. As he walked around, his cheeks flushed with dry fever, he hummed to himself, sang to himself, because in his present state he was sensitive to all things musical. He hummed a little song that he had heard sung in a light soprano voice, who knew where or when, at some party or charity concert, and that had turned up now in his memory, a gentle bit of nonsense that began:
>
> > How oft it thrills me just to hear
> > You say some simple word,

and he was about to add:

> That spoken from your lips, my dear,
> Does leave my heart so stirred!

and suddenly shrugged and said, "Ridiculous!" and cast aside the delicate little song as tasteless and insipidly sentimental—rejecting it, however, with a certain austere melancholy.[15]

At this point in Hans' education or awakening to desire and its expression, his frustration with formerly satisfactory modes of expression begins to make room for other modes of discourse. We see here another example of the double and simultaneous heightening effect which Mann describes.

As his illness progresses to a continual flush of "dry fever," Castorp is both particularly receptive to music and frustrated with the musical references available to his mind. What he seeks is some sort of musical experience that correlates better with his new and more intense feelings of desire. Mann is careful to make a distinction between the ordinary world and its banal feelings of "being in love," and the sanatorium with its more intense experiences of desire. He says that what Hans felt for Clavdia was "his infatuation (and the word is apt, even though it is a word from 'down below,' a word of the plains, and might imply that the little song about 'how oft it thrills me' was somehow applicable here)."[16] In the heightened world of the Berghof, popular music simply does not respond adequately to feelings, and thus does not fulfill its social role. It applies only "to some extent," and something, at first glance, quite different will take the place of the popular tunes on the mountain.

The next references to music within the narrative are those that establish explicit links between music and death:

> For the first time in his life he understood that he would die. And he made the same face he usually made when listening to music—a rather dull, sleepy, and devout face, his head tilted toward one shoulder, his mouth half-open.[17]

> [Joachim and Hans] stood there regarding the dead man on his bed, each in his own way—Joachim at attention, half bowing in an official, reserved pose; Hans Castorp relaxed and preoccupied, his hands clasped before him, his head tilted to one shoulder, with an expression much like the one he usually wore when listening to music.[18]

In addition to providing a foreshadowing of the link between music and death in the ending of the novel, these passages serve as moments of transition from the innocuous world of "infatuation" and its corresponding popular music and a more advanced form of desire, of illness, and eventually of death.

What most directly facilitates Hans' most advanced progression into music and desire, again within the context of a heightened illness, is the arrival of a record player at the sanatorium. It is the record player and its accompanying disks that will respond to Hans' need for a new and heightened musical discourse to replace the popular tunes that no longer give adequate expression to his desire. There is a marked progression in Hans' choice of records. At first, he plays Offenbach and Rossini; he then switches to more serious opera, Verdi's *La Traviata* and, finally, *Aida*, a work whose climax is a heightening of desire and death within a musical context, a moment of 'mise-en-abîme' which prefigures the ending of *The Magic Mountain* itself. While listening to the final scene of *Aida*, Hans has his most explicit moment of illumination, a lyric realization of the very real and concrete links among music, desire, and death:

> It required no effort of imagination for Hans Castorp to share in the tenor's ecstasy and gratitude, but as he sat there with folded hands, staring at the little black louvers, from between whose slats this all burst forth, ultimately what he felt, understood, and relished was the victorious ideality of music, of art, of human emotions, their sublime and incontrovertible ability to gloss over the crude horrors of reality. You had only to picture coolly and calmly what was actually happening here. Two people were being buried alive; their lungs full of the gases of the crypt, cramped with hunger, they would perish together, or even worse, one after the other; and then decay would do its unspeakable work on their bodies, until two skeletons lay there under those vaults, each indifferent and insensitive to whether it lay there alone or with another set of bones.[19]

Shortly thereafter, the link between music, desire, and death is made very explicitly once again, this time less lyrically: "What was the world behind [the song], which his intuitive scruples told him was a world of forbidden love? It was death."[20] Lastly, Hans goes to his death humming the "Linden Tree" melody from Franz Schubert's *Die Winterreise* that he had heard repeatedly on the phonograph player. Desire and illness both end in death; Schubert becomes the musical accompaniment.

Susan von Rohr Scaff has interpreted the ending of *The Magic Mountain* as an affirmation of the link between music and love for humanity: "A love of life brims through Castorp's departure from the magical mountain of death, and his 'ending' on the battlefield can be read as more life-affirming than the grim survival of Schubert's wanderer."[21] To support her argument, she claims that if Mann had wanted explicitly to link desire and death through music, he would have sent Hans to his death humming Wagner instead of Schubert. While Scaff's analysis may be questionable, the fact that she raises the question of Wagner within the context of *The Magic Mountain* does permit readers to ask broader questions about Schubert and Wagner in terms of nationalism's role within Mann's novelistic universe. It is a common generality to link Wagner to German nationalism and to fascism;[22] yet an examination of Mann's writings prior to the composition of *The Magic Mountain* reveal that, for Mann, Wagner and his music had vastly different connotations. In fact, it is Schubert, not Wagner, who embodies for Mann the sound of German nationalism. He writes in *Reflections of a Nonpolitical Man, 1915–1918*:

> Although he is capable of sounding a folksy German note from time to time for purposes of characterization, as in *Die Meistersinger* and *Siegfried*, this never constitutes the basis and starting point of his musical writing—is never the source from which it wells up spontaneously, as in the work of Schumann, Schubert and Brahms. […] Wagner's music is more national than popular; to the foreigner as such it may appear typically German in many respects, but at the same time it has an unmistakably cosmopolitan cachet. […] True and potent though it is, then, Wagner's Germanness is refracted and fragmented in the modern mode, is decorative, analytical and intellectual—hence its powerful fascination, its innate capacity for cosmopolitan, not to say planetary influence.[23]

So Wagner's music for the Thomas Mann of the period of *The Magic Mountain* is the music not so much of nationalism but of cosmopolitanism. The question of the role Schubert plays in *The Magic Mountain* will be considered later in more detail, but for now it is important to note that, for Mann, Schubert's is a kind of nationalist music, with its roots in German folk music which is then transformed to fit with the classical tradition. Schubert is thus a mixture of light and serious music, a popular music infused with classical trappings. In taking Schubert's melody with him to the battlefield, Hans never escapes from the snare of popular music's link with the collective as outlined by Adorno, as this essay will show. First, however, it is necessary to explore further the question of Wagner.

For Mann, then, Wagner primarily plays the role not of the nationalist composer but of the universal one. While Mann never denies at least some grain of nationalism in Wagner, he is always quick to emphasize that this was not, in his early years, how he conceived of Wagner. Mann writes in *Reflections*:

What fascinated me was not the German nationalist element in Wagner's art, nor its specifically German poeticism or romanticism—or at least, only in so far as all this appeared intellectualized therein, as decorative self-portrayal: but rather the all-powerful European appeal that emanates from it, and to which Wagner's current, almost extra-German status bears witness.[24]

There is another type of universality in Mann's construction of Wagner. In addition to a certain cosmopolitanism, there is also an element in Wagner which blends the arts and, most specifically, music and literature. Mann writes in notes in 1911:

Did Wagner bring poetry (literature) and music closer together? He treated music in a literary manner. But is it because of this that today's composers want to be more literary, and compose "literary lyrics?" And what about "literary dramas?" [...] The absolute (genuine) musical composer = unliterary.[25]

There is thus something special or unique about Wagner's music that sets him apart from other composers. It is not only because Wagner composed his own libretti that Mann characterizes him as a literary artist. Rather, it is because he treats the music itself in a literary manner. Mann retains this position in an essay of 1911:

What also gave my relationship to Wagner a certain immediacy and intimacy was the fact that secretly I always saw and loved in him—notwithstanding the claims of the theater—a great narrative artist. The recurrent motif, the self-quotation, the symbolic phrase, the verbal and thematic reminiscence across long stretches of text—these were narrative devices after my own heart, and for that very reason full of enchantment for me.[26]

Mann thus establishes an explicit parallel between Wagner's work and his own, both of which were, at the time, achieving the kind of cosmopolitan status Mann attributes to Wagner. By the time Mann writes his essay on *The Magic Mountain* in 1953, he compares his novel to a piece of music:

Just as in music one needs to know a piece to enjoy it properly, I intentionally used the word "composed" in referring to the writing of a book. I mean it in the sense we more commonly apply to the writing of music. For music has always had a strong formative influence upon the style of my writing. Writers are very often "really" something else; they are transplanted painters or architects or what not. To me the novel was always like a symphony, a work in counterpoint, a thematic fabric; the idea of the musical motif plays a great role in it.[27]

Reading these reflections together with Mann's writings on Wagner-as-narrative-artist seems to suggest that Mann is, for all intents and purposes, collapsing the distinction between Wagner's literary music and Mann's own musical literature. Mann goes on to address explicitly the lingering question of Wagner's influence: "People have pointed out the influence of Wagner's music on my work. Certainly I do not disclaim this influence. In particular, I follow Wagner in the use of the leitmotiv, which I carried over into the work of language."[28] So, upon scrutiny of Mann's extra-fictional writings, it becomes clear that Wagner is not absent from *The Magic Mountain*. Rather, he is omnipresent as a universalizing impulse and an inspiration in terms of the technique of composition.

Having established, or at least sketched out, Mann's art in terms of its relationship to Wagner's, it is time to return to the question of the relationships among music, illness, desire, and death. In addition to this list of the various discourses at work in *The Magic Mountain*, another is also present: literary language. Language has thus far played only a minor role in this analysis, as Settembrini's antidote to the dangers of half-articulate musical expression. But in talking about language, it is important to make a distinction between literary and nonliterary language. Insofar as Mann has set up the world of *The Magic Mountain* within the framework of a novel, the discourse of literary language must be considered if the reader is to make any sense of what Mann might be communicating, or, more appropriately and more to the point, how Mann is communicating via *The Magic Mountain*. Since Mann himself establishes an exact parallel between his novelistic composition and Wagner's musical compositions, it is surely fair to read his remarks on Wagner as pertaining to literary language as well. What literary language shares with the discourses of illness and of music is ambiguity, the refusal to aspire to the sort of clear communicative linguistic goal which Settembrini advocates. Insofar as literary language is ambiguous, it serves as a better means by which to communicate desire than nonliterary language; its elusiveness classifies it with illness and music as ways to give voice to desire. Because of its beautiful yet elusive qualities, literary language can indeed be as dangerous as music. What Mann says about Wagner in the following passage may just as easily be applied to Mann's own novel:

> However poetic and "German" it may like to appear, Wagner's art as such is an extremely modern and by no means innocent art. It is clever and ingenious, full of yearning and cunning; in its resources and its characteristics it knows how to combine the narcotic with the intellectually stimulating in a way that is intrinsically exhausting for the spectator. But the preoccupation with that art almost becomes a vice, a moral issue, a recklessly ethical surrender to all that is harmful and devouring, if it is merely naïve enthusiasm—and not com-

bined with an analysis whose most venomous insights are ultimately a form of glorification and a further expression, simply, of passionate devotion.[29]

It is, in fact, rather difficult to puzzle out Mann's position as he articulates it here. On the one hand, he seems to be suggesting that one must always have recourse to a sort of analysis that would serve as a corrective to art's dangerous properties. It is important to note that he uses the same word "narcotic" which appears in the description, quoted earlier, of Hans' reaction to music at the sanatorium. But analysis, on Mann's view, apparently does nothing to remove the danger of the aesthetic experience, since the analysis brings one back, finally, to "passionate devotion." Later in the same essay, Mann writes:

> Art will never be moral or virtuous in any political sense: and progress will never be able to put its trust in art. [...] An irrational force, but a powerful one; and mankind's attachment to it proves that mankind is neither able nor willing to survive on rationalism alone, as summed up in the celebrated three-part equation of democratic wisdom: reason = virtue = happiness.[30]

Here it becomes clear that no sort of corrective can be successful in reducing art's dangerous effects. In fact, Mann goes so far here as to suggest that such a corrective would be absurd because it would not do justice to the human experience, which contains irrational elements. In this statement there is a definitive rejection of the position articulated in *The Magic Mountain* by Settembrini. Art, whether in the form of music, literature, or any other form, gives expression to that which rational language cannot name. Thus, Mann's project in *The Magic Mountain* was to explore various discourses that provide alternatives to rational language in seeking to express perhaps the most irrational part of the human experience, desire. Hans' desire for Clavdia, for example, finds its expression through dreams, illness, and musical experiences. Moreover it involves literary language, since it must be noted that all of Hans' musical experiences involve text wedded to music, whether in popular songs, art songs, or opera. Here again is an affinity between Wagner's aesthetic project and Mann's: musical language and literary approaches to music find their way into Mann's novel through vocal music, the fusion of literary language and music, sung, to complete the interweaving of the discourses, by a feverish body. Music, illness, and literary language may perhaps be dangerous discourses worthy of suspicion, but both are used to great effect by Mann in his novelistic explorations of desire.

So Mann participates, through his musical prose, in that condition which he ascribes to all art, and to the cosmopolitan Wagner in particular:

a potentially dangerous yet necessary expression of the irrational elements of the human experience. Yet the specificity of Mann's use of Schubert in the ending of *The Magic Mountain* remains. If Wagner's music can, on Mann's view, be mapped onto more general ideas about music because of Wagner's cosmopolitanism, the same cannot be said for Schubert. In fact, Schubert stands in *The Magic Mountain* in total contradistinction to Wagner. If Wagner's influence pervades the whole of the composition of the novel, Schubert has a very specific thematic role to play at a very specific point in the narrative. If Wagner is invoked as the sum total of all his works, Schubert is referred to within the context of a single song. For Mann, Schubert is intimately tied to German folk music, from which he draws his inspiration, and thus to German nationalism. Moreover, the selection which Hans hears on the record player and eventually takes with him to battle, "The Linden Tree," is a reworking of a German folk tune, perhaps one that was to be found in the "sentimental folk melodies" which served as Hans' early musical source material.[31] Thus, the tune represents simultaneously both the popular music which is associated with common, superficial emotions such as "infatuation," as well as the more sophisticated expressions of desire invoked most explicitly by the Verdi opera scenes.

Schubert's song is thus a popular melody dressed up in the fancy clothes of serious music. Mann, through his use of "The Linden Tree," collapses the distinction between the types of emotion portrayed in light music and those that find expression through serious music. The statements of Theodor Adorno quoted earlier can certainly be applied to the Schubert melody. Whistling on the battlefield, Hans very effectively becomes "integrated into the community of 'fans.' In whistling such a song, he bows to a ritual of socialization, although beyond this unarticulated subjective stirring of the moment his isolation continues unchanged."[32] What stronger links to the community could there be than language, which is social and communicative in origin and purpose, and music, which represents, in this case especially, a shared national heritage? The use of Schubert at the novel's end makes clear that Hans, despite his isolation from the world "down below" because of his stay at the Berghof, is very explicitly implicated in a community of desire and of nationalism. No amount of cover provided by the trappings of high art can differentiate Hans from a community of desirers and patriots. One of the novel's many ironies is that, after such a long stay at the sanatorium, where Hans develops his individuality through a simultaneous birth into desire and into illness, he

becomes by the novel's end reintegrated perfectly into the undifferentiated, non-individualistic collective world of desire and nationalism.

   This essay has traced the parallel development of music and illness
through *The Magic Mountain*, providing context to frame the discussion
through an examination of Mann's writings on music and literature in the
period surrounding World War I. Perhaps the most appropriate conclusion to draw from this novel, which plays so effectively on ambiguity, and
which, like the illness it portrays, so successfully resists attempts to pin it
down by analysis, is that all of the discourses at play, from music to illness
to literary language to desire, lead more or less directly to the death of
the subject. Through his absorption into the collective via nationalism,
Hans dies a political death with regard to his subjectivity. Through his recourse to a popular melody, albeit a transformed one, which he cheerfully
takes to his violent death, his subjectivity yields to death by desire. Politically and emotionally, then, Hans becomes undifferentiated and silenced,
the inevitable end of the subject who engages in the dangerous discourses
of desire and illness, of which music and literature become the ideal modes
of expression.

Joseph Acquisto

Notes

1. Thomas Mann, *The Magic Mountain*, trans. John E. Woods (New York: Vintage International, 1995) 38.

2. Mann, *The Magic Mountain* 87.

3. Mann, *The Magic Mountain* 87.

4. Mann, *The Magic Mountain* 111.

5. Mann, *The Magic Mountain* 108.

6. Theodor Adorno, *Introduction to the Sociology of Music*, trans. E.B. Ashton
   (New York: Seabury Press, 1976) 25.

7. Mann, *The Magic Mountain* 36–37.

8. Mann, *The Magic Mountain* 112.

9. Mann, *The Magic Mountain* 72.

10. Mann, *The Magic Mountain* 116.

11. Mann, *The Magic Mountain* 116.

12. Adorno 26–27.

13. Adorno 27.

14. Thomas Mann, "The Making of *The Magic Mountain*," trans. H.T. Lowe-Porter, *The Magic Mountain* (Garden City: International Collectors Library, 1952) 724, my emphasis.

15. Mann, *The Magic Mountain* 138–139.

16. Mann, *The Magic Mountain* 204.

17. Mann, *The Magic Mountain* 216.

18. Mann, *The Magic Mountain* 287.

19. Mann, *The Magic Mountain* 636.

20. Mann, *The Magic Mountain* 642.

21. Susan von Rohr Scaff, *History, Myth, and Music: Thomas Mann's Timely Fiction* (Columbia: Camden House, 1998) 58.

22. An excellent, highly eloquent example of such an indictment of Wagner would be Adorno's own *In Search of Wagner*, trans. Rodney Livingstone (London: NLB, 1981).

23. Thomas Mann, *Pro and Contra Wagner*, trans. Allan Blunden (London: Faber and Faber, 1985) 54.

24. Mann, *Pro and Contra Wagner* 58.

25. Mann, *Pro and Contra Wagner* 38.

26. Mann, *Pro and Contra Wagner* 47.

27. Mann, "The Making of *The Magic Mountain*" 722.

28. Mann, "The Making of *The Magic Mountain*" 723.

29. Mann, *Pro and Contra Wagner* 52.

30. Mann, *Pro and Contra Wagner* 65.

31. Mann, *The Magic Mountain* 116.

32. Adorno 27.

2

Making Her Work Her Life:
Music in Willa Cather's Fiction

"Who marries who is a small matter, after all. But I hope I can bring back your interest in my work."

— opera singer Thea Kronberg to her long-time suitor, Fred Ottenburg, in Willa Cather's *The Song of the Lark*.

"I must have music!" Willa Cather told her friends, relaying a personal demand that found expression in the lives of many of her fictional characters.[1] For example, Cather's first short story, "Peter" (1892), unravels a conflict between the title character and his son, Antone, over a violin. Peter's reverence for the instrument—and his yearning for the "old world" Bohemian culture the family had left behind—seem incomprehensible to Antone, who considers the violin a mere commodity in the struggle for material success in the "new world." At least twenty of Cather's other short stories and all twelve of her novels involve musicians and/or music, specifically Western music, either directly or indirectly. Two of the latter, *The Song of the Lark* (1915) and *Lucy Gayheart* (1935), depend almost entirely on music and music-related concerns in their plot structure, setting, and character development. Their dénouements differ, but both novels follow the life course of a young woman who leaves her Midwestern prairie town in the 1890s to study music in Chicago.

Cather's musical preferences included symphonic works and opera—especially Wagnerian operas, which provide metaphorical grist for *The Song of the Lark* and several short stories. In her later years, she preferred German Leider to operatic arias—Schubert's song cycle *Die Winterreise* helps to tell the story of Lucy Gayheart—and Beethoven string quartets to orchestral music. Opera singers, violinists, and pianists predominate in her fiction, though a main character in "The Bohemian Girl" (1912), Nils Ericson, is a flautist. Church bells figure in *The Professor's House* (1925) and in *Death Comes for the Archbishop* (1927) while hymns appear in the text of Cather's last novel, *Sapphira and the Slave Girl* (1940).

Personal, philosophical, and literary considerations underlie these musical references. Taken together, they reveal one of Cather's primary reasons for using music in her fiction *viz.* to advance a quasi-philosophical belief. Artistic achievement demands single-minded dedication, Cather tells her readers, but the choice to so dedicate oneself inevitably involves personal sacrifice. And those who reach an artistic zenith, say, opera stars (a favorite example of hers), risk becoming not simply isolated but estranged from others.

Cather explores these claims as they affect men and women but gives especially detailed attention to their meaning in the lives of women who study and perform music. For them, the necessary sacrifice often entails rejection of emotionally binding personal relationships and/or renunciation of what might be called ordinary life. Art, exalted if not divine, in Cather's view, demands no less. First espousing this view while a senior at the University of Nebraska, Cather insisted that "an artist should be able to lift himself into the clear firmament of creation where the world is not."[2]

Although this essay is neither a psychological nor biographical study of Willa Cather, it should be said that her fiction as well as her aesthetic theories have autobiographical implications. Cather held consistently to her early views about art, and she lived them out. In short, she created a life centered on her own writing, a life with minimal intrusions and apparently with few emotional entanglements or attendant distractions. It is not the case, however, that Cather completely foreswore personal relationships. She lived in New York City for 39 years with her friend Edith Lewis, who, by all accounts, ran the household to facilitate Cather's writing. Scant evidence about the private dimensions of their relationship exists, but some feminist scholars, most notably Sharon O'Brien in her 1987 biography of Willa Cather, have speculated about a possible lesbian affair between the two and between Cather and other women.[3]

Speculations aside, the available evidence reveals that Lewis served as Cather's typist, sometimes editor, and occasional traveling companion. Also, the two women attended a variety of music events together over the course of several decades. But Cather made her work the focal point of her life. "An author's only safe course is to cling to the skirts of his art, forsaking all others, and keep to her as long as the two shall live," she proclaimed,[4] advice she not only followed herself but meted out to the men and women inhabiting her prose.

Male and female characters who are devoted to music suffer spiritual anguish when deprived of it. Female characters usually express ambivalence—and some consider renunciation—when trying to make choices about the place of music in their lives. A conspicuous exception, however, is Thea Kronberg, the protagonist in *The Song of the Lark*. Independent and self-motivated from an early age, she seems comfortable with her adult choice to put music at the literal heart of her life and to remain emotionally detached from others, even her husband. Kronberg, in fact, seems to represent aspects of Cather herself, for she fully adopts the author's beliefs about the exalted status of art and the necessity for single-minded dedication in its pursuit. Although Cather's advocacy of these quasi-philosophical beliefs, *vis-a-vis* music, is the primary focus here, her personal and literary reasons for using music in so much of her fiction cannot be ignored.

Few of Willa Cather's letters, and no personal diaries, are available, but her own behavior, along with the memories and interpretive comments of others, give evidence that she truly enjoyed various kinds of Western music. Though not a musician herself, Cather attended countless performances during her life—symphonic concerts, chamber recitals, and operas—in New York, Chicago, and elsewhere. Edith Lewis, who published a biography of Cather after her death, observed that music was "an emotional experience [for Cather] that had a potent influence on her imaginative process:[5] Similarly, Richard Giannone, author of a benchmark study of music in Cather's fiction, concluded that she was "devoted" to it "as a member of the laity...she listened to music to add to her dreams. She was an enlightened amateur, in the sense of amateur as lover."[6]

It was not only music but those who performed it—their work habits, private lives, and physical characteristics—that intrigued Cather. A newspaper music reviewer in the early stages of her career, Cather sometimes expressed herself in a manner unlikely to be tolerated by contemporary "political correctness" advocates. In an 1899 review, for example, she described Metropolitan opera soprano Lillian Nordica as "less attractive physically this season than I have ever seen her, for she happens to be unpardonly stout."[7] And Wagnerian mezzo soprano Ernestine Schumann-Heink, Cather complained, had a "peasant face" and an "absurd dumpy little figure and short arms."[8]

Six years later, in her first collection of short stories, *The Troll Garden* (1905), Cather included several narratives that reveal her intrigue with the private affairs of performing artists. In "Paul's Case" and "Flavia and Her Artists," for instance, she creates characters enraptured by romanticized fantasies not about talent or artistry but about the lives and doings of performers. Cather's friend and colleague, journalist George Seibel, missed the mark, though, when claiming that her "interest was not in music itself, but in the personalities connected with it."[9] Willa Cather's interests, as it will soon become more evident, ran far deeper and entailed philosophical reflections on the nature of art, which she employed for literary purposes, *viz.* to structure plot, to develop character, and to create ambiance and/or setting.

Glorious and divine, art is also a mysterious and ineffable master, Cather asserted in an essay on Thomas Carlyle's aesthetic theories that she wrote for a college class. Published by the *Nebraska State Journal* in 1891, the essay went on to boldly announce:

> Art of every kind is an exacting master, more so even than Jehovah—He says only, "Thou shalt have no other gods before me." Art, Science and Letters cry, "Thou shalt have no other gods at all." They accept only human sacrifices.[10]

Biographer Mildred R. Bennett quotes Cather as saying she "was going to devote her life to the worship of art."[11] Indeed, it became her religion, Bennett concluded. And music, which often serves in Cather's fiction as a bridge—to one's inner self, to other people, and to the cosmos or to God—became her ultimate art, for she conceived of it as the "discourse of the soul."[12] Characters in her fiction who yearn for music, and those who perform it, represent spiritual seekers vulnerable to defeat if not death when deprived of it. Consider, for example, the title character's father, Anton Shimerda, in the novel *My Antonia* (1918). "Jerked away" from his Bohemian birthplace and music life, Shimerda stops playing his violin after arriving in the "new world." Bereft of music and homesick, he kills himself with a rifle in exactly the same manner as his fictive relative Peter, in Cather's first short story, had done.

A later story, "Eric Hermannson's Soul" (1900), introduces a spiritual seeker born and raised in Nebraska. Eric (a variant of Peter and a precursor of Anton Shimerda) finds life's meaning in his violin, and speaks through its music. "Beauty comes to men in many guises, and art in a hundred forms," Cather opines when telling his story, but for Eric "there was only his violin. It stood for all the manifestations of art; it was his only bridge to the kingdom of the soul."[13] After giving it up, Eric becomes withdrawn, sullen, and quiet. But when Margaret, a wealthy, cultured young woman visiting from the East, plays an operatic excerpt for Eric on the piano, he "became alive" again; the music "gave him speech,"[14] and renewed vitality.

Cather empathizes with characters who seek to fill their lives with music as well as with those who hope to share it with others. She empathizes, too, with characters who respond with passionate intensity to music, Thea Kronberg, for a prime illustration. But Kate Massey, a mother of two in the short story "The Prodigies" (1897), exemplifies a distorted intensity beyond the reach of Cather's empathy. Demanding and zealous, Massey compels her children to perform musically, even when her regime seems to threaten their lives.

Cather relies on music not only to describe internal states, but to situate characters in time and place and to suggest the relationship between inner and outer worlds. This approach sometimes involves a further step, relying on music to depict geographical landscape. In *The Song of the Lark*, Cather uses Antonin Dvorak's Symphony No. 9 to speak figuratively of frontiers and pioneers in juxtaposition with homelands and native peoples. By implication, the music speaks of alienation and loss, but also of the eagerness felt by people who are "starting over," be they European farmers cultivating new soil in Nebraska or the prairie girl Thea Kronberg awakening into a new sense of herself as an artist.

Indeed, Cather makes literary use of music to reveal a variety of contrasts: between the old and the new, between what was and what will be, and between seeming polarities in sensibility, geographical location, and acculturation. Within this framework, as several later examples will show, Western classical music represents commitment to a sacred world of beauty and the lives of educated, East Coast city people, whereas its absence represents spiritual deprivation and the lives of untutored if not uncultured people in rural areas or small Midwestern towns.

Cather's interest in music and performers appears to be rooted in childhood experiences, tracing back to her Red Cloud days in south-central Nebraska. Born in Virginia in 1873, she had moved to the Midwest with her extended family when she was nine. Cather's memories of her early life suggest her kinship with the German, Slavic, Scandinavian, and Mexican immigrants in Nebraska trying to establish themselves in a "new world" of barren plains and cold winters. Feeling displaced and lonely, she yearned for familiar surroundings. Although she soon came to love the land and its mix of people, the adult Cather wrote of being "jerked away" as a child from the wooded hills and meadows of the Shenandoah Valley and stranded in a country she likened to sheet iron, "stripped bare and gray."[15]

One of seven children, Willa made friends with the four daughters of Mrs. and Mrs. James Miner; together they improvised skits and later acted in stage plays at the Red Cloud Opera House. Mrs. Miner, the daughter of a Norwegian oboe player and an accomplished pianist, introduced Willa to music and to operatic themes. In all likelihood, she was a model both for Mrs. Harling in *My Antonia* (1918), the mother of five and a skilled pianist in a small Nebraska town, and for Mrs. Nelson Mackenzie, the good-hearted friend of the zealous Kate Massey in "The Prodigies."

An avid reader, Cather learned Greek and Latin as an adolescent and studied European classics and Shakespeare. She also took piano lessons from a Professor Schindelmeisser. A drifter with German ancestry who lived briefly in Red Cloud, he appears as Professor Wunsch, Thea Kronberg's first piano teacher in *The Song of the Lark*. By all accounts, Willa was not a brilliant piano student, preferring to hear stories from her teacher about music and musicians instead of practicing or learning to read music. Nor was she a gifted singer, as Mildred Bennett reports: "She sang in a grating voice" and seemed angry when pushed by her mother to sing at a community gathering.[16]

Richard Giannone observes that Willa's earliest mentors "had a musical identity"; they included her Aunt Frank, who organized neighborhood cultural events; Mrs. Miner; and Peorianna Bogardus Sill, who had once studied under Russian virtuoso pianist/composer Anton Rubinstein (1829–1894) and who taught music in Red Cloud.[17] The life of Cather's aunt, a woman originally from the East Coast who bore five children on a Nebraska farm and then returned briefly to the East, foreshadows the plot of "A Wagner Matinee" (1904). In the story, a prairie woman suffers unmitigated anguish after attending an orchestral concert in Boston during a visit there; returning home, as she knew she must, portended cultural isolation almost beyond bearing.

But Cather herself did not experience cultural isolation in Nebraska. Wandering Italian minstrels came through Red Cloud, playing opera tunes on a harp and violin, and "Blind Boone," an African-American pianist who makes an appearance as "Blind D'Arnault" in *My Antonia*, gave performances in various homes. Touring opera companies came to Red Cloud too. As a young girl, Cather saw productions of Gilbert and Sullivan's *The Mikado*, among other light operas, and a work by Michael Balfe, *The Bohemian Girl*, at the local opera house. (The latter is also the title of Cather's 1912 story incorporating music and plot elements from the Balfe work.) While a student at the University of Nebraska in Lincoln from 1891 to 1895, she attended operas, classical music concerts, and stage plays. And, during her freshman year, she saw her first written work in print, the college essay mentioned earlier and published in the *Nebraska State Journal*. Entitled "Concerning Thos. Carlyle," this meditation on the Scottish social philosopher's aesthetic theories ("Art of every kind is an exacting master.... Art, science and letters...only accept human sacrifices,"[18]) served as Cather's own initial philosophical pronouncement on art and as a premise for her future written work—as well as for her life.

Most of Cather's early publications were nonfiction, beginning with drama reviews in 1893, written not for a college class as the Carlyle essay had been, but for the *Journal*, though she was still a student at the University of Nebraska at the time. However, by 1894 she was writing a music column and reviewing local concerts for the *Journal* and for another newspaper, the Lincoln *Courier*. Two of her columns in the *Journal* focused on contralto Helena von Doenhoff, whom she had heard sing the role of Azucena in Verdi's *Il Trovatore* when the Tavary Opera Company performed in Lincoln. The 21-year-old writer commented on Doenhoff's vocal abilities but also on her personal life, a strategy that allowed Cather to reinforce ideas originally stated in her Carlyle essay and to lay the groundwork for views that would be reflected in her later fiction.

The first column, published in December 1894, praised the quality of Doenhoff's voice and its seemingly transcendent inspiration. The second, published the following January, contained a startling message that both laments and criticizes the singer's impending marriage. Cather opposed Doenhoff's decision "to dabble in matrimony" and used the word "fatal" to describe its consequences on artistic greatness; "married nightingales seldom sing"[19] she warns her readers. Setting forth the requirements— not for "success," which she considered "empty and unsatisfying"—but for artistic fulfillment, Cather asserted that "...in art it is only the player who stakes all who wins ... complete self-abnegation is the one step between brilliancy and greatness, between promise and fulfillment."[20]

In another piece for the *Journal*, Cather reviewed the New York Metropolitan Opera Company's visit to Chicago in 1895 and its performances, among other works, of Gounod's *Romeo et Juliette*, music from which later found its way into her 1897 story "The Prodigies." It was in this same opera that Cather first heard the Australian soprano Nellie Melba, who she later unfavorably contrasted with Helene von Doenhoff. Melba's voice, as Cather described it, was capable of "transcendent miracles of tone that delight, dazzle, exalt" but "soulless," without the spiritual and emotional color; "how strange that one who has so much should yet lack the thing holier than all," she wrote, "that thing which alone gives art a right to be."[21] In Cather's assessment, even if Melba were to practice "complete self-abnegation" such as had been proposed for Doenhoff, a lack of appropriate emotional temperament would forever disallow her from reaching the exalted status of true artistry.

The commentary on Melba, although published in the *Lincoln Courier*, was written after Cather's 1896 move to Pittsburgh where she lived until 1906 and before settling permanently in Manhattan. During this period she continued to review music for the two Nebraska newspapers, taught high school English and Latin for several years, and began to write about cultural events for the Pittsburgh *Leader*. Heeding the demands of her work, Cather did not marry. But her fascination with music flourished. Along with attending symphonic concerts at Carnegie Hall in Pittsburgh, which had opened in the fall of 1895, she traveled regularly to New York City for Metropolitan Opera productions and other musical performances. These experiences, no doubt enjoyable in themselves, provided material and insights for Cather's reviews and eventually for her fiction.

Cather's reaction to a recital by the eleven-year-old Russian pianist Joseph Hoffman (1876–1957) at the Metropolitan Opera House illustrates the connection between her cultural life and her writing life. Vehement in her disapproval, she aired her views on child prodigies in a review of Hoffman's recital for the *Lincoln Courier*. Young people "could never be artists, indeed, not a musician even," Cather insisted; children who perform "go too soon into an artificial atmosphere, an atmosphere where there is no time for silence and reflection.... It kills them, that is, figuratively."[22] The imposition on young performers of the adult emotional demands is, Cather complained, not only senseless but a "sacrilege to childhood."[23]

Given fictional treatment, these angry denunciations reappeared two years later in "The Prodigies," whose two teenage characters, Adrienne and Hermann Massey, are coerced by their mother to study music and to perform, among other pieces, the duet in the parting scene from Gounod's *Romeo and Juliette*. The adult emotional demands of this piece—the intoxicating dreams of romantic love and the anguish of farewell—exhaust, drain, in fact, seem to trigger a terminal illness in 14-year-old Adrienne when her mother forces her to sing it with her brother in public. A frustrated former musician herself, this mother erred profoundly, it could be argued, by ignoring Cather's advice, i.e., foregoing single-minded dedication to her own art and choosing instead to impose her will on her family's life, thereby casting such a disastrous shadow.

Joseph Hoffman's fate, however, was not a case of life imitating Cather's fiction. After moving to the United States, he became a prominent pianist and later the director of the Curtis Institute of Music in Philadelphia. Nor did Cather's views on prodigies seem to include violinist Yehudi Menuhin, who made his debut at age seven to public acclaim. Cather met the entire Menuhin family—Moshe, Marutha, and their three children, Yehudi and his two piano-playing sisters, Hepzibah and Yaltah—in Paris in 1930. At the time, Yehudi was a 14-year-old prodigy whose later career would encourage Cather's interest in chamber music. She had, of course, been writing fictional accounts involving violinists (Peter, Eric Hermannson, and Anton Shimerda) long before her acquaintance with Yehudi Menuhin. After their meeting, Cather regularly attended his recitals, and she remained close friends with Hepzibah and Yehudi until her death in New York City in 1947.

Much earlier, she had formed a friendship with American song composer and pianist Ethelbert Nevin (1862–1901), whom she had met in 1897 after moving to Pittsburgh. Cather wrote in the *Courier* and *Journal* with intense feeling about his dedication to work and his death at age 38. Her depiction of Nevin as someone emotionally unprotected from the pain of life places him in the company of the fictive violinists mentioned above, sorrow-wounded men who find solace in music. The eternally boyish and restless composer Adriance Hilgarde, in Cather's 1903 story, "A Death in the Desert," and the discontented composer Valentine Ramsey, in her 1925 story, "Uncle Valentine," appear to be characters derived from Nevin.

In the course of writing her music columns, Cather came to know several of the singers prominent at the Metropolitan Opera in the late 1890s and early 1900s. These included Lillian Nordica, the Wagnerian soprano from Maine, who became the subject of several of Cather's non-fiction pieces, and another Wagnerian soprano, Olive Fremstad, who had immigrated with her family from Sweden to Minnesota. Nordica's voice, in Cather's estimation, ranked with that of Nellie Melba: glorious but unmatched by appropriate emotional temperament. Fremstad, on the other hand, was Cather's ideal singer, who, soon after their 1913 meeting, became a model for Thea Kronberg in *The Song of the Lark*. Fremstad's beauteous voice *and* virtuoso interpretive skills, Cather concluded, merged as true artistry, thus enabling her to fluidly evolve into the disparate women she portrayed on stage, the evil Kundry in Wagner's *Parsifal*, for instance, and the spiritual icon Elizabeth in his *Lohengrin*, a role also assigned to the fictive singer Thea Kronberg.

Cather, who had attended her first Wagnerian opera while still a college student, had, by the late 1890s, seen various productions of *Lohengrin, Tannhauser*, and *Die Walkure*. In her newspaper reviews, she lavished praise on the acting, staging, and music in the performances. But it was the themes—"fervid devotion to the Grail" in *Lohengrin*, and the conflict between the spiritual and the sensual in *Tannhauser*—that captivated her. Consistent with her own ideas about the exalted status of art and the need for single-minded dedication in its pursuit, Wagnerian themes eventually infiltrated Cather's fiction.

Tannhauser and *Lohengrin* dramatize the search for eternal meaning, symbolized by a divinely pure idea, the Holy Grail, or by spiritual love, and both operas depict the ensuing struggle when the seeker is tempted by earthly demands and/or carnal delights. Broken hearts, disillusionment, and death—but also enlightenment, and sometimes redemption—are reoccurring plot elements. In *Die Walkure*, part of Wagner's Ring Cycle, the married Sieglinde seeks love (a combination of spiritual and romantic), in Siegmund, who, she finally realizes, is her own brother. For Cather, the scene that reveals their mutual recognition of this "unholy love" is probably "the most exalted love scene ever set to music."[24] Characters driven by "lofty enthusiasm for the unattainable" in the manner of Wagnerian principals, along with references to his emotionally evocative music, appear in a number of Cather's short stories, where the protagonists who search for meaning beyond themselves are often women.

Motifs from *Die Walkure* figure in "The Garden Lodge" (1905), a narrative that also reverberates with ideas first expressed in Cather's 1895 newspaper article, "Married Nightingales Seldom Sing." The main character, Catherine Noble, who had once considered a music career but chose marriage to a Wall Street power broker instead, is thrown into turmoil by the memory of her opera-star house guest, Raymond d'Esquerré, singing Wagner. In fact, he addresses Siegmund's words to Caroline, "Thou art the Spring for which I sighed in Winter's cold embrace," as if she were Sieglinde. Stirred not simply by the hope for a spiritual connection with d'Esquerré, but by her earlier dream about a life exalted by art, by music, Caroline realizes at that moment that her "useful, well-ordered life" with Howard Noble, though happy, "was not enough. It did not satisfy, it was not even real."[25] Deciding to play excerpts from *Die Walkure* herself on the piano, she is moved to tears of desire and desperation to live otherwise, to live as an artist might.

As in many Cather stories, however, the yearning protagonist's dream grows thin, then melts away: she "felt the warmth under her heart growing cold... so heavy were the chains upon it, so many a fathom deep it was crushed down into darkness."[26] Caroline's reasons for losing touch with her dream make practical sense, for she despised the routine of practice and feared the poverty and other "sordid realities" attendant to artistic failure. Much earlier, before her married life of order and wealth, Caroline concluded that she had already "served her apprenticeship to idealism and to all the embarrassing inconsistencies which it sometimes entails, and she decided to deny herself this diffuse, ineffectual answer to the sharp questions of life."[27]

Actualizing lofty dreams requires fortitude and more, Cather reminds readers, when she depicts Caroline re-embracing marital life. Yet she reminds readers, too, of the dreary patterns of mundane life and the sometimes disastrous fate of women dependent on men. Cather presents Caroline's mother, who had "idolized her husband" (a music teacher and failed orchestral composer) as confined to "drudging bondage at the kitchen range" until she died before turning 40.[28] Both mother and daughter seem to validate Cather's prediction concerning Helena von Doenhoff, namely, that domestic bondage can "be fatal" to artistic aspirations if not to the life spirit itself.

"A Wagner Matinee," Cather's vehicle for a partial recreation of her Aunt Frank, is linked thematically and musically to "A Garden Lodge," though the former story ends on a darker note. Once again, she uses Wagner's music to convey a reawakened yearning for artistic engagement, followed by the despairing recognition that such possibility is lost forever.

Like Caroline Noble, Georgiana Carpenter had forsaken a career as a pianist for marriage. Giving up her music studies in Boston, she moved to a farm in the barren Nebraska countryside, where she cooked and ironed for her husband and six children. Thirty years later, on a visit to Boston, "the place longed for hungrily" as she put it, Carpenter is taken by her nephew Clark, now a music student, to an afternoon concert. Exhausted by her train trip, worn to old age by rural life, and benumbed by cultural/spiritual deprivation, Aunt Georgiana seems unable to put aside her worries about the farm. But "when the horns drew out the first strain of the Pilgrim's Chorus" (music in *Tannhauser* suggestive of the search for spiritual purity), she clutched Clark's coat sleeve. Gradually restored to a former sense of herself, Georgiana becomes fully engaged in the music, for it "broke a silence of thirty years; the inconceivable silence of the plains."[29]

The prelude to *Tristan and Isolde*, Wagner's exploration of longing and love that elevate and then destroy, seemed to immobilize her, but music from *The Flying Dutchman* beckoned her fingers, now swollen and knotted, to work "mechanically upon her black dress, as though, of themselves, they were recalling the piano score they had once played."[30] The concert ends with Siegfried's funeral march, wailing music from Wagner's *The Twilight of the Gods* that accompanies the demise of the spiritual seeker and hero. When the music stopped, Aunt Georgiana "burst into tears and sobbed pleadingly. 'I don't want to go, Clark, I don't want to go!'"[31]

Unlike Caroline Noble in "The Garden Lodge," who at least pretends to recover from the loss of her dream (the story ends with Caroline and her husband laughing together at the breakfast table), Georgiana Carpenter appears to be a defeated spiritual seeker. She feels she must return to her husband and family and farm, to the "tall, unpainted house, with weather-curled boards; naked as a tower, the crooked-back ash seedlings where the dish-cloths hung to dry; the gaunt, moulting turkeys picking up refuse about the kitchen door."[32] Having chosen domestic relationship, a life that Cather had so lamented on behalf of the opera singer Helena von Doenhoff, Carpenter relinquishes her moment in the "heavenly light."

Music by Wagner as well as by Dvorak and Schubert also figures significantly in Cather's novels, *The Song of the Lark* and *Lucy Gayheart*. A deeply reflective and melancholic novel, *Lucy Gayheart* traces the short life of a prairie girl who strives in vain for seemingly opposite goals: love in private life and acclaim for public piano performance. Cather scholar Richard Giannone offers an especially well-thought-out account not only of

Cather's enchantment with vocal music but of her reliance on Schubert's song cycle, *Die Winterreise* (The Winter Journey), in developing the theme and tone of *Lucy Gayheart*.[33] As Giannone observes, both the cycle (twenty-four songs) and the novel trace the painful journey of one who has lost love and hope and finally life itself. Metaphorical allusions to seasons occur in both works, though the song cycle covers a single day in contrast to the novel's one-year time span, with two winter seasons.

The title character's beloved, baritone Sebastian Clement, who sings *Die Winterreise* in a recital Lucy attends, soon dies in an apparent accident that foreshadows her own fate the following winter. Despairing a future without Sebastian, and without the exalted artistry he represents, Lucy abandons her commitment to music, though, after months of grief, she tentatively plans to revive her studies.[34] It is Lucy who lives out the youth's winter journey portrayed in Schubert's song cycle, Giannone rightly concludes. Her death, ambiguously presented as Clement's had been—is it accidental or possibly suicide?—echoes once again the warning Cather issued in her Doenhoff commentary, *viz.*, devotion to another person rather than to one's own art may be fatal to the art as well as the artist.

Antonin Dvorak's *New World Symphony*—the music itself and the themes it expresses—interested Cather from the first time she heard it, in 1894. Still a college student, Cather attended a performance of Dvorak's Symphony No. 9, given by the Chicago Symphony Orchestra in Lincoln and conducted by Theodore Thomas. In 1897 she heard the piece again, this time in Pittsburgh, and reviewed it for the Lincoln *Courier*. Dvorak, who composed the symphony while he was living in the United States during the early 1890s, drew from a variety of sources: Czechoslovakian folk melodies, African-American spirituals, and Native American song and drum rhythms. A message to his Bohemian homeland, the music suggests the diversity of life, geography, and culture in the "new world."

In her *Courier* review, Cather's words recreate the musical picture of America and its people that the symphony conveyed to her. The "Plaintive air" built upon "Negro Melodies" rises from Southern mountains, plantations, and bayous, she wrote, but depicts as well "the empty, hungry plains of the Middle West."[35] Describing the emotional as well as geographical and cultural landscapes she envisions in the Largo, or second movement, Cather continues:

> ... before you stretch the ... limitless prairies, full of the peasantry of all the nations of Europe; Germans, Swedes, Norwegians, Danes, Huns, Bohemians,

Romanians, Bulgarians, Russians and Poles, and it seems as though from
each of those far scattered lights that at night mark the dwellings of these
people on the plains, there comes the song of a homesick heart.[36]

Though she heard the yearnings of exiles in the Largo, Cather also heard
"a little staccato melody" at the end of the movement, suggesting the dawn
of a new day with "the peasant hurrying to his plow to master a strange
soil and make the new world his own."[37] And in the conclusion to the
whole work, she heard a "long, high final note on the wind instruments
that seems to rise out of that vortex of sound like an aspiration .... It is
like the flight of the dove over the waste of waters, that last note, there is
all the hope of the new world in it."[38]

Cather's interpretation of the music ("the song of the homesick heart")
can be read as a response to her own sense of otherness, for she too had
been a child deprived of familiar surroundings, having moved from the
gracious family home in the Shenandoah Valley to the bleak Nebraska
prairies. Yet her interpretation revels in hope: outsiders, immigrants from
Bohemia, Sweden, Norway, and elsewhere will transcend their feelings of
alienation in a seemingly inhospitable new land.

Speaking generally, much of Cather's fiction reflects the mix of feelings she identified in Dvorak's *New World Symphony*: the despair of immi-
grant farmers struggling to survive on arid Midwestern plains, along with
the sense of uprootedness that plagued pioneer women, but also the deep-
seated aspirations that motivated these people. My Antonia is the best
known example of this, but "Eric Hermannson's Soul" offers a condensed
version of the same "new world" motifs, complemented by Wagnerian
themes. Set in Nebraska, the story champions "poor exiles of all nations;
men from the South and the North, peasants from almost every country
in Europe ... men sobered by toil and saddened by exile, who had been
driven to fight for the dominance of an untoward soil...."[39]

At the behest of a fundamentalist preacher who ranked music with
demons from hell, the youthful Norwegian, Eric, crushed his violin "to
splinters." Morose and spiritless without it, Eric is eventually brought into
a "new world" of hope when he experiences a pure, almost transcendent
love for the unobtainable young woman, Margaret. Evidently influenced
here by Wagner's ideas about music, love, and divinity as expressed in
Tristan and Isolde and elsewhere, Cather allows Margaret to recognize
the radiant moment: She knew that the look in Eric's eyes "had never
shone for her before, would never shine for her on earth again, that such

love comes to one only in dreams or in impossible places like this, unattainable always."[40] Parted from Margaret as circumstances dictated—and in keeping with Cather's skepticism about binding human relationships—Eric is nevertheless inspired by the luminous love to return to violin playing. Luminous now himself, he looks with hope at the "new day [that] was gilding the corn-tassels and flooding the uplands with light."[41]

The "new world" motifs play out somewhat differently in Cather's fiction involving women who choose to become musicians or performing artists. Such women, she suggests, are pioneers and/or immigrants of sorts, too: Departing from traditional lives of home and family, they enter a "new world," one fraught with disparities and self-doubts. Often residents of prairie lands, they are presented as feeling displaced and conflicted yet driven by a desire to transcend their pasts and circumstances. Many of these protagonists/pioneers (as in the case of Georgianna Carpenter) are defeated or destined to grieve on various counts. The selected few who succeed on concert hall stages exhibit the courage, discipline, and hard work needed for survival in the harsh conditions of the prairies. Achievement in these "new worlds" requires an inborn gift, but also the "self-abnegation" that Cather had insisted upon when expressing her disappointment in Helena von Doenhoff's wedding plans. The stories "Nanette: An Aside" (1897) and "A Singer's Romance" (1900) bear out this set of views on women performers while also preparing the ground for *The Song of the Lark*, with its related themes, issues, and conflicts.

These stories, actually two versions of the same plot, illuminate the disjunctions between a life governed by artistic aspiration and one governed by more ordinary prospects yet enhanced by romance. In both versions, a female opera singer whose true confidante and companion is a maid (Nanette in the first story and Antoinette in the later one) faces a private crisis upon realizing she had never known an *affaire de coeur* and probably never would. Madame Tradutorri (in the 1897 story) and Frau Schumann (in the 1900 version) are married, but to men with whom they do not live and who are dependent upon their wives to underwrite their gambling habits. It is the maids who fall into heart-felt love and then want to leave their respective services to enter their own "new worlds." Tradutorri and Schumann, undeniably lonely and needy, and sometimes bitter, nevertheless come to terms with their raw emotions and choose, though not without misgivings, to renew their commitments to aesthetic striving.

Cather employs Nanette to verbalize her belief in the priority of single-minded devotion. "Had it pleased Heaven to give me a voice," the maid

says, "I should have given myself wholly to my art, without one reserva-
tion, without one regret, as Madame has done."[42] Tradutorri, in turn, espouses Cather's "theory of 'repression,'" i.e., self-abnegation: the refusing
to yield to private desire and the binding of emotion "down within one's
straining heart ... until out of this tempest of pain and passion there speaks
the still, small voice into the soul of man ...; this voice," Cather declares,
is the voice of "classical art, art exalted, art deified."[43]

Cather allows for ambivalence in Tradutorri and Schumann, women
who have entered "new worlds" often harsh and self-denying. Both singers
are depicted as weeping in regret for a life without passionate love. Yet
Cather ultimately rejects romantic encumbrance for these women in the
pursuit of artistry, presenting them in the end as self-focused—even celebratory—within their chosen spheres. Alone, drained by tears and anger,
Frau Schumann nonetheless orders for herself "a quart of Champagne."
And Madame Tradutorri, despite her "lonely tears of utter wretchedness"
feels confident that the "coronet that the nations had given her when they
called her "queen" still shines upon her brow.[44]

The conflicts and choices that Cather pondered in the two stories
about opera singers receive even closer scrutiny in *The Song of the Lark*,
published some 15 years later. Yet the main character in this novel, Thea
Kronberg, follows her elected path with far less self-doubt—though perhaps
with more self-repression—than either Tradutorri or Schumann. Defiant
and resolute, Thea cannot be found weeping before or after she enters
her "new world." In the development of this character, Cather turned to
the lives of two Metropolitan Opera singers, Olive Fremstad and Emma
Calve (along with the music of Dvorak and Wagner), for inspiration. Fremstad was not only a model for Thea but someone with whom Cather herself could identify. A creative woman who, like Cather, had defied the
strictures of life in Midwestern towns and chosen to dedicate herself to
artistic achievement, Fremstad paved the way for Kronberg. Given Swedish
ancestry to match Fremstad's, Thea sang in a Swedish church choir as
Fremstad once did, displayed intellectual and physical rigor similar to that
of Fremstad and Cather, and triumphed in the same Wagnerian roles
(Elsa in *Lohengrin*, for example) that had brought fame to Fremstad.

In her triumph, Thea's stage presence reflects that of the French soprano Emma Calve (1858–1942) whose 1897 recital Cather had reviewed
for the Lincoln newspapers. The French singer had captivated the audience in a way that "poor soulless Melba" could never do, she concluded,

in an assessment of the performance that echoed Cather's earlier pieces on Carlyle and von Doenhoff.[45] True artistry, as she explained it in the Calve review, involves a transformation from one's ordinary self to another, transcendent self. "Carried beyond herself, serene as a pole star," Cather wrote, "Calve "showed us herself to convince us how entirely she could become another."[46] But this transformation is possible only if the singer possesses a naturally magnificent voice that blends in perfect accord with finely tuned interpretive skill. So transformed, the true artist, Cather warns, risks becoming distant ("a pole star") if not alienated from others.

Cather borrows from her Emma Calve review to account for Thea Kronberg's transformation—and its consequences—when she sings the role of Elsa in Wagner's *Lohengrin* at the Metropolitan Opera. As witnessed by her childhood mentor and friend, Dr. Howard Archie, Thea, at her emotional height on stage, "becomes someone else," so much so that he feels estranged from her:

> What he felt was admiration and estrangement. The homey reunion, that he had somehow expected, now seemed foolish. Instead of feeling proud that he knew her better than all these people about him, he felt chagrined at his own ingenuousness.... She seemed much, much farther away from him than she had all those years when she was in Germany. The ocean he could cross, but there was something here that he could not cross.[47]

Thea's journey to this emotional height—and self-contained distance—had begun in the small prairie town of Moonstone, Colorado, in the 1890s, where, like Cather herself, the adolescent girl had studied piano under a drifter with German ancestry, called Professor Wunsch in the novel. Independent, with thoughts and plans of her own, Thea did not imagine herself following the traditional path of marriage and family life. She wanted to read books and to learn German so that she could sing Leider. When Wunsch spoke to her about marrying and keeping house she replied, "No, I don't want to do that."[48] Only 17 when she left Moonstone to begin music studies in Chicago, she felt little hesitation: "Thea was surprised that she did not feel a deeper sense of loss at leaving her old life behind her ..."; in fact, she felt she "lacked nothing. She even felt more compact and confident than usual."[49] Once settled in Chicago, Thea eschewed most social outings in favor of music practice and related work. Early on, then, she exhibits the traits that Cather admired in—but also demanded from— those who seek star status in music: single-minded devotion, independence of spirit, and self-directed discipline.

Thea had several music teachers in Chicago, but Andor Harsani influenced her more than any of the others, first by redirecting her studies from piano to vocal music and, later, by giving Thea a ticket to a concert that would redirect the course of her entire life. She "had been to so few concerts that the great house, the crowd of people, and the lights, all had a stimulating effect."[50] But it was the music, Dvorak's *Symphony No. 9*, performed by the Chicago Symphony Orchestra under the baton of Theodore Thomas, that drew, pulled, and then thrust Thea Kronberg into a "new world." Cather, who had heard the *New World Symphony* conducted by Thomas when she was 22, almost Thea's age, exclaims in the novel: after the first movement ended, Thea "was much too excited to know anything except that she wanted something desperately, and when the English horns gave out the theme of the Largo, she knew that what she wanted was exactly that."[51] The "that," as Cather had described it in her own response to the Largo, "is like a flight of a dove over the waste water, that last note, there is all the hope of the new world in it."[52] Expanding in the novel upon her 1897 newspaper review of the symphony, Cather paints a word picture of the music, underlaid by Platonism, to suggest its impact on Thea and the inherent nature of her destiny:

> There were the sandhills, the grasshoppers and locusts, all the things that wakened and chirped in the morning; the reaching and reaching of high plains, the immeasurable yearning of all flat lands. There was home in it, too; first memories, first mornings long ago; the amazement of a new soul in a new world; a soul new and yet old, that had dreamed something despairing, something glorious, in the dark before it was born; a soul obsessed by what it did not know, under the cloud of a past it could not recall.[53]

The concert continued with excerpts from Wagner's opera *The Rhinegold*, "about the strife between gods and men," Thea vaguely remembered. "Too tired to follow the orchestra with much understanding…she closed her eyes…and heard for the first time that troubled music, ever-darkening, ever-brightening, which was to flow through so many years of her life."[54] Thea left the concert hall in a state of ecstasy. Clarity and exhilaration merged in that moment when she choose, despite the life demands "rushing at one to crush it under," to live for this feeling of ecstasy, to "work for it, die for it; but she was going to have it, time after time height after height."[55] Transformed by the music, no longer simply an ambitious, independent-minded girl, Thea recognizes her "new" yet always destined-to-be self. Consciously and willingly, she would devote herself to her own art. And that entailed, she soon discovered, the decision to cordon herself off from others. When approached by someone—as in the case of the man who accosted her after the concert—she would often have to say, "Oh, let me alone!"[56]

Thea arrived at her distant pinnacle—an opera singer nonpareil—not only because she possessed a magnificent voice in perfect accord with finely-tuned interpretive skill, but also because she chose to follow Cather's prescription for "self-abnegation." Preoccupied with herself, with her bathing, sleeping and privacy—and fully focused on her own aims—Thea had no time for, or interest in, small talk or deep emotional engagement with others. When Dr. Archie worries, "I'm afraid you don't have enough personal life outside your work,"[57] she reveals that marriage is not on her horizon. Prepared, moreover, to lose the few friends she has for the sake of her artistic pursuit, Thea is willing "to give up for it all that one must give up for it" and to "risk everything and lose everything."[58]

Unlike many of Cather's other protagonists, Peter, in her first story, for example, and Lucy Gayheart, whose lives end in defeat, despair, and death, Thea is a survivor who becomes a star, albeit a distant, self-isolating "pole star." Romantic passion does not impede her way. She does not suffer a broken heart as did Lucy, for she did not attach herself emotionally to a man. Nor does she weep regretfully in the manner of fictional singers Madame Tradutorri and Frau Schumann.

Yet Thea does not rule men out of her life. In fact, all of her mentors and benefactors are men, beginning with Dr. Archie, who provided intellectual companionship as well as money for her career; and including Spanish Johnny, who enchanted the young Thea with his guitar music; Ray Kennedy, a railroad worker more concerned about her future than his own; various music teachers, especially the aforementioned Andor Harsanyi; Fred Ottenburg, a wealthy, long-time suitor who paves the way for her opera career; and Oliver Landry, a piano accompanist who, like all the other men, "was a good friend to a green girl," as Thea put it; "he helped me with my German and my music and my general discouragement" and "seemed to care more about my getting on than about himself."[59]

Mentors and benefactors aside, it cannot be said that Thea was shorn of desire for intimacy, affection, even sustained love, though Cather presents these desires as minimal. "I'd like to have somebody human to make a report to once in a while," Thea reveals to Fred—but she utters these words only after her Metropolitan Opera career is established.[60] On an-

other occasion, she finds herself musing about "something that had touched
her deeply," the warmth of love expressed by an old German couple in response to a Beethoven piano sonata: "Thea wanted to put her arms around
them and ask them how they had been able to keep a feeling like that."[61]

Thea finally does marry Fred, though more for reasons of respect and
gratitude than passion or love. "Who marries who is a small matter, after
all," she tells him, "but I hope I can bring back your interest in my work."[62]
Not surprisingly, Cather presents this marriage as an afterthought; briefly
mentioned in an Epilogue to the novel, it is merely something that Thea's
Aunt Tillie reads about in a newspaper.[63] After the wedding, Fred continues
"working for" and "serving" Thea, her career and her interests. When her
aunt from Colorado visits the couple in New York, it is Fred who spends
time with Tillie and takes her to dinner while Thea dines in a luxurious
solitude of her own choosing. In spite of matrimony, then, she lives in accord with Cather's prescriptions: exalting art and yielding to its concomi-
tant demands for single-minded focus and self-abnegation.

Thea, a goddess of sorts, as her name aptly implies, strives passion-
ately to transcend herself through her artistry. And she succeeds, becoming
a superlative if not divine singer, especially in the Wagnerian operas that
had so engaged Cather herself. Among other roles, Thea stars as Elizabeth in *Tannhauser*, a symbol of spiritual love, and a woman who prays for
entrance to the "blessed kingdom" when she fears she has failed to rescue
the title character from the realm of carnal desire. She triumphs as Elsa,
too, in *Lohengrin*, a woman who becomes an abbess after being left to
herself. Elsa is "made to live with ideas and enthusiasm," Thea explains
to Fred, "not with a husband."[64] The meaning of the verb "made" seems
ambiguous at first (is Elsa/Thea created to so live? Or is she compelled?).
But Cather's intended meaning becomes coherent when interpreted in
the Platonic sense suggested earlier.

Thea chose to make art her life both because she was so-created, i.e.,
she possessed the requisite gifts; and because she recognized, after hearing *The New World Symphony*, her latent and unremitting desire for the
"ecstasy" of artistic triumph. She envisioned her destiny by way of the
music, for in it she felt "the amazement of a new soul in a new world; a
soul new and yet old, that had dreamed something despairing, something
glorious, in the dark before it was born."[65] Displaced and restless on the
prairies, Thea willingly accepted the demands of her "new" life. Cather's
prescription for "complete self-abnegation" may not be possible to real-

ize just as Platonic ideal Forms remain unobtainable. And perhaps her requirements for artistic achievement are excessive, even overwrought. Yet striving for it, as Cather knew well, necessarily involves single-mindedness and thus some degree of estrangement from others. But if and when the one who strives reaches her artistic zenith, the gates to the "blessed kingdom" will—for that moment—open wide.

Marion Fay

Notes

1. Willa Cather, quoted E.K. Brown, *Willa Cather: A Critical Biography* (New York: Knopf, 1953), 301.

2. Cather, quoted Mildred R. Bennett, *The World of Willa Cather* (New York: Dodd, Mead, 1951), 214.

3. Sharon O'Brien, *Willa Cather: The Emerging Voice* (New York: Oxford University Press, 1987; reissued by Harvard University Press, 1997).

4. Quoted Bennett, 214.

5. Edith Lewis, *Willa Cather Living: A Personal Record* (New York: Knopf, 1953), 47.

6. Richard Giannone, *Music in Willa Cather's Fiction* (Lincoln: University of Nebraska Press, 1968), 4.

7. Willa Cather, "Lohengrin" and "Die Walkure," *The World and the Parish: Willa Cather's Articles and Reviews, 1893–1902*, vol. 2, William M Curtin, ed. (Lincoln: University of Nebraska Press, 1970), 620 (hereafter cited as WP2).

8. Cather, "Lohengrin" and "Die Walkure," 621.

9. Quoted in Bennett, 152.

10. Quoted in Bennett, 219.

11. Bennett, 219.

12. Giannone, 7.

13. Willa Cather, "Eric Hermannson's Soul," *Collected Short Fiction, 1892–1912* (Lincoln: University of Nebraska Press, 1965), 361 (hereafter cited as CSF).

14. Cather, "Eric Hermannson's Soul," 366.

15. Willa Cather, *My Antonia, Early Novels and Stories* (New York: The Library of America, 1987), 711.

16. Bennett, 32.

17. Giannone, 13.

18. See note 10 above.

19. Cather, "Married Nightingales Seldom Sing," *The World and the Parish: Willa Cather's Articles and Reviews, 1893–1901*, vol. 1, William M. Curtin, ed. (Lincoln: University of Nebraska Press, 1970), 176 (hereafter cited as WP1).

20. Cather, "Married Nightingales," 176.

21. Cather, "Melba," WP1, 416.

22. Cather, "Joseph Hoffman," WP1, 186.

23. Cather, "Hoffman," 186.

24. Cather, "Lohengrin," WP2, 624.

25. Cather, "The Garden Lodge," CSF, 195.

26. Cather, "The Garden Lodge," 196.

27. Cather, "The Garden Lodge," 190.

28. Cather, "The Garden Lodge," 189.

29. Cather, "A Wagner Matinee," CSF, 239.

30. Cather, "A Wagner Matinee," 240.

31. Cather, "A Wagner Matinee," 241.

32. Cather, "A Wagner Matinee," 242.

33. Giannone, cf. 213–231.

34. The 2001 Pushcart prize-winning story, "The Anointed," by Kathleen Hill, involves a twelve year old girl reflecting on Willa Cather's character, Lucy Gayheart. This music-related story probes the inner life of a sensitive independent girl who, like Lucy, grasps for an understanding of grief and unresolved desire. Hill's story and Cather's novel intersect in revealing the power of undertows, of hidden waters—be they within the self or under an ice-covered river—to change the course of life. See Kathleen Hill, "The Anointed," in *Pushcart Prize 25: Best of The Small Presses*. Ed. Bill Henderson. Yonkers, N.Y.: Pushcart press, 2001.

35. Cather, *Symphony From the New World*, WP1, 413.

36. Cather, *Symphony*, 413.

37. Cather, *Symphony*, 414.

38. Cather, *Symphony*, 414.

39. Cather, "Eric Hermannson's Soul," 360.

40. Cather, "Eric Hermannson's Soul," 378.

41. Cather, "Eric Hermannson's Soul," 379.

42. Cather, "Nanette: An Aside," CSF, 407.

43. Cather, "Nanette," 408.

44. Cather, "Nanette," 410.

45. Cather, "Calve," WP1, 409.

46. Cather, "Calve," 411.

47. Cather, "The Song of the Lark," *Early Novels and Stories*, 640 (hereafter cited as *Lark*).

48. Cather, *Lark*, 360.

49. Cather, *Lark*, 433.

50. Cather, *Lark*, 467.

51. Cather, *Lark*, 468.

52. See Note 37 above.

53. Cather, *Lark*, 468.

54. Cather, *Lark*, 468.

55. Cather, *Lark*, 470.

56. Cather, *Lark*, 469.

57. Cather, *Lark*, 678.

58. Cather, *Lark*, 680.

59. Cather, *Lark*, 661.

60. Cather, *Lark*, 688.

61. Cather, *Lark*, 690.

62. Cather, *Lark*, 688.

63. The marriage of an acclaimed woman singer to a non-musical banker is the subject of May Sarton's 1982 novel *Anger*, a work that suggests Sarton's affinity, at the very least, for Cather's themes in *The Song of the Lark* and elsewhere. In *Anger*, the tempestuous Anna is more devoted to her career than to her marriage, though she ultimately makes a truce with her husband Ned. Sarton, like Cather, opted for a personal life that allowed ample solitude and, like Cather, she dedicated herself to her work/writing/art. May Sarton, *Anger* (New York: Norton, 1982; reissued, 1996).

64. Cather, *Lark*, 648.

65. See note 53 above.

3

The Enslaving Power of Folksong in Jean Toomer's *Cane*

"Her body was tortured with something it could not let out. Like boiling sap it flooded arms and fingers till she shook them as if they burned her. It found her throat [...]. And then she sang brokenly."

— Toomer, "Fern"

"Sometimes, I feel like a motherless child
A long ways from home.
True believer, a long ways from home.
Sometimes I feel like I'm almost gone,
Way up in the heabn'ly lan'.
Sometimes I feel like a motherless child,
A long way from home."

— traditional spiritual

Jean Toomer's *Cane* (1923), one of the first significant works of both the Harlem Renaissance and American modernism, was highly experimental in form and style, combining short fiction, poetry, prose vignettes, and drama in its three-part structure. Throughout these elements, Toomer uses folksongs to explore black male anxieties about cultural identity. Faced with the pressure of assimilating into white, middle-class society, the black men of *Cane* try to regain a positive connection with their heritage through women's folksongs.[1] This association between women and an idealized folk culture, however, inverts the traditional, liberating role of music in African-American literature. In effect, a type of slavery gets reconstituted as black men use these songs and the bodies of women to maintain an *African-*American identity—ultimately alienating them further from their search for cultural and emotional wholeness.

This essay looks at the structural and thematic significance of the folksongs in *Cane*, arguing that music operates both as a tool of entrapment and resistance. For men, it embodies unrealistic expectations about romance and the past. For women, these same songs undermine male narratives and invert power structures.

Listening Without Hearing

From the opening of "Karintha" to Louisa's final song in "Blood-Burning Moon," the short fiction in Part One begins and ends with songs. They frame the vignettes "Karintha," "Becky," and "Carma"; they end all three sections of the story "Blood-Burning Moon,"[2] and two lyrical poems separate each prose section. In sum, these frames give the narrator and the community of singers narrative control, preventing female characters from articulating their own stories—Karintha "smiles and indulges," Becky remains unseen and unheard, and Carma "silences" herself by feigning suicide.

Songs are one way to preserve communal history. During the year when the sawmill burns its sawdust pile in "Karintha," for example, "the smoke was so heavy you tasted it in water. Some one made a song: 'Smoke is on the hills. Rise up'" (2). Such folksongs capture a specific moment in time, making them an active part of the town's memory. Yet this music does not always offer an objective retelling of the past. As a matter of fact, the folksongs in *Cane* typically maintain a male perspective of events and people. The recurring folksong about Karintha offers one example of how these musical narratives objectify women: "Her skin is like dusk on the eastern horizon,/ O cant you see it" (1). Its repetition by the community transform her into a symbol for male sexual desire: "Her skin is like dusk on the eastern horizon/ ...When the sun goes down" (1).

Folksongs also link women to sentimentalized images of nature and Africa. In the story "Fern," the narrator sees Fern as an embodiment of the Georgia countryside. Her broken song and face unite with "the countryside and something that I call God" (17). Like the landscape of Karintha's skin, Fern provides access to both nature and a culture that has been lost by black men who left the South. Fern's act of singing and creating song also reinforces her symbolic role as a domestic virgin-mother within the community. The local men essentially "make" her a virgin in order to preserve this ideal: "She did not deny them, yet the fact was that they were denied. A sort of superstition crept into their consciousness of her being somehow above them. Being above them meant that she was not to be approached by anyone. She became a virgin" (14). In order to perpetuate this myth, they isolate her. When Fern faints after the narrator tries to touch her, for example, he learns that "there was talk about her fainting with me in the canefield. And I got one or two ugly looks from town men who'd set themselves up to protect her" (17).

Africa also gets invoked in these folksongs as a tool for linking women to the past. In a description of the nameless girl in "Carma," the narrator conflates the woman's voice with her physical body so that her songs and dances essentially transform the goat path into a "path in Africa."

> A girl in the yard of a whitewashed shack not much larger than the stack of worn ties piled before it, sings. Her voice is loud. [...] From far away, a sad strong song. Pungent and composite, the smell of farmyards is the fragrance of the woman. She does not sing; her body is a song. She is in the forest dancing. Torches flare [...] The Dixie Pike has grown from a goat path in Africa. (10)

Her song, like her body, carries significance only as a symbol. It recalls the ceremonies and rituals of African culture, but the conflation of body and voice suggests that physical contact is the only way to access this history.

Some resistance is also possible within these musical narratives. Karintha, for example, uses song to express her anger against the men whose sexual desires forced her to "ripen" too soon: "Before any of the women had started their supper-getting-ready songs, her voice, high-pitched, shrill, would put one's ears to itching" (1). Music becomes a form of resistance, and, as Nathaniel Mackey explains, it is "a critique of social arrangements in which, because of racism, one finds oneself deprived of community and kinship, cut off" (32). Yet Karintha's marginalization stems not from racism, but from the sexual and social control of men. Later in her life, unmarried, "cut off," and pregnant, Karintha kills her child,[3] and, by juxtaposing this event with the domestic ideal of the "supper-getting-ready songs," her high-pitched shrill becomes an inarticulate cry against social hierarchies that limit and objectify women.[4]

Fern also tries to resist male oppression through music, but eventually resorts to silence as a means for protecting herself. From the outset of the story, the narrator romanticizes the landscape, seeing it ripe with folksong. "Or maybe they gazed at the gray cabin on the knoll from which an evening folk-song was coming" (15). Fern's repeated songs, "like a

Jewish cantor [...whose] singing [rises] above the unheard chorus of a folk-song," become the basis for his connection with her: "I felt bound to her" (15). Because her songs intensify his desire to regain some connection with the rural black south, the narrator idealizes her and wants her to remain in Georgia, "[listening] to folk-songs at dusk" (15). Fern's sorrowful songs break, however, when he puts his arms around her; this physical—and metaphorical—entrapment literally stifles her singing voice.

> I held Fern in my arms [...]. I must have done something—what I don't know, in the confusion of my emotion. She sprang up. Rushed some distance from me. Fell to her knees, and began swaying, swaying. Her body was tortured with something it could not let out. [...] It found her throat, and spattered inarticulately [...]. And then she sang brokenly. A Jewish cantor singing with a broken voice. A child's voice, uncertain, or an old man's. Dusk hid her; I could only hear her song. It seemed to me as though she were pounding her head in anguish upon the ground. I rushed to her. She fainted in my arms. (17)

The act of holding her becomes a metaphor for the other ways men have restricted her identity. Even though the narrator doesn't understand his role in this, his desire to hold her symbolizes this oppression.

Fern desperately tries to reject the narrator's attempt to see her as an "unnamed thing," a mythologized symbol for cultural communion. As her broken song lingers in the air, she becomes exhausted with the futility of her struggle and loses consciousness. Sadly, the claustrophobic idealizations of the narrator and the "petty gossiping people" of her community have shattered her possibilities for freedom. Toomer suggests such an interpretation in one of his letters to Waldo Frank: "The Negro of the folksong has all but passed away. [...] In those pieces that come nearest to the old Negro, in the spirit saturate with folk-song: Karintha and Fern, the dominant emotion is sadness derived from a sense of feeling, from a knowledge of my futility to check solution."[5] There is no social solution for Fern's dilemma, but, in some ways, she takes control of her identity by losing consciousness. Without her song, the narrator has no "text" to interpret, and his gaze, in the absence of her consciousness, loses its power to control.

Cracked Voices

Men may have silenced Fern's song through coercion, but their own ineffectual songs in the second part of *Cane* suggest that women have found ways not only to resist but to undermine this oppression. The music of

Toomer's male characters unwittingly communicates their frustrating failure to form lasting heterosexual relationships. At the beginning of "Box Seat," Dan tries to sing while walking toward Muriel's house, but produces only a cracked voice and harsh whistle:

> The eyes of the houses faintly touch him as he passes. Soft girl-eyes. They set him singing. Girl-eyes within him widen upward to promised faces. [...] Dan sings. His voice is a little hoarse. It cracks. He strains to produce tones in keeping with the houses' loveliness. Cant be done. He whistles. His notes are shrill. They hurt him. (56)

In addition to suggesting Dan's inability to fit into middle-class expectations, the sexualization of the houses and street[6] raises questions about the power relations between black men and women. Even though the feminine aspect of these homes inspires him to sing, he can't perform under the scrutiny of their "girl-eyes," and subsequently reacts with anger: "Break in. Get an ax and smash in" (56). The male gaze, which has permeated Part One of *Cane*, gets inverted, and its impact on Dan fully demonstrates the enervating power of objectification. As Mrs. Pribby's initial reaction to Dan illustrates,[7] "he dont fit it," and, arguably, the surrounding community's perception reinforces his orphaned status (58). Until this section of the text, male idealizations have either kept women on the margins of their communities or prevented them from advancing in the world outside Sempter. The urban North, however, has leveled the playing field to some degree. Dan feels the effect of this gaze, and his broken song, like Fern's, communicates the impact of his exclusion from both past and present.

In order to cope with his outsider status, he cultivates an "obstinate desire to possess [Muriel]" and resorts to physical aggressiveness: "Dan tightens his grip. He feels the strength of his fingers. His muscles are tight and strong. He stands up. Thrusts out his chest. [...] Dan becomes aware of his crude absurdity" (60). When he grabs Muriel's wrists, he can momentarily trap her body, but not what her body represents for him. Like most men in the previous stories, his desire to possess her seems rooted in a need to reestablish some connection with his southern past. The figure of the "portly Negress" most clearly illustrates this intersection between body and history:

> A soil-soaked fragrance comes from her. Through the cement floor her strong roots sink down. They spread under the asphalt streets. [...] Her strong roots sink down and spread under the river and disappear in blood-lines that waver south. (62)

Dan's need to interpret the negress as a symbol reflects his larger inability to relate to women. As in his relationship with Muriel, he is trapped
by his own symbolic interpretations: "Slave of a woman who is a slave. I'm
a damned sight worse than you are. I sing your praises, Beauty! I exalt
thee, O Muriel! A slave, thou art greater than all Freedom because I love
thee" (63). Frustrated with the self-imposed (and social) barriers between
them, Dan has lost his ability to relate to Muriel or to anyone.

The ineffectual songs of the narrator "Avey" offer another example
of the ways women successfully undermine male objectification. Black men
have tried to make Avey an outcast, relegating her identity to that of
either a wife—"we did agree that she'd soon leave school and marry some
one" (43)—or a prostitute—Ned's opinion that "she was no better than a
whore" (45). When the narrator tries to control her physically and intel-
lectually, however, she dismisses him by never "[taking] the trouble to call
[him] by [his] name" and treating him like a child (43). She then stifles his
passions through both aggressive physical control and maternal behavior:

> She took me in [her arms]. And I could feel by the touch of it that it wasnt a
> man-to-woman love. [...] I didnt know what it was, but I did know that I
> couldnt handle it. [...] I wanted her to love me passionately as she did him. I
> gave her one burning kiss. Then she laid me in her lap as if I were a child.
> Helpless. I got sore when she started to hum a lullaby. (43–4)

Her song is not only without words, but it also enables her to reject the role
of sexual object. She uses music to modify his image of her, leaving him
"helpless." This scene also suggests a connection with the climax of "Fern,"
setting up "Avey" as an inversion of Fern's tale: "I held Fern in my arms
[...]. She sang [...] with a broken voice. A child's voice" (17). By becoming
physically aggressive and appropriating maternal behavior ("[humming] a
lullaby"), Avey conflates the two ways men have tried to categorize women—mother/prostitute. And this duality enables her to shut out the narrator in the same ways she has been shut out from patriarchal society.

After failing to achieve physical control, the narrator then seeks intellectual dominance both through "talk," because he "could beat her at that"
(47), and folksong, which he uses to mold her into a symbol for African-
American culture. His tiresome and ineffectual "lecture" to Avey in Sol-
dier's Home Park reveals his attempt to intellectualize her life in the hope
of "reforming" her, but his words only communicate self-absorption: "I
traced my development from the early days up to the present time, the
phase in which I could understand her. I described her own nature and

temperament. Told how they needed a larger life from their expression" (46).[8] After telling her about "her own nature and temperament," the narrator frames his criticism of Avey with folksongs, suggesting the historical link he would like her to represent:

> I wanted the Howard Glee Club to sing "Deep River," from the road. [...] I started to hum a folk-tune. [...] I talked, beautifully I thought, about an art that would be born, an art that would open the way for women the likes of her. [...] I sang, with a strange quiver in my voice, a promise-song. And then I wondered why her hand had not once returned a single pressure. (46)

He views his ideas as beautiful simply because they give him control over her possibilities for growth. His quivering, uncertain "promise-song," however, is purely intellectual, never taking into account her individuality. When she doesn't respond to him (and literally falls asleep), his hopes for changing her fade. Once again, Avey's loss of consciousness, like Fern's fainting, prevents the narrator from accessing her identity, making her invulnerable to his control.

Maternal Songs and Spirituality

Cane culminates in the drama "Kabnis," and once again, folksongs are used both to categorize women (as sexual objects, embodiments of African-- American culture, and mothers) and to empower them. Early in the story, men link the songs of women to the country as a way of mitigating their cultural isolation. After Kabnis loses his job, for example, he and his friends sit in his dark cabin and listen to a woman singing outside. Toomer juxtaposes this image of darkness with the light of the woman's song and voice:

> As he opens the door and Hanby passes out, a woman, miles down the valley, begins to sing. Her song is a spark that travels swiftly to the near-by cabins. Like purple tallow flames, the songs jet up. They spread a ruddy haze over the heavens. The haze swings low. Now the whole countryside is a soft chorus. (96)

The link between her song and the land of the South reveals the narrator's and all of the men's need for women to provide a physical, earthly connection to southern culture. In a similar way, music links another woman with both the Georgia countryside and Halsey's idealized notions of love:

> I used t love that girl. Yassur. An sometimes when the moon is thick an I hear dogs up th. valley barkin an some old woman fetches out her song, an

the winds seem like th Lord made them fer t fetch an carry th smell o pine an
cane, an there aint no big job on foot, I sometimes get t thinkin that I still do.
(108)

The song and the landscape trigger Halsey's thoughts of a former lover,
but his memories do not recall a tangible, real woman. She remains unnamed because Halsey needs to see her symbolically. As these examples
suggest, this type of nostalgic yearning for a romanticized past prevents
men from forming lasting relationships with women.

Kabnis also wants to see women as embodying Southern and African
mythology, but Stella's and Cora's roles as both prostitutes and mothers
undermine this interpretation: "[The girls] are two princesses in Africa
going through the early-morning ablutions of their pagan prayers. Finished, they come forward to stretch their hands and warm them over the
glowing coals. Red dusk of a Georgia sunset, their heavy, coal-lit faces"
(112). At some level, Kabnis recognizes the incongruity between this image and their occupation as prostitutes, but even after Lewis comments on
this contradiction ("Cant hold them, can you? Master; slave. Soil; and the
overarching heavens. Dusk; dawn. They fight and bastardize you" (107)),
Kabnis looks at Stella with the hope that she (or some woman) will fill
this cultural void. She pulls back from his stare, however: "I aint got nothin
f y, mister. Taint no use t look at me" (107). By rejecting his gaze and his
notions of what she should represent, she exposes the futility of his search
for cultural communion through women. Cora and Stella also use maternal behavior to reject Kabnis' need to interpret them:

> Cora glides up, seats him, and then plumps herself down on his lap, squeez-
> ing his head into her breasts. Kabnis mutters. Tries to break loose. Curses.
> Cora almost stifles him. He goes limp and gives up. Cora toys with him. Ruf-
> fles his hair. Braids it. Parts it in the middle. Stella smiles contemptuously.
> And then a sudden anger sweeps her. She would like to lash Cora from the
> place. She'd like to take Kabnis to some distant pine grove and nurse and
> mother him." (110)[9]

As Cora shifts from being a sexual to a nurturing figure, she both sparks
Stella's maternal instincts and further enervates Kabnis.

In addition to the maternal roles that women assume in this work,
folksongs linked with motherhood also expose the need for gender equality in the black community. Several songs appear throughout the play (the
sleep-song asking for a child, the womb-song, the birth-song) that call for
community between men and women on both social and spiritual levels.

In Act One, the wind song framing this section reinforces Kabnis' feelings of racial isolation: "White man's land./ Niggers, sing" (85). In the middle of this Act, however, the sleep-song of the white winds, an African-American version of "rock a-by baby," suggests a solution: "Her breath hums through pine-cones./ cradle will fall …/ Teat moon-children at your breasts,/ down will come baby …/ Black mother" (82). Kabnis' isolation is reinforced, in part, by a racial divide in the United States, and this "sleep-song" presents fertility and interracial marriage as a way to bridge this gap: "Black mother sways, holding a white child on her bosom" (82).

At the beginning of Act Five, the same song that began the play now suggests the possible end of isolation through community: "Night throbs a womb-song to the South. […] Night's womb-song sets them singing. Night winds are the breathing of the unborn child whose calm throbbing in the belly of a Negress sets them somnolently singing. Hear their song. White man's land./ Niggers, sing" (103). This song sings of the black community's hope for equality in white America, but Toomer shows that equality needs to occur first between black men and women. In the final act, Kabnis refers to Carrie K, who calls all of the men in town "brother," as his "dear sweet little sister" (114). By labeling each other "brother" and "sister," their rapport suggests a platonic relationship that has the potential to exist on equal terms. Even though the final birth-song casts Carrie K as a mother figure for Kabnis, suggesting his need for her to mitigate his spiritual isolation, he finds some hope in this new-found relationship with her: "The sun arises. Gold-glowing child, it steps into the sky and sends a birth-song slanting down gray dust streets and sleepy windows of the southern town" (116). The birth imagery suggests Kabnis' willingness to reconnect with this community.

Love Songs

Through the poetry-songs in *Cane*, Toomer also explores the ways black men use women's bodies to reestablish a relationship with black Southern history and culture. The three love songs ("Face," "Evening Song," and "Her Lips Are Like Copper Wires,"), which examine male/female relationships, provide a thematic context that links his poetry with the rest of the work. As in the short fiction, black men silence women through their actions and idealizations, but this "silencing" often becomes a way for women to frustrate male attempts to control their identity. In the poem "Face," for example, the narrator gains interpretive control by excluding the woman's mouth from his portrait.

Hair—
silver-gray,
like streams of stars,
Brows—
recurved canoes
quivered by the ripples blown by pain,
Her eyes—
mist of tears
condensing on the flesh below
And her channeled muscles
are cluster grapes of sorrow
purple in the evening sun
nearly ripe for worms. (8)

As Laura Doyle points out in *Bordering on the Body*, "'Face' characterizes a woman according to her individual body parts, in the tradition of the blazon, but it implicitly critiques that tradition by reading the woman's experience of pain rather than the male viewer's perception of beauty in the woman's body" (86). The exclusion of the woman's mouth, however, also distinguishes Toomer's blazon from its Petrarchan and Elizabethan models—consider, for example, John Donne's "The Autumnal" Elegy, Edmund Spenser's "Ye tradeful Merchants, that with weary toyle,"[10] or William Shakespeare's parody of this convention "My mistress" eyes are nothing like the sun." By removing her mouth from this catalogue, the speaker of Toomer's poem chooses to read a silent, voiceless face as a map for the rural South and its history. Since no dialogue exists between them, silence allows the narrator to interpret her from a safe distance— where seemingly no resistance can occur. Like "Karintha" and "Becky," "Face" presents a woman who has been engulfed by the narrator's perceptions and the countryside he needs her to represent. He specifically uses archaic imagery, such as the "recurved canoes," to recall either early American or early African history. This imagery tells of a historical past filled with pain for African-American women in particular, whose stories have been silenced by male interpretation and objectification.

Another blazon, "Portrait in Georgia," appears in section one, and this poem describes the burned body of a woman who has been lynched. Through this poetic form, the speaker uses her body to depict one of the horrifying consequences of slavery for black Americans in the late nineteenth and early twentieth centuries:

Hair—braided chestnut,
          coiled like a lyncher's rope,

> Eyes—fagots,
> Lips—old scars, or the first red blisters,
> Breath—the last sweet scent of cane,
> And her slim body, white as the ash
>   of black flesh after flame. (27)

Given the comparatively small number of female lynching victims during this period, we should question the motives behind the speaker's choice to describe a woman. In *Exorcising Blackness*, Trudier Harris explains that "between 1882 and 1927, an estimated 4,951 persons were lynched in the United States. Of that number, 3513 were black and 76 of those were black women" (7). By selecting a woman's body for this portrait, the narrator, like other male narrators throughout *Cane*, invites the reader to look at her body as a way of reading black, Southern history. Her lips, for example, represent the scars and blisters that mark the bodies of those who have been tortured or killed as slaves, and, as a result, her lips ("old scars") and breath ("the last sweet scent of cane") become symbols for these African-American experiences in Georgia.

Like Toomer's use of the blazon in "Face" and "Portrait of Georgia," he also draws on imagery commonly found in Renaissance poetry to criticize black men's stereotypical perceptions of women in "Evening Song." The image of the moon and the word "charm," for example, are traditionally associated with women in Renaissance love poetry, and, by associating these images with Cloine, Toomer reveals how the narrator attempts to associate her with an idealized Southern past. In this song, he presents the moon, which rises "on the waters of his heart," as making her the object of its gaze ("Promises of slumber leaving shore to charm the moon, [...] Cloine sleeps" (19)), thus aligning nature's perception of women with his own—both see her as an object. Yet, at some level, he realizes that his connection is artificial compared with Cloine, who lies "curled like the sleepy waters where the moon-waves start." Like the parallels he makes between his heart and the landscape ("Full moon rising on the waters of my heart,/ Lakes and moon and fires"), the speaker, like the narrator of Fern, desperately tries to become part of what he perceives to be a woman's "natural" connection to the land.

Interestingly, the speaker of "Evening Song" only describes one part of Cloine's body—her lips, and, after she falls asleep, her closed lips can be read as a metaphor for the barriers black men create between themselves and black women in *Cane*. At the end of the first stanza, Cloine is

still "holding her lips apart," but, once she has fallen asleep, the narrator
has her "lips pressed against [his] heart." He holds her face against his
chest and closes her mouth in a gesture that reveals his desire to circum-
vent her ability for self-expression. Her loss of consciousness through sleep
also gives him the power to interpret and objectify her body without being
seen. The narrator's imagined control comes from his position to watch
her unobserved. At the same time, he only sees her physical beauty ("Radiant, resplendently she gleams") and eventually realizes that his access
to her is limited. Her loss of consciousness, like Fern's and Avey's, undermines his attempts at objectification because sleep provides her with an
outlet for escape.

In section two of *Cane*, another love song appears, "Her Lips Are
Copper Wires," and, as in the previous love songs, the imagery reveals the
narrator's inability to control and connect with women. The final stanza
contains one of the most disturbing images of a silenced woman in the entire work: "then with your tongue remove the tape/ and press your lips to
mine." This description of her taped lips—an image of being bound forcefully—illustrates one of the ways the narrator has reduced and sectionalized
her body; it is the only part of her that he describes. The poem's use of an
urban landscape, such as the yellow globes of the street lamps, also suggests the speaker's desire to gain power over this woman. When he makes
an analogy between the street lamps and his own eyes, which give him the
power to gaze on the objectified woman, he, like the narrator of "Evening
Song," links himself with the "natural" environment of his surroundings.
In the second stanza, he tells her to let her "breath be moist against me/
like bright beads on yellow globes," and, through this image, the speaker
becomes a panoptic light from the street lamps. For him, seeing becomes
an attempt at controlling. After becoming one of the glowing lamp posts,
his desire to fuse with her reveals his need for her—she is like an electric
wire that can recharge him:

> and let your breath be moist against me
> like bright beads on yellow globes
>
> telephone the power-house
> that the main wires are insulate [...]
>
> then with your tongue remove the tape
> and press your lips to mine
> till they are incandescent (54)

Like the male narrators in the short fiction, however, he cannot make a connection: "the main wires are insulate." Toomer associates him with the city landscape (where communication happens over telephone wires) to suggest that the artificiality of urbanization and technology contributes to the barriers existing between black men and women.

Toomer also uses particular stylistic techniques in this poem to depict the restrictions men create for women in the black community. The speaker's use of second person places a formal distance between himself and the woman he is addressing: "and let your breath be moist against me [...] remove the tape/and press your lips to mine." As a matter of fact, in all of these love songs no dialogue occurs—the men only describe and command. The speaker of "Her Lips Are Copper Wires" not only keeps this woman in a subordinate position through language (commands), but by using parenthesis, he also traps her song and words literally and poetically in the third and fourth stanza:

> that the main wires are insulate
> (her words play softly up and down
> dewy corridors of billboards)

Like musical scales, which begin and return to the same place, her words "play softly up and down" within a corridor of billboards; thus, the city landscape—which has been linked with the male narrator—literally traps her words. As a result, Toomer not only portrays the way society restricts her, but he also depicts the word "insulate."

Coda

Throughout *Cane*, black men, in their search for a tangible connection to the past, have idealized, isolated, and subjugated women in ways that further isolate them from both past and present. As we have seen, black men use the folksongs of women both to reify a romanticized Southern and African past and to construct three restrictive identities for women—virgin, prostitute, and mother. Since black men need to interpret the folksongs of women as symbols for African-American culture, they want women to embody a rural Southern life and, as a result, try to place characters like Fern, Avey, and Cloine into two or more of these categories simultaneously. In their desperate attempts to access the cultural, historical, and spiritual heritage that folksongs conjure up, they objectify black women and ultimately create an inequality in the black community that prevents

successful heterosexual relationships. As a result, folksongs, which traditionally act as a liberating force in African-American literature, enslave
the women of Sempter.

Black men, such as Kabnis, Dan, and the narrator of Avey, have moved
North both to flee racial oppression and to enter into the American middle
class, but, like the image of the black bees in "Beehive," these men lose
something after moving into white communities. Aware of these losses—
cultural, historical, spiritual—black men nostalgically turn to folk traditions
as a way of regaining their black, Southern identity. In their attempts to
idealize these traditions and reestablish some cultural connection, they sub-
jugate and silence women. Dan Moore's description of the portly Negress
offers a clear example of this: "He shrivels close beside a portly Negress
whose huge rolls of flesh meet about the bones of the seat-arms. [...]
Through the cement floor her strong roots sink down. [...] Her strong roots
sink down and spread under the river and disappear in blood-lines that
waver south" (62). Like so many other descriptions of women throughout
Cane, her body—not her individual identity—becomes the mechanism for
cultural communion. Ironically, in Cane, the power of folksongs to unite
communities ultimately fractures them. As black men continue to create
unrealistic and oppressive identities for women, they have made these
women outcasts in their own communities—a situation which parallels
black men's condition in white, middle-class America.

In order to escape the labels and objectifications of men, women co-
opt the male gaze and invert male/female power structures (particularly
through silence) in the hope of maintaining their own sense of identity.
Within the text, the tension this struggle creates keeps African Americans
in a position of social and emotional paralysis; thus, folksongs expose their
need, in this early twentieth-century work, to reestablish a meaningful,
supportive community that will allow both black women and black men to
grow into a viable future.

Thomas Fahy

Notes

1. As Bernard Bell explains, "the frustration of coping with an alien urban environment and industrial society encouraged many transplanted black Southerners
   to cling tenaciously to their folk roots" (94).

2. "In Three Enigmas: Karintha, Becky, and Carma," William Dutch argues that "the basic structural pattern in the three character sketches is a prose story enclosed in a frame. The frame is a stanza that summarizes the story or sets the mood for the story that follows" (265). By viewing these "stanzas" strictly in terms of summary, Dutch ignores their significance as folksongs, as well as the role such songs play in the tragedies of Karintha and Becky.

3. Rudolph Byrd explains that "Karintha, after several marriages, gives birth to a child and leaves it to die. [...] Karintha feels nothing for the child she leaves to die in the forest, because experience has taught her that life, particularly female life, is neither sacred nor meaningful" (27).

4. In "The Spectatorial Artist and the Structure of *Cane*," Susan Blake discusses the other ways men limit Karintha. "By regarding her as a prostitute, the men who desire Karintha limit her to an existence defined by the tangible, measurable quantities of body and money" (197).

5. Toomer, Jean. Letters to Waldo Frank. *Cane*. Ed. Darwin T. Turner. New York: W.W. Norton and Company, 1988. 151.

6. In "Jean Toomer's 'Box Seat': The Possibility for 'Constructive Crisises,'" Elizabeth Schultz argues that by feminizing houses and associating masculine qualities with the street "Toomer imagines a communion between sexual opposites, psychological opposites, and class opposites" (299). In the context of Dan's singing, however, I disagree with this assertion and her later argument that since "he nevertheless remembers his roots ... he does not suffer the disease of disassociated sensibilities as do other urbanites in *Cane*" (300). Disassociated as he is from both rural (South) and urban (North) worlds, the memory of these roots seems to mark a painful absence in his life.

7. When Mrs. Pribby answers the door, she says: "Please, you might break the glass—the bell—oh, Mr. Moore! I thought it *must* be some stranger" (57).

8. As Susan Blake asserts, "although [men] seek personal wholeness through sexual union, the conflict is clearly within the men; the women merely represent a part of life or themselves that the men cannot accept without first changing, analyzing, or idealizing, and as a consequence always lose" (203).

9. In relation to Kabnis, many references to mothering occur. Earlier in the play, Lewis "wonders what Kabnis could do for [Carrie K.]. What she could do for him. Mother him" (103).

10. In this Spenser sonnet, for example, he gives the following catalogue of his love's physical attributes: "For loe my loue doth in her selfe containe/All this worlds riches that may farre be found: If Saphyres, loe her eies be saphyres plaine;/ If Rubies, loe hir lips be Rubies sounds;/ If Pearles, hir teeth be pearles both pure and round;" (from Amoretti and Epithalamion 1595).

Works Cited

Baker, Jr., Houston A. *Singers of Daybreak: Studies in Black American Literature*. Washington, D.C.: Howard UP, 1974.

Bell, Bernard. "A Key to the Poems in *Cane*," *Jean Toomer: A Critical Evaluation*. Ed. Therman B. O'Daniel. Washington, D.C.: Howard UP, 1988.

Bell, Derrick. "The Race-Charged Relationship of Black Men and Black Women." *Constructing Masculinity*. Ed. Maurice Berger, et al. New York: Routledge, 1995.

Blake, Susan. "The Spectatorial Artist and the Structure of *Cane*." *Jean Toomer: A Critical*.

Byrd, Rudolph P. *Jean Toomer's Years with Gurdjieff: Portrait of an Artist 1923–1936*. Athens: University of Georgia Press, 1990.

Douglass, Frederick. *Narrative of the Life of Frederick Douglass*. Ed. Henry Louis Gates Jr. *The Classic Slave Narratives*. New York: Penguin Books, 1987.

Doyle, Laura. *Bordering on the Body: The Racial Matrix of Modern Fiction and Culture*. Oxford: Oxford University Press, 1994.

Dutch, William. "In Three Enigmas: Karintha, Becky, and Carma." *Jean Toomer: A Critical valuation*. Ed. Therman B. O'Daniel. Washington, D.C.: Howard UP, 1988.

Foley, Barbara. "Jean Toomer's Sparta." *American Literature*. 67.4 (1995): 747–75.

Foucault, Michel. *Discipline and Punish: The Birth of the Prison*. Trans. Alan Sheridan. New York: Vintage, 1979.

Harris, Trudier. *Exorcising Blackness: Historical and Literary Lynching and Burning Rituals*. Indiana: Indiana University Press, 1984.

Mackey, Nathaniel. "Sound and Sentiment, Sound and Symbol." *Callaloo: A Journal of Afro-American and African Arts and Letters*. 10.1 (1987): 29–54.

Schultz, Elizabeth. "Jean Toomer's 'Box Seat': The Possibility for 'Constructive Crisises.'" *Jean Toomer: A Critical Evaluation*. Ed. Therman B. O'Daniel. Washington, D.C.: Howard UP, 1988.

Sedgwick, Eve Kosofsky. *Epistemology of the Closet*. Berkeley: University of California, 1990.

Steele, Shelby. *The Content of Our Character*. New York: St. Martin's Press, 1990.

Toomer, Jean. *Cane*. Ed. Darwin T. Turner. New York: Liverlight, 1975—Letter to Waldo Frank. *Cane*. Ed. Darwin T. Turner. New York: W.W. Norton and Company, 1988.

Turner, Darwin T. "Introduction." *Cane*. New York: Liverlight, 1975.

Wagner-Martin, Linda. "Toomer's *Cane* as Narrative Sequence." *Modern American Short Story Sequences: Composite Fictions and Fictive Communities*. Ed. J. Gerald Kennedy. Cambridge: Cambridge University Press, 1995.

Waugh, Patricia. *Practising Postmodernism Reading Modernism*. London: Edward Arnold, 1992.

Whyde, Janet. "Mediating Forms: Narrating the Body in Jean Toomer's *Cane*." *Southern Literary Journal*. 26.1 (1993): 42–53.

4

Samuel Beckett's *Ping* and Serialist Music Technique

Samuel Beckett's odd and strangely emotional short work, *Ping* (1966), is characterized by a form of language that is governed almost entirely by what musicologists and linguists alike might call the "statistical arrangement of events." The development and application of this notion appeared first in the music of serialist composers in the 1950s, most notably Boulez, Cage, and Stockhausen, among others. Karlheinz Stockhausen argued, for example, that electronically controlled manipulations of multiple sounds produced an entirely new form of musical design and performance. A pioneer in the innovative uses of physical space, chance or open forms in composition, "intuitive" music, and other aesthetic and philosophical developments, Stockhausen generated new discussions on the nature of identity and intuition and their relation to music.

Pierre Boulez likewise is very much involved with the significance and impact of personal statement, with the performance as a mode arising out of an invented and seemingly open and flexible material which is, however, realizing and revealing a hard strategy underneath—a ground plan, a path, a map that is in itself a rational, poetic realization of the relationship between the acts of creating and performing, as well as experiencing, a work of art.

At play in Samuel Beckett's *Ping* is a harmonic language characterized by melodic elements that embody musical concepts similar to those of Stockhausen and Boulez. Particularly notable is how the voicing, vanishing subject expresses emotions that are unconventional in terms of ordinary human feeling. The emphasis is on structure, formalized patterns, artifice, and the undercutting of pathos. There is no doubt that Beckett's use of repetition and the re-combination of words and phrases reflect some of the same patterns found in serialist music. Essentially, serialism denotes a musical work in which linear succession, articulation, harmony, and duration (including rhythm and tempo) are strictly derived from a single, all-inclusive principle. A row of musical notes becomes a "set" of values and relationships, strictly defined not only in terms of structure but also of process. Thus the actual unfolding of the piece is a process of permutation within which all these potential relationships are revealed (Salzman 146). So, Beckett's seemingly scattered or "spastic" language is a deliberately processed and permuted system used to establish a value system between a physical environment and repeated sounds and then to register its effect on a subject's emotions. In a world of featureless white, the nameless subject in *Ping* is subjected to intrusions of sound in a confined enclosure and responds with memories of an uncertain past. In addition, he experiences doubt as to the validity of his identity.

The subject's sense of disorientation arises from the text's syntax and overall structure as well: Beckett breaks down the basic sentence or phrase structure and in this way moves toward a musically complex pattern of unfixed, or random frequency, content. The highly specified dimension of the cube ("one square yard") indicates that Beckett assigns importance to structures and their boundaries. The narrative voice painstakingly strives to describe every detail of the structure as well. The words "light," "heat," and "white" recur like the electronically generated sounds associated with the music of Stockhausen or Cage, or perhaps even related to the pulse of contemporary techno. In serialist music, it is the isolated sounds themselves that form the essential experience, just as it is in *Ping*. In many post-Cageian works, for example, a set of activities regulates a set of limitations. Instead of being conceived as sound, a work may be based on visual definitions, ideas of non-sound or silence. Instead of defining time, a piece may be defined by the random passage of time. Instead of a definable identity, there are conceptions whose essence is lack of identity. In *Ping*, the ranges of light and heat serve as a sort of metaphoric diapason for the image of the subject's beating heart as it parallels the two- and three-syllable words that break the steady one-syllable pulse of the seemingly randomly generated "pings."

In this manner, the inner articulations of *Ping* are structured by units of thought that are reduced to short phrases, partitioned by periods, and repeated and combined in new ways. These strands of expression concern the thoughts of a being that gradually realizes that he is perhaps not alone. In this work the subject's identity is reduced to a textual partnership of a memory with a single visual image: "eye black and white half closed long lashes imploring" (71). This all-perceiving, panoptic eye does not communicate; but more importantly, the pings that bounce off the walls of the confined cube provide a musical companion for the "bare white body" (69). Text and echoes thus form the serial, musical sequence that permeates, indeed constitutes, *Ping*.

The seventy lines of *Ping* contain some of Beckett's most exacting experiments in rhythm. *Ping* is the most complex of a series of similar works that include *All Strange Away* (1963–4) and *Imagination Dead Imagine* (1965). Each consists of a cumulative set of variations on a theme stated at the beginning of each section. This theme is then superimposed on its predecessor until the piece comes to an abrupt halt at its most intricate point. As a writer, Beckett has always worked assiduously with rhythm, essentially believing that the heart of rhythm is change and division. To study change and division is to study Time. Time—measured, relative, physiological and psychological—is divided in myriad ways, the most immediate of which is the perpetual transition of the future into the past. Beckett draws in other ways on music's repetitive and recursive character, observes H. Porter Abbott. "Especially in the later texts," Abbott notes, "his language seems to listen to the sounds it makes, independent of meaning, and then to redistribute them in new combinations" (18). Several questions thus arise: Does the work's title refer to a "character" known as Ping? Does it indicate an acoustic sound and echo? Does it indicate the name of the text? Or is *Ping* a "score" that plays on a theme of echo and variation? Beckett leaves these questions open-ended.

In such a world of fragments, an intermittent chaos of messages, shifting about in space, is transmitted from all angles. The pings seem to be musical "objects" emitted in order to be heard, but they do not have absolute relations to each other. Rather, the play of chance rather than logical perspective governs the relations of these linguistic objects to each other. In his classic text, *Orientations*, Boulez comments on differing types of logic:

> [G]rammatical associative logic makes it difficult for words to be interchanged without a phrase losing part of all of its meaning.... In music, on the other hand, the logic of construction is less rigorously limited in validity: the non-significance and non-direction of the musical object in its primitive state make it usable in structured organisms, in accordance with formal principles much less restricted than those that obtain in the case of words. (148)

In place of a logical fictional world, there is only an omnipresent eye
that dominates *Ping*. Instead of a story, there is only a struggle—depicted
in observations and repeated sounds. One could put forth the premise
that there is a closer relation between hearing and emotional arousal than
there is between seeing and emotional arousal. A dark world is frightening, but a silent world is even more terrifying. Is no one there, nothing going on at all? Beckett seems to suggest that at an emotional level, there is
something deeper about hearing than seeing. Silence, of course, as he
himself has made piercingly clear throughout his *oeuvre*, can sound depths
that words cannot.

With *Ping*, Beckett has etched a personage without a body, almost
surrealistic, unforgettable—and supernatural. The work is characteristic of
Beckett's compositional practice in which ideas are assembled in superimposed and juxtaposed complexes, producing dynamic contrasts of color
and rhythm rather than the organic development one associates with a
traditional story or novel. Yet how does Beckett's formula pertain to musical form? Again, we can turn to Boulez, who writes: "It is not only the
question 'what is a sound made of?' that we have to answer, but the much
harder one of 'how do we perceive this sound in relation to its constituent
elements?' So that by juxtaposing what is known with what is not known,
and what is possible with what will be possible, we shall establish a geography of the sound universe." (492)

For example, when Boulez read the poems of Mallarmé, he observed
a connection between words and music. Struck by their appearance on
the page, their actual typographical presentation, Boulez came to realize
that this formed an essential part of a new form of art. When he read of
the poet's idea of a "spaced reading," he understood that the paper itself
intervened whenever an image recurs or gives way to other images. "It is
not a question of regular musical features or lines," Mallarmé insisted,
but rather of "subdivisions of the Idea, the moment of their appearance
and their duration in association in their respective spiritual settings—the
text imposes itself at varying points close to, or far from, the latent live
wire, according to probability" (Boulez 146). This then offered Boulez a
new way of composing. He realized that such formal, visual, and physical
presentations of a poem suggested the idea of finding equivalents in music.

This interconnection of words and music is at work in the physical
presentation of *Ping*. The work has no real incidences, no plot, no climax,
and no true end. Also, there is no paragraphing, no organized sentences

with a subject, a verb and an object. Phrases are introduced at random, consisting of non-related "items": heat, light, dimension, the situation of body parts within an isolated physical space, and internal commentary. Into this enclosure are added the intermittent "pings" that provoke a chain of discomforting memories in the subject.

Ambiguity and uncertainty are at work in *Ping* at all levels. The subject responds to the erratic pings in an almost aggressive manner, but in addition, and perhaps to explain why he revolts in this environment, the scars and the "flesh torn of old" (71) suggest that he has suffered. Wondering perhaps if he is not alone, he searches for a way out. He confronts his detached and nearly figureless self and is transformed to a functional one—a bodily dimension that experiences depersonalization as though to say, "I wonder that I have lived a life without air, not enough oxygen, or light." Since the subject has no clear image of himself, he is something incomplete. Collapsing under the burden of constant questioning and repetition, he is unable to inscribe messages linguistically. Governed entirely by sound, he communicates differentially; that is, he reacts emotionally to the quantitative differences of the pings, their echoes, and their permutations on his body and discerns his identity via this indecipherable logic.

The first three phrases in *Ping*—"all known," "all white," and "bare white body"—express the opening theme of the text that constitutes a melodic order that is then subjected to a series of deductive inferences. Concurrently, this melodic order of words is constantly undermined by the intervention of the uncertainty principle. The phrases are irregular, and the wistful opening of a small figure whose legs are bound together is repeated with an unusual insistence. There is something inscrutable about a work that projects a strangely ominous quality from the outset. With the entrance of the "eye black and white half closed" (71), which later ventures in unannounced, the subject perceives a threatening element that has worked its way into the cube. Here one notes the similarity to Stockhausen's conceptualizations of conflict and opposition. The black and white eye is starkly different from the subject's eyes, which are described throughout the work at regular intervals as "holes light blue" (70).

As a musical score, *Ping* weaves together many kinds of sounds. The first third is rich in musical variety as it meditates on space—the figure's environment, and the subsidiary theme of sound—the murmurs. There is a subtle blend of tempos as well. Indeed, time is a major force and the slightly metronomic aspect of the pings and the murmurs suggests that they may also be understood as a symbol of fate. In fact, it is when the figure realizes that "all known" is also "never seen" that he begins his move towards a tentative surrender. As a result, it is hard to avoid the conclusion that the nuances of the subject's disorientation have their counterpart in his uncertainty over the role of a penetrating eye that "implores" even as it looms over him as an object of menace. With the intrusion of the eye, we find the sinister elements of the work—the elements of pain and fright. This part of the text stands in dark and violent contrast to the preceding two-thirds of the work which are given over to questions concerning the subject's identity, brief descriptions of his body, and the pings and murmurs. The eye is a great reminder of something from the subject's past that conjures up guilt and seems to be the source of his imprisonment. In this way, too, the emotions of depersonalization and intuitive knowledge are paradoxically compatible, sharing a tone that tends to balance sentimentality with more troubling and painful visions. Yet what we are left with is no sense of conclusion.

In musical terms, the notion of inconclusiveness is known as indeterminacy. It is the absence of specific instructions concerning the various elements of a composition. A mobile piece is unspecific in terms of the order of sections; a graphic score is indeterminate in notation or timing. In spite of their seeming opposition, serialism and indeterminacy have certain things in common. Both come out of philosophical attitudes about music and art—serialism contemplating the activity of the mind and its internal order, in Western determinist style; indeterminacy contemplating an Eastern-influenced philosophy of activity in the indifferent external world. Partly as a result of Cage's influence, Stockhausen experimented with "musical events" rather than formulating notes in a pattern. Then his habit of working with sound as a substance led to a period of virtual concentration on electronic pieces which gradually relinquished notation to the point where many pieces consisted only of prose poems designed to stimulate intuitive music-making.

Written when Beckett was 61, *Ping* is a work that goes against the grain. What appears as a kind of long prose poem turns into a work of great mystery and astonishing profundity, concluding with a double fugue in which the themes of doubt and acquiescence are repeated. A work of seventy semantic units, the opening is riddled with a series of grace notes, as it were, turning on the words "light," "heat," "white," and "body." In tone, the pulsating rhythm recalls a kind of march, with aspects simultaneously military and funereal. Repetitions and physical displacements everywhere abound. The core of this work lies in its emphasis on the dialectic of alternations: of body and its surroundings, of memory and meaning. That the murmurs and the eye are present suggests that the figure perhaps indeed is not alone, that there is a way out of this predicament, and that he does have an identity, a nature and a meaning.

But in place of a hero in the normal sense, we see a paradoxical figure whose environment seems to telescope his body and meaning into a single hieroglyphic effect of the cube's structure. Frederic Jameson has noted in a study on aggression that a character's **thoughts** can be fitful yet "significant characters in their own right" (49). What Jameson means is that what would seem to be a single unified character with a proper name can be an uneasy plurality of functions, a structural coexistence rather than an organic substance or "identity" (49–50). Certainly the subject in *Ping* lacks the external matter necessary to constitute him as a full subject, and he coexists reciprocally with the pings.

Ping thus forces readers to attend to a linguistic form in which a non-traditional, musical representation of a narrative text undermines the traditional, humanist notion of identity and cracks open the illusion of an autonomous, centered "self." When, in the first bars we read, "Bare white body fixed" counterpoised with "Traces blurs signs no meaning," we might be convinced that the body is a meaningless blur. But when the human traits—the scars, eyes, hands, legs, hair, and emotion—dissolve into sound, we might be more inclined to understand how the repetition of the pings paradoxically reconstruct the self even where there is no longer an apparent self. The bodily details, his nakedness in particular, make this immediately clear. The echoes become a means for the subject to re-articulate himself, and the oscillating pings and murmurs harness the subject's inner self to the outer one. This is seen in the other recurring phrases: "perhaps a way out," "perhaps a nature," "perhaps a meaning."

In his lecture, "Intuitive Music," Stockhausen asks: "When I say, I am thinking—who is saying this? ... One is not identified with the brain, but with the thinking activity, and that activity, the thinking activity, is ... responsible to a higher self" (Maconie 1). Stockhausen believed that Bach, Beethoven, and Stravinsky recognized the supremacy of intuition, based on the quality of the composer being a medium. Although the biochemical structure of *Ping* and its clever geometrical constructs reveal a nearly lifeless scene with minimal traces of active existence, the traces of human passion and intuition are present. When the "long lashes" of the observing eye implore, Beckett's friction against total failure for even the merest of vanishing selves becomes apparent. It is the subject's uneventful fate that finally helps him intuitively come to terms with his existence.

At the work's beginning, it is announced to the subject in his augury of innocence: "All known all white bare white body fixed one yard legs joined like sewn." Gradually, the figure begins to see the truth of his existence in the cube. Given a choice between two different types of philosophical argument, one based on analytical logic, devoted to resolving contradiction, the other on a dialectical approach, accepting of contradiction, the subject chooses the dialectical approach. At last he realizes that the pings bring other pings into the cube, and that his summoning of memory is an attempt to rectify his earlier misgivings about the possibility of finding a way out of the cube. The subject concludes that his fumblings and the pings are the only way he has of signaling to an other. As with the return echo, which symbolizes the necessary Other, it is the sound of the echo itself that signals the possibility for his own recovery or his will to continue. In this regard *Ping* espouses the Eastern philosophical approach.

One question remains: if language binds the outer self to the inner, then *Ping* must surely seem to be an autistic examination of identity, for no linguistic system seems to function very well in the cube. Where ideas of light and sound lurk, the central characteristic lies in its slow, unyielding tempo—and so its sense of an inexorable clock—against which the musical gestures of the pings propose more fluid and human ways of telling time. These musical gestures emerge under conditions of extremity, even panic, which is then dramatically expressed, but the pressures of the pings are so severe that they stifle any sound that the subject might make in response to them. These sounds are centered on precision, acting with maximum intensity and immediacy and resonating at the edge of silence, or rather, at the boundary where the barely audible draws the keenest attention. They do not "speak" to the subject. Rather, they suggest the sounds of breathing, of panting and of heartbeats. Consequently, the text is on the verge of being sound effect, but the pings are so rigidly sounded with such frightening accuracy, they mean more. One might imagine that they are watching the subject in expectation, observing his body by surveillance, waiting to overtake it with the aid of the penetrating eye.

As the piece proceeds, the pings become more continuous and arrive at something like a fragment of music that the subject cannot get out of his head. They grow more disturbing with repetition and suggest finally in the last sentence a sound that the subject has been acquainted with all along: the bottled-in voice of his own self, no longer able to verbalize: "that much memory henceforth never"; "old ping last murmur ... ping silence ping over" (72). These unlikely, even preposterous, events are brought to imaginative life through the narrator's memory and are told in the accents of an individual voice, such accents heard in the remarks: "That much memory almost never"; "Ping murmur"; "ping silence." These are the ritual phrases produced by an insistent voice, emitted without fuss, and yet emotionally explosive, ruthlessly striving to be a direct, spoken expression. These moments are thematically linked to the premise out of which the piece is written—that memory is life and its lapsing a foretaste of death. The connection it bears to Beckett's other works is another example of the author's inventiveness, his ability to make memory linked to identity by connecting those images through the improvisations of a musical voice.

Since consciousness of one's identity has always been Beckett's essential subject, so too the end of the work reveals the subject's "mind" as becoming more uncertain of its own powers and virtue. Overwhelmed by the "unlustrous eye" (72), it expires—never finally—to a conclusion in which nothing is concluded, but is appropriate to the overall pitch and voice of this canny narrative framework. The terrain mapped out by *Ping* indeed lacerates and exposes a wound of memory, but the mechanisms of the echoes and repetitions are those very devices that compensate for loss and pain. The phrase "ping perhaps not alone one second with image always the same that much memory almost never ping silence" (70–1) is rephrased several times but in the intervals the reader's knowledge of the subject is enhanced. After a "ping" is sounded, brief descriptions of the subject's body follow, which suggests that there is a relationship between sound and the body. The head is "haught"; the legs and feet are "joined like sewn"; the eyes are blue and the hair is long and white. The ping is "elsewhere always there" (70) and yet its origin remains unknown.

The somewhat unnerving effect of the pings is a complex textual description of defamiliarization, in which the subject makes an acquaintance with panic and attempts to resolve his turmoil by concerning himself with trying to understand sound as language, language as sound, sound as content, and sound as musical structure. In this way *Ping* resembles the new music of the post-war composers who built their works from the simplest and barest of premises. The initial premises of Cage, Boulez and Stockhausen were the individual and isolated sound events. In the works of

Cage, for example, there is no clear line of distinction between his writings and his musical works. Eventually, he abandoned all rational control over many aspects of the musical event. He threw dice, used the *I Ching*, plotted charts on a piece of paper, and ultimately relinquished all activity, as with his famous *4'33"* for open piano and a silent performer. In Cage's later works, sounds are a series of unpredictable disturbances, just as the pings are noise and interference in Beckett's work.

One also could cite the linguist Daniel Vanderveken's comments on semantics as they relate to musical performativity and the coming to terms with one's identity. Vanderveken, like Stockhausen, observes that communication can be accomplished through "thought alone without any public use of language ..." (Vanderveken 56). Thus, for example, the subject in *Ping* can mentally conjecture that he in fact exists, or recommend to himself to be courageous, or express pain without uttering orally or writing any sentence, and sometimes without even having the slightest intention of communicating these thoughts to any other speaker.

Moreover, unlike speech acts, which are necessarily conscious, mental states can be either conscious or unconscious, according to Vanderveken (57). In this manner, Beckett can be said to employ the text itself as the subject's public speech acts, while the reader becomes the public hearer of his unconscious mental state. Further, the entrance of the penetrating eye becomes a public audience as well. These dual facets of the territory of language and memory, overlapping and in parallel, usher in the musical methods by which the subject determines his identity and they enable the reader to discover the subject's search for communication.

From another perspective, the so-called "nonsense" language in Stockhausen's collection known as *Licht* operates with obscurity, as do the echoes in *Ping*. In *Licht*, language is pulverized into fragments, affecting the balance of sense and sound. It used to be thought that syllables on their own had no meaning; now we understand that nonsense-talk has a fundamental layer of meaning related to its acoustic and gestural nature. This dimension of speech was of musical interest to Stockhausen. His higher purpose in playing with sounds was to reveal the process by which they acquire a musical meaning. In other words, meaning is not something that is here one moment and gone the next, but rather the shift from meaning to music is a gradual process the more the text is cut up. Even if a text is reshuffled word by word, something of its original meaning remains evident in the choice of vocabulary, the texture of words, and the ratio of short to long words, and so on. Stockhausen remarked that there were long stretches in his *Hymnen* where "[I] simply heard inside me while composing, and which I was unable to incorporate into the musical structure at the time I received them. They had to be 'inserted' into the preconceived design" (Maconie 2). The figure in *Ping* offers a similar pattern, discerning his surroundings piecemeal in order to arrive at the central point of the work: that his memory is a long forgotten knowledge. By the last line, the subject comes to feel less anxious about the pings and acquiesces to what is now beyond his reach: "old ping last murmur ... long lashes imploring ping silence ping over" (72).

The work of other psycholinguists, notably Van Dijk and Kintsch, may also help one to understand what is going on at the *deep* structure of *Ping*. They distinguish two different sorts of knowledge systems that are engaged in processing information: semantic memory and episodic memory. On the one hand, semantic memory consists of concepts interconnected by different kinds of associations. The interrelations of associations are of various sorts, such as cause-effect, or purpose-result, among others. On the other hand, episodic memory is arranged in a completely different manner. Episodes or events involving the subject in situations arising along temporal-spatial dimensions organize it in terms of the subject's lived experience. These situations, if built up from repeated experiences of similar events, become part of episodic memory, available there as "scripts" (303). This is particularly evident when the text engages itself in emotion and feeling, as it does in *Ping*.

The use of episodic memory, whether consciously applied or not, is one reason why the textual voice in *Ping* is so unexpectedly musical and moving. In the last sentence the reader gets the impression that he has heard a short operatic tragedy in which a subject strives to find meaning in the hand that fate has dealt him and loses the battle, but not without first having expended a tremendous amount of emotional energy. In *Ping*, Beckett writes as if mind, heart, body, eye and emotion were all fused with language, lending to the verbal sign an incontrovertible musical authority. Since all Beckett's writing is a form of erasure, the musical form in *Ping* is all the more critical and original.

Mary Catanzaro

Works Cited

Abbott, H. Porter. "Samuel Beckett and the Art of Time: Painting, Music, Narrative." *Samuel Beckett and the Arts: Music, Visual Arts, and Non-Print Media.* Ed. Lois Oppenheim. New York: Garland, 1999.

Beckett, Samuel. *Ping. First Love and Other Shorts.* New York: Grove, 1974.

Boulez, Pierre. *Orientations: Collected Writings.* Ed. Jean-Jaques Nattiez. Trans. Martin Cooper. Cambridge: Harvard UP, 1985.

Jameson, Fredric. "Agons of the Pseudo-couple." *Fables of Aggression: Wyndham Lewis, the Modernist as Fascist.* Berkeley: U California P, 1979.

Maconie, Robin. "Stockhausen Discussion Page." http://www.jimstonebraker.com/maconiefaq.html: 1–10. 27 March, 2000.

Salzman, Eric. *Twentieth-Century Music: An Introduction.* Englewood-Cliffs, NJ: Prentice-Hall, 1974.

Van Dijk, Teun A., and Walter Kintsch. *Strategies of Discourse Comprehension.* New York: Academic Press, 1983.

Vanderveken, Daniel. Mea*ning and Speech Acts. Principles of Language Use. Vol. I.* Oxford: Cambridge UP, 1990.

5

I Gotcha! Signifying and Music in Eudora Welty's "Powerhouse"

With its funky syncopations and smoky lyrics, jazz takes center stage in Eudora Welty's story, "Powerhouse." We almost hear the pounding beat of the piano, an upright bass, and a wailing horn. The character of Powerhouse seems larger than life as he improvises and wields words and music with flamboyant style. Jazz musicians, with their improvisational style, delight in experimenting with rhythm, lyrics, and tempo, whatever it takes to transpose traditional music into their own music. Powerhouse's resilience springs from the control he feels when on stage; in addition to determining which requests to play, he can also lead the band this way or that, depending on his mood. A daring performer, Powerhouse signifies as he leads his white and black audiences and readers with his improvisational music and stories.

In *The Signifying Monkey*, Henry Louis Gates Jr. uses the term "signifyin(g)" to represent the rhetorical strategies in which black speakers make non-native language their own; signifyin(g) promotes bonding and community and preserves a black heritage that spans several hundred years. The Signifying Monkey, a trickster figure, toys with language and audience to revise traditionally oppressive discourse. Geneva Smitherman argues that "through boastful talk, pungent rhymes, verbal repartee, and clever 'signifyin' (indirect language used to tease, admonish, or disparage), the rapper establishes himself or herself as a cultural hero solely on the basis of oral performance" (qtd. in Gates 104).

Signifyin(g) through indirection functions in two ways: it allows the speakers to even the playing field against their white, governing audience and it enables the speakers, who ordinarily have no voice, to engage in revisionary tactics for the benefit of themselves and their community. Gates states that

rhetorical naming by indirection is when one writer repeats another's structure by one of several means, including a fairly exact repetition of a given
narrative or rhetorical structure, filled incongruously with a ludicrous or in-
congruent context. (103)

Signifyin(g) tricksters do not operate in a vacuum; rather, in a defiant movement, they revise traditional narratives and dominant expectations with a
passion and ingenuity that escapes censure.

After seeing Fats Waller perform in Jackson one night, Welty went
home and wrote "Powerhouse" in one sitting, something she claimed she'd
never done before. Improvising a story shortly after experiencing a master
of improvisation, she writes:

> Everything I wrote is made up except the program itself and the impression it
> made on me, both hearing and seeing it.... But I was so excited by the eve-
> ning that I wrote it after I got home. And the next day when I woke up I said,
> 'How could I have had the nerve to do something like that?' but I did have
> the sense to know that there was no use in me trying to correct or revise any-
> thing. It was that or nothing, because it had to be written at that moment, or
> not at all. I could not have gone back over it and tried to shape it or do some-
> thing constructive like that. You know, I just left it. But that was a one time
> thing. (Prenshaw 328)

This is as close to performance as Welty can come. Although she later revised "Powerhouse" for *A Curtain of Green*, she did not immediately revise, thus mimicking the performance concept of "being in the moment."
She views the experience as a "one time thing" because, however inspired,
she can only mimic black "forms," not maintain them. Thus, in improvisation, a song or story differs with every telling; it is always a "one time
thing." Although she imitates a jazz musician's improvisation, Welty nods
to the difference between written and musical expression and only discusses jazz from a writer's standpoint. Yet, the vibrancy of "Powerhouse,"
attests to her skill in incorporating the form of jazz into her fiction.

"Powerhouse" reads unlike any other Welty story; it conveys a sense
of rhythm and movement that we generally associate with poetry or music. As Welty strings a single melody, the telegram riff, throughout the
story and changes the harmonies, different audience's responses, with each
movement, her efforts result in a dynamic and distinct final composition.
Loretta Lampkin argues that Welty pushes and pulls the reader through
"carefully selected tropes and schemes, all functioning in disjunctive, syncopated, and fragmented forms to create the illusion of changing, dou-

bling, and skipping beats—the illusion of jazz improvisation" (25). Indeed, both the plot and the language of this story display signs of jazz improvisation, from the start-stop action of the characters to the animated dialogue:

> his hands over the keys, he says sternly, 'You-all ready? You-all ready to do some serious walking?' waits then, STAMP. Quiet. STAMP, for the second time. This is absolute. Then a set of rhythmic kicks against the floor to communicate the tempo. Then, O Lord! say the distended eyes from beyond the boundary of the trumpets, Hello and good-bye, and they are all down the first note like a waterfall. (132)

Welty also moves her reader along a waterfall as she combines short and long sentences, sounds and visuals to make us feel like audience members observing an actual performance. Thomas Getz argues that "reading 'Powerhouse' is like listening to good jazz, and it is only the fact that we are reading that makes the simile necessary. Welty has listened closely to 'Fats' Waller's music, and her story is the expression of that act of listening" (41). Welty urges us to be effective listeners, to tune in to Powerhouse's jazz. Respectfully aware of the differences between her own skill and that of black musicians, Welty conflates the oral tradition of jazz with the written tradition of fiction.

Jazz, like signifyin(g), centers around orality and exemplifies music that blacks can claim both as their own distinctive voice, their discourse, and a representation of their heritage. Black musicians were interested in "jazz performance as a powerful metaphor for larger issues such as the historical experience of racism, group solidarity, the expression of intensely felt emotions, and the development of African-American culture" (Panish 96). Jazz breaks from tradition, from basic rhythm, lyrics, and tempo and moves toward syncopation and originality, in other words, toward distinctness and difference. Gates argues that in both blues and jazz, the musician makes musical phrases that are elastic, that

> stretch the form rather than articulate the form. Because the form is self-evident to the musician, both he and his well-trained audience are playing and listening with expectation. Signifyin(g) disappoints these expectations; caesuras, or breaks, achieve the same function. This form of disappointment creates a dialogue between what the listener expects and what the artist plays. (123)

The musician's ability to "stretch" rather than merely "articulate" the form suggests an inclination to revise, to take the known and make it new, unexpected, and nontraditional. Powerhouse, a consummate jazz musician, bends notes and changes keys on impulse and expects his audience to follow him. If they fail to comprehend, he contemptuously leaves them behind. Like Powerhouse, Welty wields her instrument, the pen, in her characteristic style; she uses the device of the unreliable narrator to guide and mislead us in order to help us to be the kind of audience both she and Powerhouse craves.

Welty's narrator differs from any other character in the story. An early typescript version of "Powerhouse" shows an entirely different narrator, one who used the derogatory rhetoric of bigotry. Welty changed the line, "he has big nigger feet size twelve" to "he has African feet of the greatest size" (131). She eliminated two references to "Jews" and replaced the words "niggers" and "niggertown" with "Negroes" and "Negrotown" (131–135). She may have made these revisions to make "Powerhouse" more palatable to readers, or she may have wanted her narrator to reflect a less prejudiced sensibility. Unlike any of Powerhouse's audiences, the narrator of the story reveals an openness toward and appreciation for Powerhouse and his music that invites our participation. Radiating excitement and naiveté, the narrator introduces Powerhouse: "Powerhouse is playing! He's here on tour from the city. 'Powerhouse and His Keyboard' 'Powerhouse and His Tasmanians' think of the things he calls himself!" (131). The narrator's final words make us aware of Powerhouse's difference, his magic:

> What is it? Listen. Remember how it was with the acrobats. Watch them carefully, hear the last word, especially what they say to one another, in another language—don't let them escape you; it's the only time for hallucination, the last time. They can't stay. They'll be somewhere else this time tomorrow. (132)

Aware that black musicians speak a different, exclusive language, this narrator encourages readers to open themselves to an alternative discourse that manifests itself in jazz and its signifying practices. We cannot articulate this otherness, but we can listen and celebrate. Meanwhile, black performers enjoy a distinctive voice, a riff on the dominant discourse of white society.

The stage acts as a powerful forum for black signification; not only are there back-up players to lend support, there are audience members just waiting for the trickster. No matter which stage Welty offers Powerhouse, he always speaks from a platform because that is the only place he may freely tell his stories. Performance, then, defines Powerhouse and shapes jazz. Jon Panish argues that

> performance is essential to jazz ... jazz emphasizes improvisation—invention during the act of performance—over either composition or reproducing a written score. Jazz is part of a cultural tradition in which live performance is central to the creation of music. (79)

The performative nature of jazz allows the musician a freedom and flexibility that, say, a recorded version of the same music does not. During a jazz performance the musician's improvisation asserts primacy over the written or recorded piece of music which in any other discourse would not hold true. Generally, the written word has a finality and unalterability that no speaker may challenge.

Powerhouse shapes his show by the audience's response; through his music, he responds with either disdain or interest. James Lincoln Collier notes that "most jazz musicians like to work in front of a live audience, especially a dancing audience. They get something from an audience that is reacting, that is involved with the music" (qtd. in Panish 80). Though a dancing audience may be ideal for the jazz musicians, they are often met with an empty dance floor. Powerhouse's white audience merely observes the band; they do not respond by calling out, encouraging, or applauding. They hardly dance, "only a few straggling jitterbugs and two elderly couples. Everybody just stands around the band and watches" (133). The performer essentially ignores and resists connecting with the audience. When audience members who, "laughing as if to hide a weakness ... sooner or later hand him up a written request" (132), Powerhouse translates the songs into his own language through the use of signals; he always shouts out a number, never a name to designate a song. When he makes a decision about a song, "a light slides under his eyelids, and he says '92!' or some combination of figures *never a name*" (emphasis mine 132). He needs no written song list, nor does he choose to call out the songs by name; he and his band mentally transpose a song to a number, a number to notes on a piano or bass. As the music begins, it "marks the end of any known discipline" (132).

Bored with his audience's requests, Powerhouse begins a telegram ad-lib or improvisation that continues through the rest of his evening. Welty makes this impromptu central to her story and connects Powerhouse with Waller, who was known for his skillful improvisation. She also draws parallels between Powerhouse who "has African feet of the greatest size" and Waller who wrote a song entitled "Your Feets Too Big." Richard Albert argues that "Waller's oral improvisations included altering the lyrics of popular songs, changing words and syllables here and three, and injecting humorous asides, frequently with sexual innuendo" (67). A master revisionist, Waller transformed popular music and made it his own. Morrow Berger notes that Waller changed lyrics like "you went to my head" to "you went to my cranium" or "you grabbed my knowledge pump" (7). Waller alters and elevates "your feets too big" by explaining, in his injured manner, "your pedal extremities are colossal" (Berger 7). Likewise, Powerhouse brushes off the "insipid love song," entitled "Pagan Love Song," which has lyrics like "come with me when moonbeams are high/like Tahitian skies and starlit waters linger in your eyes" by improvising a wild riff, a sordid story about his wife Gypsy, who goes splat on the sidewalk. Powerhouse groans, "you know what happened to me? … I got a telegram my wife is dead … Telegram say—"here the words: your wife is dead" (133). Whether Powerhouse's words are true or fabricated, the content of his story signals some loneliness within him, the loneliness of the traveling musician. According to Ralph Ellison, a "signifying riff" functions as a "melodic naming of a recurrent human situation … played to satirize some betrayal of faith or loss of love observed from the bandstand" (231). Powerhouse's story about his wife, however, goes beyond mere "loss of love."

Powerhouse's telegram rap dominates his performance and allows him a forum for his criticism. Within two lines of dialogue, Welty suggests the potency of the written word and alludes to Powerhouse's major grievance: Scoot asks him, "what name has it got signed, if you got a telegram," and Powerhouse replies, "Uranus Knockwood is the name signed" (134). His band member replies, "'why don't you hear it straight from your agent? Why it ain't come from headquarters? What you been doing, getting telegrams in the corridor, signed nobody?' They all laugh. End of that chorus" (134). Later, in the World Cafe, he conflates Uranus Knockwood to Bing Crosby by calling him a "no-good pussyfooted crooning creeper, that creeper that follow around after me, coming up like weeds behind me… bets my numbers, sings my songs" (138). By naming someone else, Uranus Knockwood, as the person who signs a telegram bringing him supposed news of terrible loss, Powerhouse suggests another level of narration to his story.

Through this telegram story, Welty responds to white musicians who were appropriating black music forms much to the frustration of black musicians. White musicians like Benny Goodman, known as "The King of Swing," and Paul Whiteman, known as "The King of Jazz," became famous by performing black musicians' songs (Adams 58). Timothy Adams argues that Waller's tune "Whiteman Stomp" "was a joke on not only Paul Whiteman, but on white man everywhere" (58). Adams goes on to say, "black innovators of blues and jazz naturally resented the appropriation and simplification of their music by whites" (58). Musicians like Waller or the fictional Powerhouse sought to undermine music of dominant society by creating music unique to their African heritage. They did so by revisionary tactics such as borrowing bits and pieces from childhood songs, family stories, and throwing neighborhood raps into traditional songs to transform the sound and meaning of lyrics or melodies. Powerhouse's telegram rap attempts to subvert the white lyrics of "Pagan Love Song" and, at the same time, ridicule white musicians.

Accompanied by the lolling notes resonating from the piano, this rap might sound like just another bewildering song to his unenthusiastic audience. His band, however, instantly absorbs the rap and follows his lead by asking questions and testifying at the appropriate times:

> "You know what happened to me?"
> Valentine hums a response...
> "I got a telegram my wife is dead."
> "Uh-huh?" (135)

Bearing witness to Powerhouse as if he were a preacher on a Sunday afternoon, the band members urge him on as part of the performance. While Scoot may question him or Little Brother soothe him by saying, "she wouldn't do that ... you ain't going to expect people doing what they says over long distance," they never call Powerhouse on the truth of his assertion (135). The band members recognize his rap as signifyin(g), and they play their appointed role as chorus members.

As Welty shifts Powerhouse and his band to another setting, she contrasts how the same story affects a black audience. Through Welty, Powerhouse performs for several disparate audiences: the white audience, the black audience, his band and the reader. Although his band acts as a chorus, he still entertains them. As he declares "it going to be intermission" and the band heads "down yonder where it say World Cafe," they merely change stages; now they will have a new crowd to dazzle. While he and his band expect to feel at home in Negrotown, they quickly discover that they are once again misfits.

The World Cafe, located in Negrotown, does not seem so different from the place the musicians have just left except for the evidence of dominant discourse. The inside of the cafe contains admonishing "Not Responsible" signs, calendars with black subjects, a phone labeled "Business Phone, Don't Keep Talking," and "circled phone numbers written up everywhere" (136). Earlier, through the white audience's written requests, Welty situates writing as the dominant form of discourse; here she splashes examples of written messages all over this black cafe. However, the humor behind the sign "Not Responsible" for what? and the telephone sign, "Don't Keep Talking" rather than typical instructions such as, "Please keep all calls to three minutes," suggests the black occupants' attempt to signify regardless of the white boundaries imposed on them. The writing in the World Cafe suggests restraint and rules, two notions that Powerhouse and his musicians struggle against.

The influence of dominant society extends to the music in the World Cafe. For instance, Valentine and Scoot go over to the nickelodeon and *"read all the names* of the records out loud" (emphasis mine 136) negotiating the written world as well as the oral or musical world. Within an all black environment, they speak names and songs instead of using numbers or hand signals. Powerhouse asks which version of a song the jukebox contains, and when not to his taste, he requests, *by name*, "Empty Bed Blues." Even in Negrotown the nickelodeon contains songs by white musicians, much to Powerhouse's dismay:

> 'Whose "Tuxedo Junction"?' asks Powerhouse.
> 'You know whose.'
> 'Nickelodeon, I request you to please play "Empty Bed Blues"
> and let Bessie Smith sing.'
> Silence: they hold it like a measure.
> 'Bring me all those nickels on back here,' says Powerhouse. (136)

Valentine and Scoot do not respond to his request because they do not find Bessie Smith on this nickelodeon; it only contains songs by white singers. Upon leaving an audience who requests white songs, the band faces the same music selection in their own milieu. Welty sets this second stage with many of the same trappings as the earlier stage to depict the overarching reach of white authority. This should serve as an early warning to Powerhouse that this black audience may not respond like his band members to the stories he weaves; these people have been influenced by the same white musicians as the white audience.

Powerhouse's rap takes on a different sound in the World Cafe as his black audience encloses the band to listen to the story. This audience initially responds with wide-eyed interest as he whispers about his wife's going "ssst! Plooey! What she do? Jump out and bust her brains all over the world" (137). His audience now sighs and "burst[s] into halloos of laughter" as he jokes about Uranus Knockwood "walking round in" Gypsy's "brains all scattered round" (138). As the crowd "moans with pleasure" and testifies, "uh-huh," "ya! ha!," "yeahhh!," and "you know him," they encourage Powerhouse and are in awe of him. While this audience may seem ideal for Powerhouse as they laugh at the right moments and give him their attention, they, nevertheless, reveal how dissonant their views are with Powerhouse's. Recognizing him as a hero, the crowd offers their own hero, Sugar-Stick Thompson, who "dove down to the bottom of July Creek and pulled up all those drownded white people fall out of a boat. Last summer, pulled up fourteen" (139). This man, this sugar stick, doesn't melt in water because he saves white people. Yet, unlike the loquacious Powerhouse, Sugar-Stick, "their instrument, cannot speak; he can only look back at the others" (139). This boy cannot tell his own story, and even if he could, Powerhouse would scoff at a story about the rescue of fourteen white people. Even this crowd has been appropriated by white society. As Powerhouse resumes his telegram rap, a waitress questions his story; for the first time, he must address the issue of truth.

> 'It's awful,' says the waitress. 'I hates that Mr. Knockwoods. All that the truth?'
> 'Want to see the telegram I got from him?' Powerhouse's hand goes to the vast pocket.
> 'Now wait, now wait, boss.' They all watch him.
> 'It must be the real truth,' says the waitress, sucking in her lower lip, her luminous eyes turning sadly, seeking the windows.' (139)

Like Phoenix Jackson, in "The Worn Path," this waitress views the written word as unparalleled proof and a sign of great importance. The waitress's doubt reflects just how the primacy of white written discourse forces a dominant melody over all dissonant chords. The band, who knows that no telegram exists, cringes at what Powerhouse might do to sustain his story. His threat to show written proof of a telegram results from his frustration with these non-believers who don't fail to understand his signifyin(g). Though his intent does not seem as malicious with this audience, he weaves his story to tease a reaction from this audience. Finally, the doubting waitress says, "it must be the real truth" (139). When Powerhouse acts as if he has proof, she accepts his word. She requests written evidence, but, because she is still rooted in the oral nature of her community, she believes his words alone. By addressing the issue of truth in such a direct manner, Powerhouse underscores the weight of his words. He says to the waitress, "no, babe, it ain't the truth .... Truth is something worse, I ain't said what, yet. It's something hasn't come to me, but I ain't saying it won't. And when it does, then want me to tell you?" (139). The band, his chorus, responds by howling "don't boss, don't, Powerhouse!," and the waitress screams, "Oh!" (139). While he admits that he has lied and that Gypsy has not killed herself, he also implies that he must find the ideal balance of truth and lies to find real power. For Powerhouse and his band, the truth "is something worse" (139).

The musicians feel marginalized in both a white and black setting because pages of written white discourse covers their heritage. White audience members request their own versions of jazz tunes, the jukebox in the World Cafe contains songs by white musicians, and the black audience consists of individuals swayed by a dominant society. While Powerhouse experiences all of these enclosures, he constantly resists his oppression through performance. The possibility of the true story frightens the band members and the waitress because they realize that if they believe the lie, then they are free.

In the meantime, Powerhouse continues to signify and to improvise, always seeking to revise the traditional. As he and his band leave the World Cafe, with "The Goona Goo" blaring on the nickelodeon, he resumes his telegram rap. Finally, his story winds down; he has told this story over several hours and several beers in a syncopated, disjointed manner, just like a jazz song. He shouts, "Take a telegram! ... Take an answer," (139) and his band members "get a little tired" (139). However, he orders his crew to spell Uranus Knockwood's name, and "they spell it all the ways it could be spelled. It puts them in a wonderful humor" (140). By spelling Knockwood's name many different ways, the band acts like Powerhouse to a lesser degree: they attempt to revise language in the form of a name. By changing the name, they negate the man, erasing him from the story. Powerhouse's response to Knockwood, "I gotcha. Name signed: Powerhouse," reveals his awareness of his oppression; perhaps he does know the truth. Although he has created Knockwood, he must impose his name as the final word of the story. He has revised the telegram rap just as he revises songs and lyrics to reflect himself and his heritage.

Powerhouse emerges as a strong, conquering character because while the band members occasionally improvise, he, "teacher," "musician," shows that overcoming oppression must be a constant, enterprising endeavor. He calls on his African heritage to signify and provoke indirection by tricking his audiences, altering songs, and weaving astonishing stories. The narrator says, "who could ever remember any of the things he says? They are just inspired remarks that roll out of his mouth like smoke" (141). Powerhouse may appear to be nothing but smoke and mirrors; however, his words have substance. The stories he tells and the music he plays may dazzle or confuse, but, for him, these words enable him to present an alternative discourse, another truth about what he finds detestable in his world, whether it is white or black.

Reine Dugas Bouton

Works Cited

Adams, Timothy. "A Curtain of Black: White and Black Jazz Styles in Powerhouse," *Notes on Mississippi Writers* 10 (1977): 57–61.

Albert, Richard. "Eudora Welty's Fats Waller: Powerhouse," *Notes on Mississippi Writers* 19 (1987): 63–72.

Berger, Morrow. "Fats Waller: The Outside Insider," *Journal of Jazz Studies* 1 (1973): 3–20.

Ellison, Ralph. "On Bird, Bird-Watching, and Jazz." *Saturday Review* July 20, 1962. Reprinted in *Shadow and Act*. New York: Random, 1964. 231.

Gates Jr., Henry Louis. *The Signifying Monkey: A Theory of African-American Literary Criticism*. Oxford: Oxford UP, 1988.

Getz, Thomas. "Eudora Welty: Listening to 'Powerhouse,'" *The Kentucky Review* 4 (1983): 40–48.

Lampkin, Loretta. "The Musical Movement and Harmony in Eudora Welty's 'Powerhouse,'" *CEA* 45 (1982): 24–28.

Panish, Jon. *The Color of Jazz: Race and Representation in Postwar American Culture*. Jackson: UP of Mississippi, 1997.

Prenshaw, Peggy, ed. *Conversations with Eudora Welty*. Jackson: UP of Mississippi, 1984.

Welty, Eudora. *The Collected Stories of Eudora Welty*. San Diego: Harcourt Brace, 1980.

6

"Listening, listening": Music and Gender in
Howards End, Sinister Street and *Pilgrimage*

What does Beethoven mean? It is a strange question, one which would usually receive a hesitant answer. Still, it has been intriguing people for two centuries and continues to do so. This musical icon of almost mythical proportions has not lost any of its fascination, which is partly due to the fact that there is no direct correspondence between the name and Beethoven the man. Most people would probably associate the composer with his music whereas for others the name is more or less synonymous with genius. Beethoven the signifier has more than one signified. As a consequence, the question is not who Beethoven was but what he is.

The arbitrary nature of the relation between the name and its many connotations makes it virtually impossible to arrive at one single definition. Not even an attempt to give a diachronic survey of the changing, modified and accumulated meanings will be made, but Beethoven will be situated in a context of cultural practice. Today listeners can enjoy his music in DVD players at home or almost anywhere thanks to portable CD players. Beethoven's genius is even embodied in a clever dog on film. The composer is undoubtedly part of a contemporary cultural context, and his status in it says as much about contemporary listeners as about the artist himself. As Martyn Evans points out in *Listening to Music*, music does not exist in a cultural vacuum. There is no such thing as an innocent ear; it is always "tainted" by practical, political, spiritual and other factors.[1] Hence, "musical experience is not transparent, but highly directed. And the form that this direction takes is learned as part of the perspective of the society we inherit."[2]

In the thin slice of time critics call Edwardian, listening to Beethoven's music amounted to an implicit acceptance of an inherited male discourse. The male ear was thus much better tuned in to his symphonies and sonatas than the female ear which was being made subject to penetration or even rape. Thus, paradoxically, the more a woman enjoyed Beethoven's music, the more she endorsed her own inferiority and subjection. As a result, music made her conscious of herself as a split subject. However, having become aware of her inferior position, she could start elaborating a listening of her own. E.M. Forster's *Howards End*, Compton Mackenzie's *Sinister Street* and Dorothy Richardson's *Pointed Roofs* (the first book of the *Pilgrimage* sequence) are three novels that deal with the listening act through Beethoven's music, all emphasizing the gender negotiations involved. Where Forster and Mackenzie display the difficulties of the woman's position, Richardson goes even further, suggesting a possible method of escape.

"Only Connect." The famous epigraph of E.M. Forster's novel *Howards End* has set critics speculating as to what values should be connected. Most of them agree that the central ones are male/female, prose/passion, the middle class/the masses, rural/urban and English/German. It has been taken more or less for granted that such connections can be achieved, and, consequently, the characters have mostly been discussed and analyzed from the point of view of these binary opposites. Since the novel is an important contribution to the "condition of England" discussion, however, it is more likely that it is built on the impossibility of connection in a society characterized by huge socio-political problems.

There is no doubt that music is an important ingredient in the novel. Critics have pointed out that Beethoven's Fifth Symphony is a theme running through the whole book.[3] True, Helen Schlegel is impelled by the power of Beethoven's music to achieve a sexual union with the poor clerk Leonard Bast, and this union results in a child which is often seen as symbolizing the new England where the gulf between the opposites mentioned above is bridged to some extent. However, such a reading seems to simplify matters. In order to arrive at the more complex role music plays in *Howards End*, it needs to be seen as a gendered and ideological discourse that thwarts the much desired connections the novel appears to espouse.

Although this reading of *Howards End* testifies to the impossibility of connection, little attention has been paid to a key chapter in which the binary opposites are deconstructed. Chapter V, dealing with the Beethoven concert, reveals a whole web of inconsistencies characteristic of a transitional phase being experienced by Edwardian society. To judge from the opening paragraph of the chapter, it would appear that Beethoven's Fifth Symphony is accessible to everyone. In a good-humoured tone, Forster is concerned to show that, irrespective of individual attitudes, people come together in Beethoven's music; it indeed breaks down barriers between them:

> It will be generally admitted that Beethoven's Fifth Symphony is the most sublime noise that has ever penetrated into the ear of man. All sorts and conditions are satisfied by it. Whether you are like Mrs Munt, and tap surreptitiously when the tunes come—of course, not so as to disturb the others; or like Helen, who can see heroes and shipwrecks in the music's flood; or like Margaret, who can only see the music; or like Tibby, who is profoundly versed in counterpoint, and holds the full score open on his knee; or like their cousin, Fräulein Mosebach, who remembers all the time that Beethoven is 'echt Deutsch'; or like Fräulein Mosebach's young man, who can remember nothing but Fräulein Mosebach: in any case, the passion of your life becomes more vivid, and you are bound to admit that such a noise is cheap at two shillings. It is cheap, even if you hear it in the Queen's Hall, dreariest music-room in London, though not as dreary as the Free Trade Hall, Manchester; and even if you sit on the extreme left of that hall, so that the brass bumps at you before the rest of the orchestra arrives, it is still cheap. (44–45)[4]

The first two sentences establish the general appeal of the Fifth Symphony. It is music which satisfies everyone, as the list of responses in the rest of the paragraph is supposed to exemplify. But does the text itself support this reading? In that case, Beethoven's music is unique in being truly democratic since, irrespective of nationality, class or gender, everyone can relate to it. In order to find out whether this is really so, or if, by contrast, the music cements existing prejudice and inequality, readers need to focus on the act of listening in which interesting things happen to the dichotomies mentioned above.

The effect of the music is said to make the passion in every listener's life more vividly felt. It is surprising to find, though, that no matter what response the music elicits, it is invariably classified as an expression of passion. If passion means a strong emotional reaction, partly or completely disconnected from the sobering influence of reason, then prose may be , no obvious opposite of the musical experience. Evans' definition of a listener's response as a mixture of the two contrasting categories of prosaic technicalities and poetic expression may shed some light on the dichotomy.[5] The opposition is thus between what must always be limited by the ordinary, everyday world of musical scores, technicalities and instruments and that which cannot be restricted by it but evades it in sublime transcendence. However, since Forster claims that irrespective of response (prosaic or poetic), passion (poetic capacity) is strengthened, he dismantles the binary opposition of prose and poetry; it is nothing but an illusion and as such meaningless.

Consequently, music is an indeterminate sign. In *Classical Music and Postmodern Knowledge*, Lawrence Kramer argues that music embodies sensitivity, thus encouraging the listener to introspection.[6] However, when turning the attention inward, the listener does not find the qualities that triggered off the process. There is simply no connection between the signifier and the signified. What is found instead, according to Kramer, is "a creative 'energy of mind,'" which a male listener can claim as his own, but a woman has no access to. Hence, there is no feminine listening. Kramer's line of reasoning about women and music recalls Jonathan Culler's theory, put forward in "Reading as a Woman," that female reading is nothing but an illusion. According to Culler, female reading is impossible since there is no female experience to serve as the basis of such a theory. Since women are socialized into male culture, they are divided: "For a woman to read as a woman is not to repeat an identity or an experience that is given but to play a role she constructs with reference to her identity as a woman, which is also a construct, so that the series can continue: a woman reading as a woman reading as a woman."[7] Kramer cites Helen Schlegel as an example that there is no feminine listening, which is mainly due to her having been socialized into male culture. Her response to Beethoven's Fifth Symphony testifies to sensitivity being disconnected from contemplation, or, in Forster's terms, passion from prose.

However, although the prose/passion dichotomy topples as well as the male/female one intimately related to it, the reason is not that passion outweighs prose. Studying the novel closely, readers will find the opposite case to be more true. Some responses are not really worth looking into; Mrs Munt's tapping is a negation of passion, and Fräulein Mosebach and her fiancé represent a trivialization of it. What about Helen, Margaret and Tibby then? Interestingly, none of them is actually listening to the music. The two sisters see things in the music, and their brother is busy reading the score. They all respond in ways that are characteristic of their historical, social and cultural milieu. In "Hearing Is Seeing: Thoughts on the History of Music and the Imagination," Leon Botstein draws attention to the connection between listening and visualization in late nineteenth and early twentieth-century responses to music.[8] But he also makes the important distinction between visualizing through music and reading music as a highly abstract and structured form of expression which could only be deciphered by "an aristocracy of elite cognescenti."[9]

Tibby's attitude to the music can be safely placed in the category of prose. It is dependent on reason, language, structure and form; he does not seem to visualize anything. He is mainly preoccupied with checking how faithfully the notated text is rendered musically, neither seeing nor actually listening to the music. Margaret, "who can only see the music" (*HE* 44), seems to represent the opposite of this unimaginative response. The question is, though, what she sees. Strongly against the idea of the interchangeability of the arts, she is no advocate of programme music with the rather indistinct border between music and literature that Helen favors.

> 'Now, this very symphony that we've just been having—she won't let it alone. She labels it with meanings from start to finish; turns it into literature. I wonder if the day will ever return when music will be treated as music. Yet I don't know. There's my brother—behind us. He treats music as music, and oh, my goodness! He makes me angrier than anyone, simply furious. With him I daren't even argue.' (*HE* 52)

Margaret is at a loss as regards the meaning of music, but it is fair to assume that her strong emotional reaction is an expression of a more far-reaching confusion than appears at first. Hiding behind the untenable idea that music is primarily an aesthetic principle free from social or political implications, Margaret wants to defend the purity of music. It is ironic that she, who will try to persuade Henry Wilcox of the necessity of connection later, cherishes the illusion of separateness when it comes to music. Margaret feels caught between the attitudes of her brother and sister, seemingly approving of neither. Her only reason for rejecting Helen's view of a connection between music and literature is that nothing is gained by it. It is the thought of mixing things up that is repellent to her. Being in favor of change by means of a connection, Helen may be seen to represent what Raymond Williams calls the "emergent" principle in society whereas Tibby embodies the "dominant" in his insistence on absolute music. Far removed from the male center of things as he may be, he identifies with the idea of patriarchal power in Edwardian society through his attitude towards music. As Marcia J. Citron points out in "Feminist Approaches to Musicology", music is indeed a gendered discourse:

> Absolute music inscribes a male psychological profile of growth that stresses quest and transcendence. The socialization process encourages separateness,

exploration, and adventure, which result in personal change. Whether original or derivative, the crucial point is that absolute music, particularly the
symphony, was grounded in a gendered process reflective of one sex and
alien to the other.[10]

It is the rigidity of this power structure represented by music which makes
Margaret "furious." The futility of protest is felt when Margaret admits
that she "daren't even argue" (*HE* 52). In short, the discourse of music is
alien to her sex.

This proves that the self-regulating ideology works beautifully. Margaret intuitively knows that England is at a crucial point socially and politically. She enjoys discussing issues such as democracy and the vote for
women, both of which are absolute necessities in her opinion. Still, when
it comes to music, her dauntless outlook is less obvious. Although Tibby's
approach is narrow-minded and repressive, Helen's stance appears too
uncertain for her to embrace. Instead she seeks safety in the past or the
"residual" as Williams terms it: "I wonder if the day will ever return when
music will be treated as music" (*HE* 52). This is an interesting statement
since it implies that there is an absolute definition of music which is based
on the idea that it is self-contained and totally unconnected. Thus, when
Margaret sees the music and nothing but the music, she cannot visualize
it by referring to anything outside it.

Is there, then, a great difference between what she sees and what
Tibby reads? She is certainly not contemplating the music in terms of reading the score. But her attention does not seem to be turned inward either;
she fails to find the "energy of mind" Kramer claims is the privilege of
men. Rejecting visual associations of the kind Helen favors, Margaret quite
simply hears the various notes that make up the musical composition.
These, however, do not signify anything. The only thing she sees is the
empty sign of music. Listening to the "music as music" amounts to having
a musical signifier but no signified. Margaret does not realize that music
has meaning only within the cultural context in which it is performed.
Ironically, for all her fine talk of equality and the vote for women, her
views on music show that she subscribes to the norms of patriarchal society.
Her reluctance to see anything but the music itself is a passive acceptance
of the political Establishment. Citron claims that it was common for women composers around 1900 to avoid, when composing music, features
that were considered inferior from a patriarchal point of view in order to
gain acceptance from the male Establishment.[11] As a listener, Margaret
engages in a similar denial of marginalized elements without realizing

that the price for such an acceptance may be a split subjectivity and a struggle for selfhood which is unknown to men.

So far the problematic nexus music/woman has been outlined in fairly broad terms. Since neither genre nor composer has really been taken into account, music has been dealt with from a general point of view. Reference has been made in passing to the historical context of the performance but the full implications of the typically Edwardian responses are yet to be discussed as is the significance of the actual place where the concert is performed. As has been implied above in the analysis of Margaret's approach, music is meaningless when placed outside its cultural context. After a discussion of Helen Schlegel's response to music, this will become even clearer.

However, before the way in which she perceives the music is examined, it may be of importance to try to define her preconceived ideas of the Beethoven symphony since they most likely influence her actual response to it. The very name of the composer commanded respect, as Citron points out: "If we take the name of Beethoven, for example, attributes such as great, genius, and powerful might come to mind. Beethoven's name would imply a giant in Western art music, and therefore someone whose music is first rate."[12] As keywords in imperialist England of the first decade of the twentieth century, greatness and power were by definition male. Thus, to actually go to a Beethoven concert could be seen as an implicit corroboration of the established political order.

Acknowledging Beethoven as a genius would strengthen a similar interpretation. In *Gender and Genius: Towards a Feminist Aesthetics*, Christine Battersby traces the origins of the genius cult, claiming that it has been defined as male throughout history although this male foundation is not as solid as it may seem. In fact, many of the laudable features of a genius would not automatically be labeled male but seem stereotypically female. The great paradox is that while qualities that are necessary for artistic creation, such as intuition, emotion and imagination, had come to be considered "feminine," women were not allowed to create. "A man with genius was like a woman ... but was not a woman."[13] Interestingly, E.T.A. Hoffmann felt a need to strike a balance between intuition and prudence in his view of Beethoven's genius. In fact, he argued that Beethoven's talent was due to a rare combination of these two components. In his opinion, the enormous upgrading of the intuitive insights that the Romantics had engaged in needed to be tempered by schooled introspection, criticism and revision. Moreover, as Citron points out, since the composer was dis-located from the court and Church in the early nineteenth century, the concept of genius added authority and legitimacy to the composer's sta-tus.[14]

Significantly, the insistence on the male gender of the genius seems to have been particularly strong in the early years of the twentieth cen-tury. In *Sex and Character* (1903, English transl. 1906) Otto Weininger claims that "female genius is a contradiction in terms, for genius is simply intensified, perfectly developed, universally conscious maleness"[15] and that "the man of genius possesses like everything else, the complete female in himself; but woman herself is only a part of the Universe, and the part can never be whole; femaleness can never include genius."[16] The imperialist undertones of a conquest are not only applicable to matters of territory but also to gender; the man conquers the woman, denying her an exis-tence in her own right.

Furthermore, Andreas Huyssen has argued that in the nineteenth cen-tury women were marginalized through an exclusion from high culture which was envisaged as male, whereas the female gender was reserved for the masses and popular culture.[17] The concrete manifestation of this margin-alization was the concert hall. In Carl Dalhaus's opinion, concert halls in which symphonies were performed functioned as temples of art whose very shape underscored male power and transcendence just as much as churches did.[18] While music had been performed and enjoyed by men and women alike in the sheltered private sphere, men were more used to pub-lic surroundings. Therefore, the public character of the concert hall was better suited for and more supportive of male experience than female. According to Citron, it is possible that around 1900 the salon began to be seen as a place of female power since music was performed within the private sphere.[19] The concert hall, erected for performances in public, brought an end to this unfortunate blurring of the borderline between the private and public spheres. At ease in this temple of art, men could more easily experience a metaphysical transcendence so that attention was shifted from the composer as subject to the listener's exaggerated notion of self. This is a feature particularly noticeable in Beethoven's music and has been important in the construction of the cult of genius.[20]

Helen Schlegel's behavior at the Beethoven concert in Queen's Hall is a good illustration of a woman's difficulty in making the concert hall a natural environment for listening to music. Capricious and emotional as she is, Helen's inability to conform to the discipline of concert-going should perhaps not be entirely ascribed to mere whimsicality. Listening to the Andante, whose gender implications will be discussed later, she starts evaluating the architecture, finding little of which she approves: "Much did she censure the attenuated Cupids who encircle the ceiling of the Queen's Hall, inclining each to each with vapid gesture, and clad in sallow pantaloons, on which the October sunlight struck" (*HE* 45). Helen is certainly not experiencing metaphysical transcendence here. The architecture annoys her, eliciting a rather prosaic statement: "'How awful to marry a man like those Cupids!'"

After the last note of Beethoven's Fifth Symphony, Helen rises and leaves the concert hall hurriedly. This creates some confusion since, according to the programme, there are more pieces to be performed. She is so wrapped up in her own thoughts that she seems to forget that she is in a public place, and, when leaving, inadvertently takes the umbrella belonging to Leonard Bast, a young clerk. Tibby, as the male member of the family, is the one who is supposed to set things right. He, in contrast to his sister, respects the discipline of the concert hall: "Tibby rose to his feet, and wilfully caught his person on the backs of the chairs. By the time he had tipped up the seat and had found his hat, and had deposited his full score in safety, it was 'too late' to go after Helen. The Four Serious Songs had begun, and one could not move during their performance" (*HE* 48).

There is another incident that shows that women fail to live up to the expectations of public life while men find it easier to adjust to it. Fräulein Mosebach, the German cousin, leaves her bag behind when leaving the concert hall. The contents of the bag (address-book, pocket dictionary, map of London and money) symbolize the young lady's means of coping in the public sphere. Interestingly, this time it is Leonard Bast who is the man to restore the forgotten object. As a poor clerk, Leonard is not familiar with the gentlemanly behavior of the leisured class. He is a member of the masses and, as such, associated with the female gender. However, he finds himself in a place dedicated to high culture which, according to Huyssen, is classified as male. Bast manages to bridge this gap, but not without considerable embarrassment. When offering to catch up with the German couple, he "got very red" but, in contrast to Tibby, succeeds in his task and "return[s] to his seat upsides with the world" (*HE* 50).

A common subject in Edwardian music journals was the behavior of the English concert audience which, according to critics, left much to be

desired. It was, however, reported to be improving, which was largely due
to the imitation of the admirable Germans. The English/German rivalry
in political as well as social matters is a characteristic feature of the Edwardian period although, from an English point of view, it was in many
ways a construction designed by the English to uphold their supremacy
and prevent social change. This seems to have been the case with the
question of audience behavior. In *The Bourgeois Experience*, Peter Gay
shows that appalling concert behavior was a general problem in both Europe and America throughout the nineteenth century. Germany seems to
have been no exception. Furthermore, the picture Gay gives of the audience implies that the worst behavior was to be found at the top of the
social hierarchy, while "the less affluent, less snobbish concertgoer sitting
in the orchestra and the poverty-stricken music student standing in the
top balcony were far more likely to have developed listening into a high
art."[21] The impression given by Gay does not at all correspond with the
one gleaned from contemporary English music journals in which English
and German audiences were treated as opposites. The latter was an alleg-
edly democratic group composed of all social classes, whereas the former
had been an exclusive entity, considered a race apart, a peculiar people,
to be spoken of by their fellows with awe "not altogether unmixed with
contempt."[22] Still, although this is not a very flattering picture of the privi-
leged class of concertgoers, it was not until the composition of the audience changed and members of the masses were admitted that the insistence
on concert discipline became more evident.

As a consequence, the ideological distance between the audience and
the composer grew and came to be seen not only in musical but also in
political terms of the masses and their leader. Therefore, it is not surprising that words such as composer, genius and imperialist weave an intricate web of patriarchal dominance, while the Other becomes synonymous
with woman and the masses. At the Beethoven concert in *Howards End*,
conflicting values clash in the drama enacted in the public sphere of the
concert hall which marginalizes women and a male member of the masses.
Helen Schlegel flees from this patriarchal sanctuary, and Leonard Bast
has to prove that he is entitled to sit down "upsides with the world."

Listening to a Beethoven concert in public is an activity implying patriarchal oppression that does not seem to disturb Helen's passionate and
spontaneous response to the music in the least. Rather than just ignoring
this seeming incongruity, it may be asked wherein the passion lies. Critics
often take the prose/passion dichotomy as a starting-point when discuss-

ing the novel in order to establish where a connection can be achieved. Peter Widdowson, for instance, in *"Howards End*: Fiction as History" emphasizes the opposition: "Helen's passion and idealism 'connect' with the spirit of 'adventure' and of unquenchable individual life in Leonard—that potential for true 'wholeness' of culture hinted at, but unborn, in him and the huge class he represents."[23] However, Widdowson leaves this statement totally unconnected with the novel's important musical implications. This is surprising since it is the Beethoven concert that actually brings Helen and Leonard together, leaving such a strong imprint on Helen's imagination that she makes the music the theme of her life.

As has been demonstrated, however, the musical theme is not one of connection, but of disillusionment, resulting from the failure to achieve a connection. This is where the actual form of the music becomes significant. In addition to the patriarchal features of the public concert hall and the genius myth evoked by Beethoven's name, the sonata form to which the symphony belongs may now be added as the highest and most complex achievement a composer can reach. The sonata aesthetic is built on a multi-movement form carrying interesting gender associations as A.B. Marx was the first to point out in *Die Lehre von der musikalischen Komposition* (1845): "The second theme ... serves as contrast to the first, energetic statement, though dependent on and determined by it. It is of a more tender nature, flexibly rather than emphatically constructed—in a way, the feminine as opposed to the preceding masculine."[24] Similar ideas, focusing on masculine strength and female tenderness, were put forward by later musicologists such as Hugo Riemann and Vincent d'Indy around 1900.[25]

Thus, the sonata form can be seen as a male discourse of the ideological domination of man over woman. Against this background, Margaret Schlegel's wish to have music treated "as music" is both pathetic and ironic. The first theme of a symphony represents the male thrust and is intimately associated with power, hegemony, opposition and competition.[26] The second feminine theme functions more or less as a contrast to the male one, and, although the two themes may seem engaged in playful struggle, the second mainly serves to set off the first. It is absolutely crucial that the male order is restored in the final movement:

> The tonic of the masculine must close the movement, otherwise deeply inculcated patterns of narrative desire will be frustrated. As Susan McClary has pointed out, such desires must not be denied, and thus the feminine has to be

sacrificed, as it were. She believes that Western art music seems to have a
need for the construction of an Other within a work, whether it be associated
with the feminine or some other object of ideological subordination.[27]

The Other is quite clearly female in the sonata aesthetic, but what "other
object of ideological subordination" can be found? As has been argued
above, women are categorized with the masses, which seems a likely combination in the case of the Beethoven symphony in *Howards End*. Helen's
response to the music is made complex by the fact that she is divided in
her identification with the Other; she perceives the note of the marginalized woman as well as that of the marginalized masses.

It is difficult to understand exactly what Kramer means when he argues
that Helen responds to Beethoven's music "as a kind of young man."[28]
The main distinction, which he argues very convincingly in favor of, is between male and female listening. To add further divisions, however, only
creates confusion. In what ways does a young man respond to music differently than one who is considerably older? Maybe he wants to imply that
Helen's readiness to acknowledge new and disturbing elements commu-
nicated through the music is the feature of a young and impressionable
man. In addition to being vague, such a supposition is sexist since it suggests that women lack the faculty for perceiving signs of social change.
Whichever generation she is associated with, Helen's response is to be
understood in an Edwardian male discourse of power and strength. She is
completely enwrapped in the music of the first movement which she visu-
alizes in terms of heroes and shipwrecks. Thus, she has incorporated the
gender values of the sonata aesthetic. The heroic note is dominant and
persuasive, representing a corroboration of an imperialist stance, and can
be defined as that of the Establishment.

Compared to the strong and unique first movement, the second is a
disappointment: "For the Andante had begun—very beautiful, but bearing a family likeness to all the other beautiful Andantes that Beethoven
has written, and, to Helen's mind, rather disconnecting the heroes and
shipwrecks of the first movement from the heroes and goblins of the third"
(*HE* 45). Whereas the male theme is strong, unique and independent, the
female is only one of many similar beautiful themes with a damaging effect
on the former to which it is subservient. Since the second theme is that of
the female Other, Helen does not identify at all with it. On the contrary,
the second theme annoys and bores her. In fact, like her sister, Helen
tries to distance herself from what was considered inferior in patriarchal
society. Listening to the Andante, her eyes and mind wander to the tradi-

tionally feminine subject of marriage, rejecting it forcefully. She would much rather continue listening to the heroic theme. This shows to what extent Helen has incorporated patriarchal society into her mindset, a society from which she is, ironically, excluded.

With the next movement, the male theme returns slightly modified. Helen is both intrigued and frightened to identify an unheroic note in the music. Transferring the power of the hero to the goblins who, in contrast to the imperial hero, are frightening in their passivity is a means of introducing the "other object of ideological subordination": "They were not aggressive creatures; it was that that made them so terrible to Helen. They merely observed in passing that there was no such thing as splendour and heroism in the world" (*HE* 46). In a culture where the predominant ideology is based on an assertive disposition a character merely observing the world becomes the shadowy but threatening Other. The goblins are creatures not quite human; they are as distant from human heroes as the masses are from the Establishment. They can be scattered easily but have an anarchic impact on reality: "Panic and emptiness! Panic and emptiness! The goblins were right" (*HE* 46).

Then the goblins go away, and the imperialist ideology prevails again. Interestingly, they do not disappear of their own accord, but they need to be told off by the strong authoritative leader. Beethoven is here given the characteristics of an artistic imperialist: "For, as if things were going too far, Beethoven took hold of the goblins and made them do what he wanted. He appeared in person. He gave them a little push, and they began to walk in a major key instead of in a minor, and then—he blew with his mouth and they were scattered!" (*HE* 46). The focalizer here is most likely Tibby since he has asked the rest of the company to look out for the transitional passage of the drum indicating this change, whereas Helen is more intrigued by the return of the goblins. As a representative of a patriarchal ideology based on strength, Tibby wants the threatening Other to disappear. Helen is again swept away by the power of the music. Listening to the heroic note, she imagines gods and demigods fighting. The only thing that counts is the belligerent spirit, not the actual outcome; "… conqueror and conquered would alike be applauded by the angels of the utmost stars" (*HE* 47).

The imperialist note is so insistent that when the goblins return Helen is not quite sure they have really been there and even identifies with the Establishment ideology when passing them off as "phantoms of cowardice and unbelief" (*HE* 47). But, as she knows herself, this is just a way of undermining the power of the lower classes. They represent courage and belief by their mere presence, and they are the ones who can undermine the whole established social structure. Dehumanizing the masses is not a means of reducing their power. It is rather the opposite; in their other-ness they constitute a potent threat:

> They might return—and they did. It was as if the splendour of life might boil over and waste to steam and froth. In its dissolution one heard the terrible, ominous note, and a goblin, with increased malignity, walked quietly over the universe from end to end. Panic and emptiness! Panic and emptiness! Even the flaming ramparts of the world might fall. (*HE* 47)

Helen is left with the impression of a subversive Other. However, accord-ing to the sonata aesthetic, male order must be restored at the end, and Beethoven's Fifth Symphony is no exception:

> Beethoven chose to make all right in the end. He built the ramparts up. He blew with his mouth for the second time, and again the goblins were scat-tered. He brought back the gusts of splendour, the heroism, the youth, the magnificence of life and death, and, amid vast roarings of a superhuman joy, he led his Fifth Symphony to its conclusion. (*HE* 47)

Listening to the music, Helen intuitively understands that national char-acteristics do not form a vertical cleavage. Instead, she feels that there is a socio-political split horizontally which cuts across national differences. This means that English and German values are not, as has been suggested earlier, the binary opposites Forster implies they are. In fact, the dividing-line between English and German features may be blurred to such an ex-tent that it is of no consequence. The socio-political implications of the music, by contrast, are so strong that, irrespective of national identity, they may reveal a hollowness at the core of a hierarchically ordered society like the English. Despite the fact that Helen Schlegel identifies a note in Beethoven's Fifth which challenges hierarchical thinking, the subversive reaction is contained. Distinguishing the goblin note, she acknowledges the potential of the social and political Other, but, in her contemplative approach, she adheres to the male norm while the female Other remains shadowy.

Ultimately, then, Helen Schlegel fails to listen to the symphony out of her female self. A more successful step towards a uniquely female listen-ing is taken by Miriam Henderson in Dorothy Richardson's *Pilgrimage*. However, before this feminine approach to listening is examined, the case of a man engaged in male listening may serve as an interesting contrast. Compton Mackenzie's bildungsroman *Sinister Street* (1913) portrays the protagonist Michael Fane's maturity into adulthood largely in terms of music. Throughout his childhood and most of his adolescence, Michael is virtually shut out from the world of music. His visual impressions are sophisticated, whereas auditory ones are characterized as mere noise. Since Michael's sister Stella is a very talented pianist with access to the world of music, this polarization is exaggerated in order for Michael to construct a male identity that qualifies Stella as Other.

Stella conforms to the stereotypical pattern of the musical woman. She performs the social function of playing to please other people in the private sphere. Moreover, she enjoys playing the piano because it is her way of expressing herself emotionally, thus creating a sense of female mystery. Her brother, by contrast, excels in verbal means of expression and does not feel anything when listening to music. Having completed her formal education in music, Stella wishes to give a public recital in King's Hall, an event which coincides with Michael's leaving school and launching into university life at Oxford (the chapter dealing with the concert is, in fact, the final one in Book Two out of the novel's four). This place in the novel's structure suggests that the concert is of crucial importance for both Stella and Michael, but, contrary to what might be expected, it marks the end for the former, while the latter feels it is a beginning. The public performance is a climax in Stella's career; she then marries, and music becomes of secondary importance. Michael, on the other hand, is actually born into male adulthood through his sister's performance of Beethoven's Fifth Symphony. Stella, however, is only the necessary means to an end.

Before she comes on stage, Michael fails to respond to the music. The Third Leonora Overture is only "a blur" and totally incomprehensible to him. The German tone poem that follows is similarly without other meaning than as noise for him:

> It seemed to go on forever in a most barbaric and amorphous din; with corybantic crashings, with brazen fanfares and stinging cymbals it flung itself against the audience, while the woodwind howled and the violins were harsh as cats... The tone poem shrieked and tore itself to death. The world became very quiet. (368)[29]

Neither Beethoven's Leonora overture nor the German tone poem, possibly Richard Strauss' *Also Sprach Zarathustra*, promotes contemplation through male listening. This effect is reserved for the Fifth Symphony. Stella enters "tall and white" and is "handed across the platform" (*SS* 368). It does not take long, however, before she is forgotten:

> It was not until Beethoven's sombre knock at the opening of the Fifth Symphony that Michael began to dream upon the deeps of great music, that his thoughts liberated from anxiety went straying into time. Stella, when for a little while he had reveled in her success, was forgotten, and the people in this hall, listening, listening, began to move him with their unimaginable variety. Near him were lovers who in this symphony were fast imparadised; their hands were interlaced; visibly they swayed nearer to each other on the waves of melody. Old men were near him, solitary old men listening, listening ... old men who at the summons of these ringing notes were traversing their past that otherwise might have stayed for ever unvoyageable. (*SS* 369)

Michael's account of the response to the symphony is very close to the one described by Forster in *Howards End*. It does indeed seem to make "the passion in your life more vividly felt." The difference is, though, that Forster is at pains to prove that there is a general and unanimous response to the music before he gives the detailed description of Helen Schlegel's reaction. In *Sinister Street*, the male perspective is clear from the start, and, although Michael is impressed by the "unimaginable variety" of the audience, the experience of listening to this piece is an important stage in a young man's process of coming to terms with himself in patriarchal society. Michael is certainly listening as a young man.

He is struck by the homogeneous audience but mentions only two categories: lovers and old men. Having been romantically entangled with a young girl called Lily, he can identify with the male lover. To some extent, he also identifies with the old men since they can look back on an active and adventurous life that he feels is about to begin: "He would travel through the world ..." (*SS* 371). After listening to the music for a little while, Michael drops all amorous associations since love is not noble enough to be linked with it: "There was something more noble in this music than the memory of a slim and lovely girl and of her flower-soft kisses. The world itself seemed to travel the faster for this urgent symphony. Michael was spinning face to face with the spinning stars" (*SS* 369).

Thus, Michael restricts the associations evoked by the music to the male world. Going back through his past, he feels that the music corroborates a traditionally patriarchal outlook on life. He finds, for instance, support in the music for the teaching methods of a highly eccentric male tyrant. Whatever subject he thinks of, the common factor is a "sensation of finality," which, as we have seen, is an important male element in the concluding movement of a symphony. The music is a faithful summing up of Michael's life so far. Listening to the music, he feels the "energy of mind" which Kramer claims is a male prerogative:

> Men contemplating music can freely claim this active, synthesizing faculty as a distinguishing mark of their gender; women (officially, at least) cannot. Precisely, then, by not harboring the Hegelian 'broad expanse ... of a richly filled conscious life,' music allows the subject to discover in himself the under-lying principle by which that expanse is possessed and filled. Through the co-alescence of the musical empty sign and feminine lack, the self secures its proper masculine position.[30]

The symphony brings one stage of Michael's life safely to an end, investing it with a final meaning, but, what is more, it also marks the beginning of a new phase. Michael is an impressionable young man and, as such, differs from the old men in the audience. As has been suggested in connection with Helen Schlegel's response, malleability may be the feature distinguishing the young man from the old although they share an interest in leading active, purposeful lives. The music makes Michael question his values. He does not believe in the principle of equality but "as he surveyed the audience he was aware from time to time of a great longing to involve himself in the web of humanity" (*SS* 370). And, preparing himself for an active life, he is all of a sudden uncertain as to its driving principle: "He would travel through the world and through the underworld and apply always his standard of ... of what? What was his standard? A classic permanence, a classic simplicity and inevitableness? The symphony stopped" (*SS* 371).

The moment the music stops, he becomes aware of Stella again. She has been excluded from his preoccupation with male values in a patriarchal world. Since the Fifth Symphony has served the purpose of strengthening his own identity, he sees her through the eyes of the superior and possessive male: "What a possession she was; what an excitement her career would be. How he would love to control her extravagance, and even as he controlled it, how he would admire it" (*SS* 371).

Michael has listened to the music as a male. The connection between signifier and signified has not been established, but the symphony has had a direct bearing on his identity. He has been able to summarize his past life and, in doing so, has found enough pleasure in it to part with it ready to continue. The music has also provided him with the opportunity to question his ideological foundation and prepared him for the future. In short, Michael has engaged in creative introspection; what he has identified in the music is a clear view of self.

This is what Helen fails to do. Instead, the music helps her to formulate vague notions of the Other. The effect the music arguably has on Michael Fane as a male in a patriarchal society, she explicitly states that it has on her too: "The music had summed up to her all that had happened or could happen in her career" (*HE* 47). However, there is an important difference. Helen leaves the concert in an agitated state of mind "push[ing] her way out during the applause." Michael, by contrast, is happy and at ease: "The concert was over, and as Michael came swirling down the stairs on the flood of people going home, he had a strange sensation of life beginning all over again" (*SS* 371). This positive final effect is in striking contrast to the ominous note Helen feels the music leaves her with: "She read it as a tangible statement, which could never be superseded. The notes meant this and that to her, and they could have no other meaning, and life could have no other meaning" (*HE* 47). Like Michael, she has a sense of finality. In his case, however, it is one which engenders hope whereas she feels nothing but doom.

The patriarchal Fifth Symphony strengthens Michael's sense of self because he is a man; it strengthens Helen's feelings of being the Other, a marginalized woman, while simultaneously also shattering all attempts to construct a self. Thus, she listens neither as a woman nor as a young man. She does not listen to the music at all. Ironically, while Michael finally breaks out of his world of unintelligible noise and actually learns what male listening is, Helen is reduced to the auditory level of hearing "sublime noise" only.

Michael has his male identity confirmed through Beethoven's Fifth Symphony. Identity is a keyword also for Miriam Henderson in *Pointed Roofs*, the first book of the first volume of Dorothy Richardson's *Pilgrimage*. Miriam's search for individual fulfillment is a more complicated process than Michael Fane's, though. *Pilgrimage* is an attempt to define female experience and justify its very existence. As Gillian E. Hanscombe argues, the novel is "explicitly feminist, not in the sense of arguing for equal rights and votes for women, but in the more radical sense of insisting on the authority of a woman's experience and world view."[31] In order to get at the very core of female experience, vague and elusive as it may be, Richard-

son avails herself of music as a suitable means. The close connection between a search for a female self and music is emphasized by Richardson
herself in the "Foreword" to the novel in which she states that "in 1913,
the opening pages of the attempted chronicle that became the first chapter
of 'Pilgrimage,' was written to the accompaniment of a sense of being
upon a fresh pathway."[32] This search is very different from and much more
thoroughgoing than the one which leads to the rather superficial notion
of identity in *Sinister Street* where, as has been suggested earlier, the music has the function of confirming an already existing outlook rather than
constructing a completely new and challenging one.

Forced to go to Germany as a student-teacher due to her father's disastrous financial speculation, Miriam is without an identity. Socially, her
sense of self has collapsed completely. She has lived with the illusion that
she is the daughter of a gentleman and as such belongs to the leisured
classes. Genderwise, she also feels insecure; she has been taught to think
independently but is all of a sudden deprived of the means of acting freely.
Her father has influenced her to such an extent that she despises women
and cannot get on with men. She envies girls in her acquaintance who
have been trained and certificated and are truly independent but they are
"trade" and are thus passed off as "sharp" and "knowing."

Her national identity is more or less the result of these social circumstances, which is why the German setting has such a strong impact on her.
Her English set of opposites such as male/female, cultivated/common and
modern/old-fashioned appears totally useless in Germany where these contrasts are mixed and reduced to the one main pair of English/German. In
England, she felt very strongly that she was "different," she aimed at de-
signing an identity which would diverge from the norm. Arriving in Germany, she vaguely realizes that what she believed to be her true self is
nothing but her own construction of the established norm. When she starts
to fashion a strong and independent identity, music becomes instrumental
in side-stepping the male norm.

Miriam has been brought up to believe that her father's ambition to
be "a person of leisure and cultivation" is reconcilable with a modern and
radical approach to music. She gradually comes to understand, though, that
those two interests are mutually exclusive. Her father is so preoccupied
with the idea of being an English gentleman that he sacrifices everything
to it, including his family. Despite various attempts to appear modern
musically, he subscribes to the taste of the Establishment by passing off
everything else as "new-fangled music". Thus, when saying that Miriam

has "to finish her education abroad," he is right. In fact, Miriam's very first auditory impression in *Pointed Roofs* is that of the piano-organ which she hears while reluctantly packing in her room: "It was the Thursday afternoon piano-organ, the one that was always in tune" (*PR* 15). Ironically enough, the mechanical music is the only thing "in tune" in this dysfunctional English setting. Music is reduced to the status of predictable and comforting sound in a socially insecure family.

The very first evening in Germany "there had been a performance that had completed the transformation of Miriam's English ideas of 'music'" (*PR* 36). The nationalities represented at the performance are German, English and Australian. It is particularly the singing of the Australian girl, Gertrude Goldring, which has an enormous impact on Miriam. It is the falseness of pitch that attracts her since it reminds her of the cry of a London coal-man. Miriam's English notions of music are built on a social foundation that excludes working class features. All of a sudden she realizes that what appears to be English about her ideas can be defined as such in comparison with a foreign approach, in this case Australian, but is after all intimately related to domestic social issues. She had to get away from the music of the patriarchal Establishment which is always in tune, like the piano-organ, in order to find out that her notions of music are socially and culturally determined. To be out of tune may, in fact, be more musical.

In this process, her picture of Germany is essential and acts as a driving force. German professionalism and efficiency are important components reflecting the commercial climate of the period. Her idealization of Germany leads to a total dismantling of English self-confidence, which is noticeable in the playing of the English girls. E.E. Williams's advice that the English should learn the imitative art is a solution which Miriam ponders but rejects.[33] She sees that some of the other English girls try to imitate the German way of playing the piano "with expression" but that is no alternative for her. "The two she had just heard playing were, she felt sure, imitating something—but hers would be no imitation. She would play as she wanted to one day in this German atmosphere" (*PR* 45). This atmosphere is a construction of hers which she is proud of; it is complex, contradictory and challenging. She calls it German, thus seemingly establishing an opposition to English values:

> If only she could bring them all for a minute into this room, the wonderful Germany that she had achieved. If they could even come to the door and look in. She did not in the least want to go back. She wanted them to come to

> her and taste Germany—to see all that went on in this wonderful house, to
> see pretty, German Emma, adoring her—to hear the music that was every-
> where all the week, that went, like a garland, in and out of everything, to hear
> her play, by accident, and acknowledge the difference in her playing. (*PR* 66)

However, the English/German dichotomy is founded on a simplification
that veils more fundamental differences. She takes over an imperialist discourse without really acknowledging the need for clear-cut nationalist definitions. Her strategy may, in fact, be to undermine the whole imperialist
edifice by adopting the dividing-line between German and English characteristics but blurring it to such an extent that it becomes meaningless
for the creation of identity. Judged from a feminist point of view, her use
of the established patriarchal structure can be seen to show the hollowness of it.

The transformation of Miriam's English ideas of music is then not as
complete as she may think. She has still a long way to go before she has
shed her notions tainted by patriarchal oppression. Like Helen Schlegel,
Miriam intuitively defines the Other in the music, but, while Helen leaves
it at that, Miriam feels the urge for a redefinition which would acknowledge the marginalized elements in their own right. This is a process that
entails a total dismantling of the traditional activities of performing, listening and, ultimately, of composing music.

The gender aspects of performing music are intimately connected with
the division between the public and private spheres. To perform at home
before a known audience was a woman's task comparable to her other domestic duties. This is one of the absurdities Miriam becomes conscious of
in her process of musical transformation: "She soon discovered she could
not always 'play'—even the things she knew perfectly—and she began to
understand the fury that had seized her when her mother and a woman
here and there had taken for granted one should 'play when asked,' and
coldly treated her refusal as showing lack of courtesy" (*PR* 58). The public
performance, by contrast, was generally seen as a male activity. This is
partly due to the reasons discussed earlier of the concert hall as a male
construction promoting an exaggerated notion of the self. Another important factor is the similarity between the gifted godlike pianist and the
composer-genius resulting from the almost non-existent ideological distance between the two. A large number of Edwardian novels, Henry Han-
del Richardson's *Maurice Guest* to name one, testify to this link.

Significantly, the female performer of Beethoven's Fifth Symphony
in *Sinister Street* is of no real importance; she is the instrument conveying

the composer's genius so that the male listener may identify with it. She is
nothing but a medium and certainly not powerful and godlike but rather
stereotypically angelic in her innocence and self-consciousness. In *Howards
End* the performing function is more or less left out of account. Apart
from the listener's response, the brilliance and power of the composer is
repeatedly mentioned. Thus, the listening act is reduced to a one-way
communication; the male composer is addressing the listener authorita-
tively. In Michael Fane's case, the result is a strengthening of male identity through a corroboration of a patriarchal outlook. Helen Schlegel is
expected by the situation to join forces with the composer in a similar way
but fails to do so and is disturbed by the lack of attunement. To be able to
really listen to the music, Miriam understands that the artificial divisions
between composer, performer and listener have to be discarded to pave
the way for a more creative redistribution of these roles.

A role which has been reserved for men is that of the critic. Citron
draws attention to this fact while at the same time emphasizing the difference between reception and response:

> Reception operates more directly in canon formation than does individual
> response. Generally articulated in written form, reception focuses on collec-
> tive response and its relationship with history. A class of professionals—the
> critic—has occupied the center of reception and this forms an interesting
> contrast with the social plurality of the individual respondent.[34]

By stressing such features as an established canon, which by tradition is
male, and the professional nature of the criticism through an act of writing,
the picture Citron gives of male dominance in music reception is applicable
to Edwardian England. This becomes even more evident when the significance she ascribes to cultural metaphors is considered. She argues that,
although music reviews did not directly encourage colonizing attempts,
they reinforced already existing expansionist tendencies by focusing on
musical metaphors for magnitude and transcendence.[35]

Citron establishes a polarization between male public reception and
female private response. But is it possible to talk of female response in the
absence of female listening? Such a response, as has been noted in Helen
Schlegel's case, is nothing but a thwarting of genuine listening. Moreover,
the reception/response dichotomy cannot be directly translated into the
male/female one. The Other in Edwardian fiction is definable not only in
gender terms; the socio-political dimension is equally important. This dimension explains, for instance, why Leonard Bast is marginalized in a

patriarchal society of high culture with very slim chances of ever gaining entrance.

Another factor which renders the reception/response opposition problematic is the difficulty in actually respecting the borderline, as Citron is well aware: "Critics are professional listeners, as it were, whose main goal is to propagate their own points of view, their own aesthetic paradigms."[36] The inverse case is perhaps more often experienced by women since, in their private roles of daughters and wives, they are often exposed to the highly individual opinions of men on music. Miriam, for instance, gradually realizes that the personal views of her father and her former music teacher in England are products of conventional, established music reception. It is really irrelevant whether these ideas are categorized as reception or response. Either way they marginalize female response, listening and experience.

What Miriam engages in is a revaluation of listening as actively creative rather than passively receptive. This new creation of the well-known piece does not, however, replace the composer's established version but exists side by side with it in a dual ontology.[37] As to the performer, this figure becomes "a crucial presence between maker and listener. No mere static relay point, the performer serves as (re)creator and respondent all in one."[38] This process, in which all the roles have equal importance, reshuffles the order of the three functions. The creative composition is not the first and necessary stage although the mechanical aspect of it, the notated version, is. Thus, the listening act follows the performance but precedes the composition.

It is all a matter of technique, as Miriam soon realizes: "'It's *technique* I want,' she told herself, when she had reached the end of her collection, beginning to attach a meaning to the familiar word" (*PR* 57). The technical aspect of music is often associated with absolute music and as such with a male approach. Miriam is aware of this and thus feels the need to redefine the word that, paradoxically, despite being familiar, has had no meaning for her as a woman. Miriam's technique is to "unlearn" traditional technique, which, as will be shown, serves to reinforce female subordination through music.

The process has its pitfalls, though; the first is genre. Helen Schlegel and Michael Fane respond to the same piece of music; she as the female Other and he as the male norm. Miriam Henderson has a greater selection of musical compositions to choose from in her attempt to fashion a

uniquely female form of listening. She is not exactly aware of the importance of genre but feels intuitively that musical categories are important
in her search for a female self; some are obstacles that prevent her from
reaching it while others are felt to be a sounding-board for a female way
of perceiving the world. With the exception of a few lieder, vocal music is
an example of the former category and the sonata of the latter.

Does Miriam's response to the sonata form then entail a re-valuation
of it in terms of gender? For all her intuitive capacity, this is not the case.
Like Helen Schlegel, she has problems breaking out of the rigid patriarchal paradigm. The first case of self-delusion becomes evident in her very
choice of music to practice. It testifies to the power of the established patriarchal canon in Edwardian England rather than an independent and
unprejudiced mind, as Miriam believes: "She would play something she
knew perfectly, a Grieg lyric or a movement from a Beethoven sonata ...
It must be Beethoven ... Grieg was different ... acquired ... like those
strange green figs pater had brought from Tarring ... Beethoven had always been real" (*PR* 56). However, her statement that "Beethoven had
always been real" can be put to the test. Indoctrinated by the imperialist
ideology of Edwardian England, she may easily perceive Beethoven as
real since his music sanctions this political outlook. Similarly, Grieg is
"acquired" by the mere fact that he is different. The question is, though,
whether Grieg's music and the figs are strange for the simple reason that
they deviate from the norm, just as women differ from the male norm.

As has been pointed out before, the sonata is a gendered discourse
since the male and female themes form a pattern according to which the
former is invariably presented as the superior. Miriam's choice of the Sonata Pathétique exemplifies this with great clarity as does her execution
of the first masculine movement associated with vigour and power:

> She chose the first part of the first movement of the *Sonata Pathétique*. That
> she knew she could play faultlessly. It was the last thing she had learned, and
> she had never grown weary of practising slowly through its long bars of chords.
> She had played it at her last music-lesson ... dear old Stroodie walking up
> and down the long drilling- room ... 'Steady the bass'; 'grip the chords,' then
> standing at her side and saying in the thin light sneery part of his voice, 'You
> can ... you've got hands like umbrellas' ... and showing her how easily she
> could stretch two notes beyond his own span. And then marching away as she
> played, and crying out to her, standing under the high windows at the far end
> of the room, 'Let it go! Let it go!' And she had almost forgotten her wretched
> self, almost heard the music... (*PR* 56)

This is technique in the traditional sense of the word. The music-teacher communicates the patriarchal imperialist ideology through his teaching, an action which has similarities with military drilling. The piano and Miriam herself are both obedient instruments. She cherishes the illusion that she "had almost heard the music."

The new technique, however, will enable her to actually hear the music without "forg[etting] her wretched self" and, by contrast, reinforcing her notion of a strong and independent female self. One step in this direction is to break the dominance of the tonic, the central musical sign in male musical discourse since the tonic, as has been shown above, must always be reaffirmed in order to reach finality and resolution. In the following passage, Miriam identifies in the first male movement of the sonata a dominant which, refusing to be resolved by the tonic, holds it in equilibrium. In noting that presence, she discovers a female identity pressing against the boundaries of a traditional discourse of imperialist expansionism which is intent on reducing her to a mere sounding-board for this ideology:

> She felt for the pedals, lifted her hands a span above the piano, as Clara had done, and came down, true and clean, on to the opening chord. The full rich tones of the piano echoed from all over the room, and some metal object far away from her hummed the dominant. She held the chord for its full term ... Should she play any more? ... She had confessed herself ... just that minor chord ... any one hearing it would know more than she could ever tell them ... her whole being beat out the rhythm as she waited for the end of the phrase to insist on what already had been said ... Grave and happy she sat with unseeing eyes, listening, for the first time. (*PR* 56–57)

Cecilia Björkén-Nyberg

Notes

1. Martyn Evans, *Listening to Music* (Houndmills: Macmillan, 1990) 100.

2. Evans 101.

3. See, for instance, Anne Foata, "The Knocking at the Door. A Fantasy on Fate, Forster and Beethoven's Fifth," *Cahiers Vicoriens and Edouardiens* 44 (1996): 135–45.

4. E.M. Forster, *Howards End* (London: Penguin, 1989). This novel will subsequently be referred to as *HE* in parenthetical references.

5. Evans 1–2.

6. Lawrence Kramer, *Classical Music and Postmodern Knowledge* (Berkeley: University of California Press, 1995) 53.

7. Jonathan Culler, "Reading as a Woman," *On Deconstruction: Theory and Criticism after Structuralism* (Ithaca, 1982) 58, quoted in Marcia J. Citron, *Gender and the Musical Canon* (Cambridge: Cambridge University Press, 1993) 176.

8. Leon Botstein, "Hearing is Seeing: Thoughts on the History of Music and the Imagination," *The Musical Quarterly*, 79.4 (Winter 1995): 581–89.

9. Botstein 584.

10. Marcia J. Citron, "Feminist Approaches to Musicology," in *Cecilia Reclaimed: Feminist Perspectives on Gender and Music*, ed. Susan C. Cook and Judy S. Tsou (Urbana and Chicago: University of Illinois Press, 1994) 23–24.

11. Citron, *Gender and the Musical Canon* 68.

12. Citron, *Gender and the Musical Canon* 115.

13. Christine Battersby, *Gender and Genius: Towards a Feminist Aesthetics* (London: Women's Press, 1989) 8.

14. Citron, *Gender and the Musical Canon* 184.

15. Otto Weininger, *Sex and Character*, quoted in Battersby 115.

16. Weininger, quoted in Battersby 113.

17. Andreas Huyssen, *After the Great Divide: Modernism, Mass Culture, Postmodernism* (Bloomington: Indiana University Press, 1986), quoted in Battersby 6.

18. Carl Dalhaus, *Nineteenth-Century Music*. Trans. Bradford Robinson (Berkeley: University of California Press, 1989), quoted in Citron "Feminist Approaches to Musicology" 22–23.

19. Citron, *Gender and the Musical Canon* 108.

20. Citron, "Feminist Approaches" 23.

21. Peter Gay, *The Bourgeois Experience: Victoria to Freud. Vol IV: The Naked Heart* (New York: Norton, 1995) 21.

22. "The English Amateur," *The Musical World*, 25 Feb. 1905: 132.

23. Peter Widdowson, "*Howards End:* Fiction as History," E.M. Forster, *Howards End* (Boston: Bedford Books, 1997) 365.

24. A.B. Marx. *Die Lehre von der musikalischen Komposition*, quoted in Citron, "Feminist Approaches" 20.

25. See, for instance, Hugo Riemann, *Katechismus der Musik* (Leipzig: Max Hesse, 1888) and Vincent D'Indy, *Cours de composition musicale* (Paris: Durand et Cie, 1902–9).

26. Citron, "Feminist Approaches" 19.

27. Citron, *Gender and the Musical Canon* 139.

28. Kramer 53.

29. Compton Mackenzie, *Sinister Street* (London: Penguin, 1960. This novel will subsequently be referred to as *SS* in parenthetical references.

30. Kramer 53.

31. Gillian E Hanscombe, "Introduction," Dorothy Richardson, *Pilgrimage 1* (London: Virago, 1979) 1.

32. Dorothy Richardson, *Pilgrimage 1* 10. This novel will subsequently be referred to as *PR* in parenthetical references.

33. Donald Read quotes E.E. Williams, *Made in Germany* (Heinemann, 2nd ed., 1896) 172–75 in *Documents from Edwardian England 1901–1915* (London: Harrap, 1973) 129–31. Williams presents a list of possible ways of dealing with increasing pressure from foreign competition in trade.

34. Citron, *Gender and the Musical Canon* 178.

35. Citron, *Gender and the Musical Canon* 168.

36. Citron, *Gender and the Musical Canon* 180.

37. Citron, *Gender and the Musical Canon* 172–73.

38. Citron, *Gender and the Musical Canon* 173.

7

Ernest J. Gaines and *A Lesson Before Dying*:
The Literary Spiritual

In *A Lesson Before Dying*, Ernest J. Gaines tells the story of a significant event in the community of Bayonne, Louisiana in the 1940's, using the spiritual as analogy. The story revolves around Jefferson, a young man unjustly tried and sentenced to death by electrocution, and Grant Wiggins, a schoolteacher who is enlisted to help him die with dignity. Like the spiritual, the novel is emotive, much the same as a musical experience. *A Lesson Before Dying* is a Passion book,[1] complete with musical setting and full of core symbolism for a Louisiana community, indeed for the African Diaspora. Through the tension/release suggested by complex counterpoint, repetition of questions, and call-and-response, *A Lesson Before Dying* presents an allegory to the crucifixion of Jesus with specific emphasis on the crucifixion spiritual, "Were You There?" paired with "He Never Said a Mumblin' Word."[2]

"Were You There" relates the entire story through call-and-response, repetition, and melody. Each of the verses of "Were You There?" describes a stage of the event: 1. "Were You There when they crucified my Lord," 2. "Were You There when they nailed him to the tree?" 3. "Were You There when they pierced him in his side?" 4. "Were You There when they laid him in the tomb?" Each line, repeated, is followed by the chorus: "Oh, sometimes, it causes me to tremble, tremble, tremble." This first line of the chorus is followed by a restatement of the appropriate verse. In other words, chorus one ends with "Were You There when they crucified my Lord?" Chorus two ends with "Were You There when they nailed him to the tree," and so on through every verse. Through the lens of "Were You There," which turns on the Bible story, Gaines raises philosophical questions about the dominant culture and the implications of its attitudes toward issues such as the death penalty, manhood, and sacred laws of the divine. These questions, combined with direct references to what can be called "Jefferson's Theme," "He Never Said a Mumblin' Word," are specific to the overall themes of the novel, and serve as the signposts which guide this discussion. Although much more can be written about Gaines's use of the spiritual, only two primary uses will be explored here: cultural signification[3] and structure.

Cultural Signification

Since the sixties, the uses of African American vernacular music as literary devices have become studied strategies in poetry and fiction. With the renascence of Zora Neale Hurston, the blues poetry of Langston Hughes, the musicality of Ralph Ellison, the works of Alice Walker, Ishmael Reed, Gayl Jones, and most revered *Jazz* diva, Toni Morrison, many writers explore this musico-literary intersection, adding their own expository contributions to those of African-American scholars. Scholars such as Houston A. Baker, Jr., LeRoi Jones (Amiri Baraka), Arthur Jones, Bernice Johnson Reagon, Albert Murray, Henry Louis Gates, Cornel West, bell hooks, Angela Davis, Paul Gilroy and Barbara Fields have offered perspectives from their various fields of study.

Vernacular theories proposed by these scholars have several elements in common which can be applied to readings of African American literature. Aspects such as double consciousness, riddles (or questions), the trope of the Talking Book, worrying the line, or playing the dozens contribute to authenticity and/or re-constructionist theoretical inquiries, or, as Robert Stepto suggests, "a methodology for an integrated study of Afro-American folklore and literature."[4] An integrated study requires an understanding of idioms and views unique to the African American experience, especially the cultural legacy resulting from this experience. The legacy of African American music is well-known, and its inter-textual resonance elevates the meaning of the text.[5] The free voice, an important part of any cultural legacy, contributes to the reconstruction of identity without diluting its folklore.

Gayl Jones, in *Liberating Voices: Oral Tradition in African American Literature*, has discussed Gaines's *The Autobiography of Miss Jane Pittman* in this light. She has stated that Gaines may be discussed as a writer whose black speech breaks out of the narrative frame, tells a story within a story and frees the voice of Miss Jane. As Jones remarks about *The Autobiogra-*

phy, "The oral aspect and the "I" are integral parts of Gaines's story and the storyteller's creative and regenerative energy."[6] *A Lesson Before Dying* follows this same strategy, but the schoolteacher's voice in *Lesson* isn't the only one that is liberated. The voice of the hero, Jefferson, a condemned yet innocent man, is freed as well, and the concept of the "defeated hero" (which could also describe Jesus at the moment of crucifixion), the story-within-a-story, and the use of cultural idioms such as dialect combine to create a chorale suggestive of the spiritual or gospel music. No doubt Gaines's acoustic environment is filled with music because the spiritual is a part of the African American oral tradition which evokes slavery, religion, sufferings, and transformations and provides authenticity to *Lesson*. The words, "I was not there, yet I was there" spoken by the schoolteacher, Grant Wiggins, as narrator, open *Lesson*. This allusion to the spiritual "Were You There?" signals the reader that, 1) the African American community is present, and 2) central to the story are the themes of persecution and redemption or transformation.

The transformative power and archetypal immediacy of "Were You There?" is explained by Arthur C. Jones in his book, *Wade in the Water: The Wisdom of the Spirituals*. Jones states that both the melody and the words require our attention:[7] ("Oh, sometimes it causes me to tremble, tremble, tremble; were you there when they crucified my Lord?"), repeated over and over, guides us into the spiritual recesses of our souls; and the symbolism of crucifixion, so similar in physical and emotional impact to the daily life of people in slavery, assists the singer and listener in understanding the suffering that was present in that experience. It provides listeners with a glimpse of a transformative process in which singers can experience hope that their present suffering is not the end of the story."[8] "I was not there, yet I was there,"[9] not only answers the question of the spiritual "Were You There?," but also begs (worries) it, for the first chapter rattles with the brutal injustice of Jefferson's trial.

After introducing the phrase, "I was not there, yet I was there," Grant Wiggins tells the story of the trial, weaving the facts of Jefferson's experience with the arguments of the prosecutor and the defense lawyer. Jefferson is innocent, but his naive action of accepting a ride from two men, Brother and Bear, who rob a liquor store and kill the owner, results in heavy circumstantial evidence which points toward his guilt. The defense lawyer, who compares him to a hog, states as Jefferson's defense that he is too much of a fool to have been involved in the crime. And so the first verse of Gaines's literary spiritual ends with the judge ruling that Jefferson is guilty: "Death by electrocution. The governor would set the date."[10]

Gaines's sub-theme of hope that there is a life beyond the suffering enters after the date of the execution is set, as narrator Grant Wiggins and his fiancé walk around the quarter:

> We left the house. Up at the church, Reverend Ambrose had just started his 'Termination song, 'Amazing Grace.' We went down the quarter.
> Most of the people who had not gone to church were indoors. Seldom was someone sitting out on the porch, and no one worked in the gardens or chopped wood in the yard. Horses and mules were grazing in the pasture beside and behind the houses...the entire plantation was deadly quiet, except for the singing coming from the church up the quarter behind us.[11]

Determination Sunday, or 'Termination Day, according to Zora Neale Hurston, is an aspect of a 'love-feast' (Methodist) or 'experience meeting' (Baptist) that is held once a month before Communion.[12] Gaines, choosing "Amazing Grace" at this moment, places Reverend Ambrose in his role as healer for the community's grief. The preacher helps them find meaning in a seemingly meaningless world. Gaines's narrator, Grant Wiggins, has difficulty grading school papers because he can't concentrate due to his Tante Lou's practicing of her "determination song." As Tante Lou practices her song in a high soprano voice, preparing for "Determination Sunday" or "Termination (judgment) day:"

> I went back inside. I had started correcting papers a couple of hours earlier, but I hadn't done very much. On Sunday, my aunt began getting ready for church as soon as she woke up, which was around six o'clock. Until eleven o'clock, there was nothing I could do but listen to her singing her 'Termination song.'
> Determination Sunday was the third Sunday of each month, when members of the church would stand and sing their favorite hymns and tell the congregation where they were determined to spend eternity. My aunt started warming up at six in the morning, whether it was 'Termination Sunday or not, and didn't quit until eleven, when she walked out of the house. I would be forced to put away the work until after she had gone, or I would go for a walk through the quarter and back into the field.[13]

This form of Protestant confessional, known as testimony, says Hurston, has a variation in which the person who wants to testify sings a verse or two of a hymn, then: "speaks expressing (a) love for everybody, (b) joy at being present, (c) tells of the determination to stay in the field to the end. Or, (2) sings a 'hot' spiritual, giving the right hand of fellowship to the entire church, and a shouting, tearful finish that (3) (a) expresses joy at being present, (b) recites an incident of conversion, telling in detail the visions seen and voices heard, and (c) expresses determination to hold out to the end."[14] Grant finally stops to listen:

> I pushed away the papers and listened to the singing [from the church]. Miss Eloise was singing her 'Termination song, 'Were You There When They Crucified my Lord?' You could hear that high shrill voice all over the plantation. I had been hearing it all my life, all my life. After her there would be someone else, then someone else. It would go on for three or four hours. And it was impossible to do anything but listen to it or leave.[15]

As Arthur Jones sees it, the people who sang these songs were people of profound self-understanding and awareness who had the ability to transcend their suffering, and the spirituals are a testament and "an historical record of the reality of their oppression, unparalleled in the history of human civilization."[16]

As hero, Jefferson, searching for transcendence, finds some refuge in his knowledge of the story of the crucifixion of Jesus. The spiritual "He Never Said a Mumblin' Word" frames his transformation. He asks Grant Wiggins if he believes in God, to which the teacher replies that he does. Jefferson continues his philosophical questioning, asking Grant Wiggins the simple question "How?", to which the teacher replies that he thinks it's God that makes people play and sing, makes the trees and food grow from the earth.

> Then Jefferson asks, 'Who make people kill people, Mr. Wiggins?'
> 'They killed His Son, Jefferson.'
> 'And He never said a mumbling word.'
> 'That's what they say.'
> 'That's how I want to go, Mr. Wiggins. Not a mumbling word.'[17]

For Jefferson, the spiritual is his "harmony of despair"[18] after the date for his execution is set. At Christmastime, Wiggins tells Jefferson about the children at school rehearsing their Christmas program. While he is speaking, Wiggins realizes that Jefferson is thinking of something else:

> 'It's Christmas?' he asked. But he was not thinking about Christmas; he was thinking about something else. And he knew that I knew he was thinking about something else.
> 'No, Christmas is still a few weeks off, 'I said. 'but we're getting ready.'
> 'That's when he was born, or that's when he died?' he asked.
> 'Who?' I said. He looked at me, knowing that I knew who he was talking about.

'Born,' I said.
'That's right, 'he said. 'Easter when they nailed him to the cross and he never said a mumbling word.'[19]

According to the Bible, as Arthur Jones points out, Jesus actually did utter a few words.[20] These words illustrate that the theology in the spirituals is core symbolism, not fundamentalist religion; it speaks to the oppression of the people. Jones comments that although the African people were forced to endure the physical and emotional agony of slavery and could not control the outward circumstances of their abuse, they could definitely control the extent to which they acknowledged their pain. To be silent was one powerful form of resistance.[21]

Structural Aspects

The structural aspects of the novel, call and response, repetition, and counterpoint, emphasize such a silent resistance. Call-and-response patterns of the spiritual appear throughout *Lesson*. Immediately following the trial, where Jefferson has been called a hog by his own (white) lawyer in court, his godmother, Emma, wants Grant Wiggins to teach Jefferson to become a man before he dies. The silence accents her request as she calls upon Grant to help her godson gain his dignity:

> 'Called him a hog.'
> She said that, and it was quiet again. My aunt looked at me, then back down at the table. I waited.
> 'I know he was just trying to get him off. But they didn't pay that no mind. Still give him death.'
> She turned her head slowly and looked directly at me. Her large, dark face showed all the pain she had gone through this day, this past weekend. No. The pain I saw in that face came from many years past.
> 'I don't want them to kill no hog,' she said. 'I want a man to go to that chair, on his own two feet.'[22]

Grant's reluctant response to Emma's call that he shoulder the burden of Jefferson's lessons in dignity indicate his acknowledgement that his responsibilities to the classroom lessons reach far beyond reading, writing and arithmetic. He knows he must teach those in his charge the important lessons of survival in an unfriendly society as well as academic knowledge. Therefore, he teaches his students to respond clearly to the white superintendent of schools: "Please respond loudly: 'Thank you, Dr. Joseph.' Which they did, loudly."[23] Looking over the classroom, Dr. Joseph singles out specific children from each grade and calls on them:

> 'Did you say your bible verse this morning, Gloria?'
> 'Yes, sir, Dr. Joseph.'
> 'Well, what did you say?' he asked her
> 'I said, "Lord is my shepherd, I shall not want," Dr. Joseph.'
> 'Hummm,' Dr. Joseph said. 'Seems I've heard that one before...'[23]

Dr. Joseph then calls on the one boy in class whom Grant wishes had stayed home that day. This boy answers "Yazir," to Dr. Joseph's question and pledges allegiance to the flag: "Plege legen toda flag. Ninety state. 'Merica. Er—er—yeah, which it stand. Visibly. Amen."[25]

The children each respond as they have been taught, appropriately in unison or individually, and in the oppressive air of the schoolroom hang stifling echoes of slavery. The children chop their own wood for heat, the schoolroom is an old plantation church, the chalk is a premium item, and the textbooks are marked and torn from previous use. Gaines emphasizes these similarities through Grant's observations during the half hour that follows.

> Dr. Joseph would call on someone who looked half bright, then he would call on someone whom he felt was just the opposite... And besides looking at hands, now be began inspecting teeth. Open wide, say 'Ahhh'—and he would have the poor children spreading out their lips as far as they could while he peered into their mouths. At the university I had read about slave masters who had done the same when buying new slaves, and I had read of cattlemen doing it when purchasing horses and cattle.[26]

These call-and-response patterns, interwoven with cultural conflict, build a counterpoint, a third structural tool shared with music. Grant Wiggins tells us this story from the present, thus is conscious of himself as the story-teller as well as a character in the story. Alternating between his present and his earlier life as a child in the quarter and a student at the University, he tells us much more than the story of Jefferson. This volleying of inner/outer worlds, reminiscent of the spirituals, which often contained coded messages, raises many of the philosophical questions that inform *A Lesson Before Dying*. As a binary construct, this shape can be seen as a crossroads, a railroad crossing, and perhaps most specifically, a cross. Its simultaneous themes run in contrast to each other, and its continuous form is similar to a long-meter hymn or the crucifixion spirituals such as "Were You There" and "He Never Said a Mumblin' Word." These contrasts orchestrate a story that oscillates between past and present, draws parallels between them, and examines the interstices of black/white, urban/agrarian, educated/uneducated, and sacred/profane.[27]

The sacred/profane dialectic is easily traced in the novel. Questioning the degree to which this music influences Jefferson's soul, the character of Reverend Ambrose calls attention to the age-old controversy between gospel music and secular music.[28] Grant Wiggins tells Jefferson he likes to listen to those "lowdown blues" and talks honestly to the Reverend about his own agnosticism while he reinforces his argument that Jefferson needs the radio in his cell.

The tenuous yet honest relationship between Reverend Ambrose and Grant Wiggins explores this polarity, one that demonstrates the universality of *Lesson*. Grant, the non-believer, is associated with the stuff of blues—car wheels on crushed seashells, bars, lying to his Aunt, fist-fights, and love for Vivian, who is in the midst of a divorce. On one visit to Jefferson's cell, before Grant buys the radio, (in fact his inspiration for it) he vies for Jefferson's attention:

> 'Inez is still giving her fairs up the quarter,' I said, trying to get him back. 'But no music. No dancing. She calls that sinning. If you want your music at a fair, you have to go down to Willie Aaron's house. Willie still has that stack of old low-down blues—Tampa Red, Mercy Dee—you know, all of them....'
> 'I just thought of something.' I told him. 'Let me bring you a little radio. You can have music all the time. You can listen to Randy's Record Shop late at night.'
> 'Randy still on?' he asked, looking at the wall, not at me.
> 'Yes, he's still on,' I said. 'I was listening to him just the other night.
> I have to play the radio low so Tante Lou can't hear it. These old people, you know,—all music except church music is sinning music....'[29]

In response to the secularity of Grant's beliefs, Reverend Ambrose admits to Grant that he lies to his people. He lies about his own pain and suffering in order to help others. Grant has told Ambrose that he will not lie to Jefferson about his belief in heaven. It is at this point that Grant learns more about his obligations, as Preacher Ambrose, building to a crescendo, reminds Grant how his Aunt's hands bled for him through her hard work. Indirectly, this repetition of crucifixion imagery keeps the tension of Jefferson's fate at the forefront of the novel, and again evokes the spiritual. The sheriff has told Grant that if any problems arise, he will take the radio and stop the visits. After the radio has been given to Jefferson, Grant arrives home to discover:

> ...All three of them were sitting around the kitchen table when I came in. They had already finished their coffee. The cups were still on the table, but empty.

> 'You know what you done done?' my aunt asked me...
> 'What did I do?' I asked.
> 'Why?'
> 'Why what, Tante Lou?'
> 'That radio!' she said. 'That radio!'
> 'What's wrong with the radio?'
> 'What's wrong with it?' Reverend Ambrose cut in. 'What's wrong with it?
> that's all he do, listen to that radio, that's what's wrong with it."
> 'And what's wrong with that?' I asked.[30]

As they sit around the table glaring, Grant fights back.

> 'Tante Lou, that radio has nothing to do with turning Jefferson against God,'
> I said. 'That radio is there to help him not think about death. He's locked up
> in that cage like an animal—and what else can he think about but that last
> day and that last hour? That radio makes it less painful....'
> 'No, I said. 'You can have it your way. You can take it from him. But you
> won't reach him if you do. The only thing that keeps him from thinking he is
> not a hog is that radio. Take that radio away, and let's see what you can do
> for the soul of a hog.'[31]

Running simultaneously with the language of the spiritual, Gaines's contrapuntal techniques solve an age-old problem that occurs when a writer
cross-pollinates with music: how does one create a chorale developed from
simultaneous voices within a story line? It is impossible, when using musical structures in literature, to reproduce, for example, a chord. Words are
linear, and require the active participation of the reader and the resulting
variables. Gaines's multi-layered narrator, Grant Wiggins, feels, describes,
dialogues, questions, thinks, and informs the reader. In the aural textures
of Grant's visit to Jefferson in his cell, Gaines manages this complex musicalization[32] technique. After Grant purchases the radio, Jefferson listens to
"those lowdown blues" and sad cowboy songs from Randy's Record Shop.
However, Grant narrates as "You Are My Sunshine" plays on the radio in
descant to "Were You There," which is "Grant's Theme." The opening
notes of these two classic songs synchronize: the first three notes of "Were
You There," the interval of a fourth, followed by a minor third, and the
beginning notes of "You are My Sunshine," a fourth followed by a major
second, followed by another major second, coincide rhythmically and har-
monically. Example 1 is a notation of the first four measures. In common
time, "You are my Sunshine" begins on beat two, "Were You There" begins on beat three. "There" and "sun" fall together on beat one of the second measure. "when" and "shine" on the third beat, etc.

Ex. 1 Qhodlibet fragment (notated by the author)

Although the quodlibet[33] that results from the combination of these two songs is poignant and not amusing, its construction represents synchronous events in *Lesson*. At times the melodic contours are in contrary motion, at times parallel, at times unison, alternating between tension/release and consonance/dissonance. Jefferson listens night and day and is always searching for stronger stations.

In African-American vernacular music, repetition holds an important position. Speaking of the spiritual "He Never Said a Mumblin' Word," Jones states the repetitive melody line "leads us progressively into the inner reaches of the spirit, deepening that inner journey with each repetition."[34] The emphases engendered by repetition is a particular characteristic of "worrying the line." This "worrying" or repetition, is a structural technique Gaines reclaims from the spiritual:

> I was not there, yet I *was there*. No, I did not go to the trial, I did not hear the verdict, because I knew all the time what it would be. Still, I *was there*. I *was there* as much as anyone else *was there*.[35]

Other repetitions used as analogue to the spiritual occur when Grant Wiggins learns of the legal verdict from his Tante Lou and her friend Miss Emma, Jefferson's godmother, "although of course, he knew, as everyone knew, what the outcome would be." He wants to avoid Miss Emma, but his Aunt forces him, saying he has to sit and talk with them or she will throw him out of the house. Both Grant Wiggins and his Aunt repeat themselves:

> I stood back from the table and looked at the both of them, I clamped my jaws so tight the veins in my neck felt as if they would burst. I wanted to *scream* at my aunt; I was *screaming* inside. I had told her many, many times how much I hated this place and all I wanted to do was get away.... But she had not heard me before, and I knew that now matter how loud I *screamed*, she would not hear me now.[36]

Miss Emma and Tante Lou insist that Wiggins will teach Jefferson to become a man. Their relentless insistence—their repetition—their worrying the matter—also echoes the structure of "Were You There" with its four verses each followed by the same refrain and ending with the restatement of the verse. Miss Emma, according to Grant, "repeated the old refrain I had heard about a hundred times the day before."[37]

Repetition also occurs in the life of the community in the day-to-day routines which never change. Grant Wiggins grows tired of the sameness, and at times shows his unhappiness. His student, Inez, notices it at the Christmas play and tells him he looks unhappy.

> 'She was right; I was not happy. I had heard the same carols all my life, seen the same little play, with the same mistakes in grammar. The minister had offered the same prayer as always, Christmas or Sunday. The same people wore the same old clothes and sat in the same places. Next year it would be the same, and the year after that, the same again.[38]

And Jefferson repeats himself when he talks about his last meal.

> 'I want me a whole gallona ice cream,' he said…. 'A whole gallona vanilla ice cream. Eat it with a pot spoon. My last supper. A whole gallona ice cream.' He looked at me again. 'Ain't never had enough ice cream. Never had more than a nickel cone…. But now I'm go'n get me a whole gallon. That's what I want—a whole gallon. Eat it with a pot spoon.' "I can bring you some ice cream anytime, Jefferson," I said. 'I'm go'n wait,' he said. 'I'm go'n wait. I want a whole gallon. Eat is with a pot spoon. Every bit of it—with a pot spoon.'[39]

In the weeks prior to his death, Jefferson reveals his thoughts in a note-book. Changing in pulse, texture, and form, the staccato rhythms relate emotionally to the spiritual, and resonate contextually with slave narra-tive. Gaines's architecture of the spiritual as literary "sorrow song"[40] cul-minates in Jefferson's notebook. In response to Grant's suggestion that he write, Jefferson plays an expressive improvisation that recalls a slow blues:

> mr wigin you say rite somethin but I dont kno what to rite an you say I must be thinkin bout things I aint telin nobody an I order put it on paper but I dont kno what to put on paper cause I aint never rote nothin but homework I aint never rote a leter in all my life cause nanan use to get other chiren to rite her leter an read her leter for her not me so I cant think of too much to say but maybe nex time[41]

This first entry is followed by a gradual development of Jefferson's revela-tion, as he begins to describe his experiences:

> I dont know what day it is but las nite I coudn sleep an I cud yerned down the way snoin an I laid ther and thot bout samson sayin if the lord love me how com he let my wife die an leave ma an them chiren an how come he dont come here an take way people like them matin brothers on the st charl river stead of messin wit po ol foks who aint never done nothin but try an do all they kno how to serv him[42]

Still listening to the radio, Jefferson makes an important comment not only about the spiritual, but music itself, when he writes, "I can yer randy but I aint listnin no mo cause he for the livin an not for me."[43] Jefferson's melisma, or coded melody, continues until the morning of his scheduled execution. His last few phrases are shorter. Just as a jazz soloist when exploiting a theme might use diminution, augmentation, and poly-rhythms, Gaines improvises Jefferson's notebook:

> day breakin
>
> sun comin up
>
> the bird in the tre soun like a blu bird
>
> sky blu blu mr wigin
>
> good by mr wigin tell them im strong tell them im a man good by mr wigin im gon ax paul if he can bring you this
>
> sincely jefferson[44]

In what could be "Jefferson's Blues," the improvisational tone builds to a climactic moment in the hero's journal.

Coda

On the day of the execution, Grant Wiggins, the teacher, asks questions of himself, "worrying the line" of "Were You There?":

> Where was he at this very moment? At the window, looking out at the sky? Lying on the bunk, staring up at the gray ceiling? Standing at the cell door, waiting? How did he feel? Was he afraid? Was he crying? Were they coming to get him now, this moment? Was he on his knees, begging for one more minute of life? Was he standing? Why wasn't I there? Why wasn't I standing beside him? Why wasn't my arm around him? Why?[45]

Using the structure of questions that parallel the text of the spiritual requires the reader to imagine answers. These words recapitulate two primary themes of *A Lesson Before Dying*—injustice and oppression, combined with a message of hope. After Jefferson's notebook, Gaines's coda follows the model of the spiritual by encoding a hopeful message. The day's events are told as directly experienced by Grant Wiggins and his class, Miss Emma, the Godmother, Tante Lou, Reverend Ambrose and Paul, the deputy. Paul, the (white) deputy, has been helpful to Grant Wiggins throughout the ordeal. Importantly, he is the bearer of the news that the event is over. He relays the message from Jefferson, "Tell Nannan I walked." He is the one person in the white community who crosses the color barrier. He is transformed, just as the Biblical Paul, because *he was there.*

> 'You're one great teacher, Grant Wiggins,' he said.
> 'I'm not great. I'm not even a teacher.'
> 'Why do you say that?'
> 'You have to believe to be a teacher,' I said...
> 'I saw the transformation, Grant Wiggins,' Paul said.
> 'I didn't do it.'
> 'Who, then?'
> 'Maybe he did it himself.'
> 'He never could have done that. I saw the transformation. I'm a witness to that.'[46]

Although he has helped Grant Wiggins, Paul has never been in the quarter until the day of Jefferson's execution, when he brings Grant the notebook. However, he sticks out his hand in an effort to make friends with Grant. He says to Grant:

> 'Allow me to be your friend, Grant Wiggins. I don't ever want to forget this day. I don't ever want to forget him.'
> I took his hand. He held mine with both of his.
> 'I don't know what you're going to say when you go back in there. [to the school] But tell them he was the bravest man in that room today. I'm a witness, Grant Wiggins. Tell them so.'
> 'Maybe one day you will come back and tell them so.'
> 'It would be an honor.'
> I turned from him and went into the church. Irene Cole told the class to rise, with their shoulders back. I went up to the desk and turned to face them. I was crying.[47]

Just as the spiritual contains hope, *A Lesson Before Dying* ends with hope followed by tears of grief and release. As Ernest Gaines constructs his Passion story, he reconstructs the spiritual. The universal themes of suffering, oppression and transformation contain the music which has been born of them: blues and spirituals. His soundscapes meter the emotional content and infuse authenticity into the prose of *A Lesson Before Dying.*

A Lesson Before Dying fulfills the requirement of authenticity in the African American novel. It is a story which accomplishes the difficult task of remaining racially authentic, while integrating the polar oppositions of progress and dilution.[48] Gaines derives elements from spirituals, blues, the Bible and the political and social legacy of African American culture, and incorporates them into a story which liberates the liminal voices of the new/old order, the defeated hero, the dual consciousness of the narrator, and even the possible conversion of the "other," Grant/Paul, who, through seeing the transformation of Jefferson, has a transformation of his own. In *A Lesson Before Dying*, Gaines "explicates the trope of the Talking Book"[49] through his architecture of the reconstruction of identity, representation of the oral within the written, literary signifying upon the Bible and slave narratives. The result is the construction of a literary spiritual analogous to "Were You There?" which re-mythologizes the crucifixion and lifts the text beyond words.

Sarah E. Baker

Notes

1. Credit must be given to Dr. Julia Allen for use of the term 'Passion book' in this context.

2. For the music and complete words to both these spirituals, see *American Negro Songs and Spirituals*, Ed., John W. Work, (New York: Bonanza/Crown, 1940), 103 and 105.

3. I define "cultural signification" as the indication of a particular culture through the use of idioms and expressions unique to the culture, and identified with same.

4. Robert Stepto quoted by Houston A. Baker, Jr. in *Blues, Ideology and Afro-American Literature: A Vernacular Theory*, Chicago: The University of Chicago Press, 1984, 91.

5. Roland Barthes, citing Julia Kristeva, discusses *geno*-text and *pheno*-text in his essay "The Grain of the Voice." He suggests, along with scholars such as Bettina Knapp, that music elevates text beyond the meaning of the words (162–163). Discussing qualities of certain text as music, Barthes places listening into three categories and draws boundaries between hearing and listening. Hearing, Barthes says, is a physiological act, but listening is a psychological act. He distinguishes these three kinds of listening: "alert listening," "deciphering," and "signifying." On the level of signifying, the third kind of listening, the ear seizes upon who

speaks, or emits, and creates an "intersubjective space where 'I am listening' also means 'listen to me' and depends upon a general 'signifying' no longer conceivable without the determination of the unconscious and its endless interplay of transference" (246). This is the level of listening that we experience as the inner voice that speaks when we are reading silently.

Barthes's divisions of listening can be connected with the schema of R. Murray Schafer, who also separates hearing into three categories. *Soundscape* (italics mine), a term coined by Schafer in his book, *The Tuning of the World*, describes the study of acoustical environment and also elucidates a design for listening. In the twenty years since Schafer first published this comprehensive work on "heard events," new sounds have entered the environment. Yet, Shafer's theories have rarely been applied to the analysis of sound in literature and the relevance of time when using sound images. Schafer proposes that hearing aural images of a past time which resound from the silent page depends largely upon choices made by writers which stimulate an inner hearing.

6. Gayl Jones, *Liberating Voices: Oral Tradition in African American Literature* (New York: Penguin Books 1992), 166.

7. Arthur C. Jones, *Wade in the Water: The Wisdom of the Spirituals* (Maryknoll, NY: OrbisBooks, 1993), 30.

8. Arthur Jones, 30.

9. Ernest Gaines, *A Lesson Before Dying* (New York: Vintage/Random House, 1993), 3.

10. Gaines, 9.

11. Gaines, 106–107.

12. Zora Neale Hurston, *Mules and Men*, 1935. (New York: Harper & Row, Publishers, Inc., 1990), 247–248.

13. Gaines, 97–98.

14. Hurston, 247.

15. Gaines, 102.

16. Arthur Jones, 34.

17. Gaines, 223.

18. Arthur Jones, 34.

19. Gaines, 138–139.

20. See *The Holy Bible*, New Testament: Luke 23. The following specific verses are quoted from the King James Version, New York: Oxford University Press. Scolfield Edition 1969:

> Luke 23:34 "then said Jesus, Father, forgive them; for they know not what they do."

Luke 23:43 "And Jesus said unto him, 'Verily I say unto thee, Today shalt thou be with me in paradise.'

Luke 23:46 "And when Jesus had cried with a loud voice, he said, Father, into thy hands I commend my spirit, and having said this, he gave up the [spirit]."

A point relative to *Lesson*: one of the thieves who was crucified with Christ had "done nothing amiss." He is the person to whom Jesus is speaking in verse 43.

21. Arthur Jones, 32.

22. Gaines, 12–13.

23. Gaines, 53.

24. Gaines, 54.

25. Gaines, 56.

26. Gaines, 56.

27. Reingold Hammerstein discusses this dichotomy in two articles in the *Dictionary of the History of Ideas*. "Music as a Divine Art," and "Music as a Demonic Art," 264, 267–268.

Two pertinent excerpts:

Music as a divine or a demonic art is music that is not considered on its merits alone, but points beyond itself and man. Music as divine is connected with religion, and may be interpreted as an image, imitation, or anticipation of divine or heavenly music.

When music resonates the core of being; when it connects on a level beyond logic or reason into pure emotion; when it triggers complex psychic phenomena, it may be categorized as holy/unholy.... Such conceptions are encountered both in magical and in mythical eras, throughout cosmological and theological-metaphysical forms of thought, indeed well into structured philosophical systems. They possess a strongly thematic character...)

28. This sacred/profane dialectic is common ground the black and white community shares when concerned with music of the popular culture. Thomas Dorsey struggled with this split, playing with Ma Rainey, Mother of the Blues' as "Georgia Tom," while also writing some of the greatest hymns ever written, such as "Precious Lord, Take My Hand." In the white community an example of this sacred/profane split exists with Jerry Lee Lewis and Jimmy Swaggart— cousins who took different paths, both plagued with scandal.

29. Gaines, 171.

30. Gaines, 180–181.

31. Gaines, 182–183.

32. William Freedman, *"Tristram Shandy: The Art of Literary Counterpoint,"* in *Literature and Music: Essays on Form*, ed. Nancy Gluck, (Provo, Brigham Young University Press, 1984). Aldous Huxley first coined the term "musicalization of fiction" and wrote a novel *Point Counter Point* which demonstrates his technique. Mr. Freedman quotes *Point Counter Point*.

33. Quodlibet in the *New Grove Dictionary of Music and Musicians* is defined as a composition made of two or more well-known (usually) songs played polyphonically with each other, usually for purposes of amusement.

34. Arthur Jones, 31.

35. Gaines, 3.

36. Gaines, 14.

37. Gaines, 44.

38. Gaines, 151.

39. Gaines, 170.

40. Although W.E.B. DuBois refers to the spirituals as "sorrow songs," Zora Neale Hurston did not agree with this mournful way of describing the spirituals.

41. Gaines, 226.

42. Gaines, 227.

43. Gaines, 234.

44. Gaines, 234.

45. Gaines, 250.

46. Gaines, 254.

47. Gaines, 255–256.

48. Paul Gilroy, *The Black Atlantic: Double Consciousness and Modernity*. Cambridge: Harvard University Press, 1993), 94.

49. Henry Louis Gates, *The Signifying Monkey: A Theory of Afro American Literary Criticism* (New York: Oxford University Press, 1988), 131.

Works Cited

Baker, Houston A. Jr. *Blues, Ideology and Afro American Literature: A Vernacular Theory*. Chicago: The University of Chicago Press, 1984.

Gaines, Ernest. *A Lesson Before Dying*. New York: Vintage/Random House, 1993.

Gates, Henry Louis, Jr. *The Signifying Monkey: A Theory of Afro American Literary Criticism*. New York: Oxford University Press, 1988.

Gilroy, Paul. *The Black Atlantic: Modernity and Double Consciousness*. Cambridge: Harvard University Press, 1993.

Hammerstein, Reingold. "Music as a Demonic Art." *Dictionary of the History of Ideas*. ed. Philip P. Wiener. 4 vols. Vol. III. New York: Charles Scribner's Sons, 1973. 264–267.

———. "Music as a Divine Art." *Dictionary of the History of Ideas*. ed. Philip P. Wiener. 4 vols. Vol. III. New York: Charles Scribner's Sons, 1973. 267–271.

Hurston, Zora Neale. *Mules and Men*. 1935. New York: Harper & Row, Publishers, Inc., 1990.

Jones, Arthur C. *Wade in the Water: The Wisdom of the Spirituals*. Maryknoll, NY: Orbis Books, 1993.

Jones, Gayl. *Liberating Voices: Oral Tradition in African American Literature*. New York: Penguin Books, 1992.

Jones, LeRoi. *Blues People*. New York: William Morrow & Co., 1963.

Kirk-Duggan, Cheryl. *Exorcising Evil: A Womanist Perspective on the Spirituals*. Maryknoll, NY: Orbis Books, 1997.

Knapp, Bettina L. *Music, Archetype, and the Writer*. University Park, Pennsylvania: Pennslyvania University Press, 1988.

Morrison, Toni. *Playing in the Dark: Whiteness and the Literary Imagination*. New York: Vintage/Random House, 1993.

Spencer, Jon Michael. *Re-Searching Black Music*. Knoxville: The University of Tennessee Press, 1996.

West, Cornel. *Race Matters*. 1st Vintage Ed. New York: Vintage Books, 1993.

Work, John W., Ed., *American Negro Songs and Spirituals*. New York: Bonanza/Crown, 1940.

8

A Quartet that is a Quartet:
Lawrence Durrell's *Alexandria Quartet*

Just as the term "symphony" denotes both an orchestra and the form of work performed by an orchestra, so the musical term "quartet" denotes both "a composition for four solo performers" and the four performers themselves. The technical term for the quartet form is "sonata," which "refers to the structure of an individual movement" within a work, rather than "the overall form of a multi-movement work."[1] Unlike other literary works (such as *The Raj Quartet*, which merely has four parts, Tolstoy's "Kreutzer Sonata," which is merely named for the sonata performed by a character in the work, or the movie *Intermezzo*, which has no relationship to music form, Lawrence Durrell's *Alexandria Quartet* is indeed a literary application of the musical sonata (quartet) form.

Durrell's letters to Henry Miller indicate that he had given a great deal of thought to the application of the musical quartet form to literature. In September, 1937, Miller suggested to Durrell the idea of creating a quartet of writers—Alfred Perlés, William Saroyan, Durrell, and himself.[2] Years later Durrell wrote to Miller that he had supplied the title for Eliot's "Four Quartets." By calling the work a quartet, he indicates that he is aware that a work with four movements may be called a "quartet." Also by suggesting the title "Four Quartets" (in the plural) rather than simply "Quartet," Durrell shows that he is aware that "quartet" refers to a movement rather than a complete work. According to Ian S. MacNiven, "Durrell had no (or very little) formal musical training, although Miller had at one time considered a professional keyboard career and may have talked music theory to him. [Also] Durrell remained a lover of classical music and became friends with Yehudi Menuhin, who always saw to it that Larry received free tickets whenever he performed near Sommières." Durrell "was fascinated by Beethoven's quartets" and even "carried recordings of some of them to Corfu in 1935."[3]

Durrell wrote to Eliot that the four poems which make up *Four Quartets* "remind me of that gruesome last quartet of Beethoven. So arid, so abstract, and so dry, and yet so rich in another way." In a 1970 interview he said, "At that time ... [Eliot] hadn't in mind uniting all those four poems up." Durrell explained that Eliot had not given much thought to the poems, but said "I truthfully believe that the idea of the Beethoven quartet struck him. He didn't write me to say thank you for the title, but the correspondence is all about Beethoven's last quartets." Durrell also said, "I was thinking of *The Alexandria Quartet* as novels, but I was also struck by the relevance of the musical comparison."[4] Apparently he was also thinking of his quartet in relationship to four-dimensional reality, a concept which is analogous to the musical concept of a form which presents three different movements and then incorporates and goes beyond them all in the final movement.

Most quartets have four movements, all in sonata form except the third movement, which is often a rondo or scherzo. In presenting the many characters, complexities of plot, and contradictions of subjective truths which make up the world of his fictional Alexandria prior to and during World War II, Durrell follows this pattern. *Justine, Balthazar,* and *Clea* are thematically consistent and follow sonata form. Movement I, *Justine,* is a relatively straightforward twentieth century vision of a declining civilization, of a filthy, seedy, and often violent metropolitan city, and of its impoverished and despairing inhabitants. *Balthazar* presents a different view of Alexandria. Unlike the Europeanized Alexandria which Darley describes, Balthazar's Egypt is oriental, subversive, occult, primitive, often rural, and, ultimately unknowable. A breeding ground for political intrigue, betrayal, and murder, this Egypt is part of a world in a downward spiral toward world war. Balthazar is a second, slower movement in a minor key. Melissa, Scobie, and Toto de Brunel die. Darley is confused and disillusioned, and simple resolution of the plot of *Justine* is impossible. In a similar vein, *Clea* parallels the structure, incorporates the themes, and repeats the motifs of Justine and Balthazar with many variations. *Clea* provides new perspectives on the themes and characters from the previous novels at a later point in time. *Mountolive* functions as a simpler third movement with seven chapters of rising action followed by two of climax and seven of falling action. Standing in stark contrast to the complex— even convoluted and deceptive—polyphonic plot of the other novels, *Mountolive*'s plot is analogous to the simple melody of a monophony.

Durrell calls *Mountolive* "a straight naturalistic novel,"[5] which is "tame ... but the fulcrum of the quartet."[6] He also calls it "the third movement (rondo) of a symphonic poem"[7] and implies an analogy to Eliot's *Four Quartets*. Unlike the complicated forms of the other novels in Durrell's quartet, *Mountolive* is a single, simple, linear, chronological chronicle of the professional career of a simple protagonist. Its monophonic plot is without harmonic complexities or polyphonic melodies. Durrell's *Quartet*, like Browning's *The Ring and the Book*, Joyce's *Ulysses*, and Woolf's *To the Lighthouse*, utilizes many different points of view. Unlike the above mentioned authors [who usually just present various characters' narrations sequentially], Durrell employs a complicated and obscured layering of those narrations, many of which are imbedded within and distorted by a second- or third-hand narrator—a narration of "sliding panels ... like some medieval palimpset where different sorts of truth are thrown down one upon the other, the one obliterating or perhaps supplementing another."[8] *Mountolive* dramatizes a vision similar to those of Browning's "Half Rome" and "Other Half Rome" in *The Ring and the Book*—the simpler, even simple-minded vision, of an ordinary popular novel. Like newspaper reports, it presents simple straightforward "facts," superficial and erroneous explanations of motives, but no consideration of multiple causes and effects or causal sequences. Its interpretations are oversimplified. But its simplicity does provide a fulcrum for The Quartet. *Mountolive* has the unity and simplicity—almost superficiality—of many rondo and scherzo movements. Like many of those movements, its progression is orderly and speeds up toward the climax. Just as those monophonic movements usually follow one simple melody at a time, *Mountolive* follows one simple plot at a time.

The musical sonata (quartet) form is constructed of three parts—exposition, development, and recapitulation. It may also have an introduction and a coda. Eugene K. Wolf explains that "sonata form is ... [a] binary form in which an initial modulation from the tonic to a new key" (the dominant or relative minor) is followed by "a coordinated return of the main theme and the tonic key ... producing a rounded or recapitulating binary form." The following figure demonstrates this form.

A = Tonic V = Dominant or Other Related Key C1 = Closing Material

Part 1   Part 2
‖:A   (Cl.):‖:A'   (Cl.):‖
1——▶V————┤ V——▶1——┤

Two main parts of the sonata form are the exposition, "which modulates to the new key" and a longer second part, made up of the development
and recapitulation. The development "ordinarily modulates still farther
afield and provides varied and often dramatic treatment of material already heard in the exposition. The recapitulation ... is based thematically
upon the exposition but now ends as well as begins in the tonic" coordi-
nating tonality and theme. The following figure shows the full sonata form
of a movement:

N = new key   Pr. = primary material
Sec. = secondary material → = modulations   Tr. = transitional material
Cl = closing material   Retr = retransition

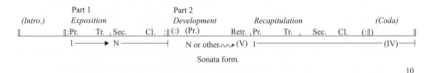

Sonata form.

10

Introductions: The introduction of a sonata form is a relatively short
passage, in slow tempo that introduces the movement.[11] Such introductions are present in *Justine, Balthazar,* and *Clea.* Chapters 1 through 10 of
Justine introduce Alexandria and establishes the mood of malaise which
permeates the city. Part I of *Balthazar* resketches the landscape and presents general ideas about the lovers and love affairs of Justine. Part I of
Clea, reviews Darley's memories of Alexandria, introduces Nessim and
Melissa's child, shows Darley's return to and describes wartime Alexandria, and reintroduces the major characters—especially Darley and Clea.

Expositions: Expositions have various structures, in which tonality (the
tonic key and its scale), thematic material (the musical idea, usually the
melody, but often including thematic variations), and large-scale rhythmic motion (the rhythm or pattern of movement in time, including tempo
(the speed at which the music is performed), and the duration of time of
sounds or silences. Exposition also establishes the primary harmonies of
the work.

Tonality in music corresponds to theme and mood in literature. Thematic materials in music, including melodies, "coherent succession[s] of
pitches,"[12] are analogous to narrative plot. The rhythmic motions of music, which include the rhythm or pattern of the movement in time, the

tempo, and the duration of notes and silences are analogous to the pace, duration, and frequency of the narrative events of a novel. And just as it is richness of tonality, interest, and complexity of melody and its attendant harmonies, and variation of rhythmic motion which makes for a satisfying work of music, so too, the significance of theme, the interest and variations of mood, and the pace, duration, and frequency of narrative make *The Alexandria Quartet* a satisfying reading and—unlike much other fiction—rereading experience. Literary harmonies would include the relationships between characters, relationships between plots, settings, and imagery, and the interactions of character, plot, setting, imagery, and mood.

Although individual episodes and tableaus of Durrell's *Quartet* are usually represented in normal chronological order, the sequence of the overall narrative of *Justine, Balthazar,* and *Clea* are anachronous. Durrell regularly utilizes analepse (recalling earlier events) in the same manner that melodies or melodic fragments may be presented anachronously and be interrupted by other melodies in music. Analepse is essential in music to recall earlier melodies and motives and to provide unity and interest to the work. Like all great composers and many novelists, Durrell employs and exploits the fictional possibilities of analepse of events as well as repetitions of quotations, dialogue, episodes, tableaus, and relationships. When Durrell employs repetitions and variations, it is never merely to recollect previous events but always to provide different motivations and interpretations of those events and of the characters whose influence was significant in motivating those events.

When quotations and dialogue are repeated like musical leitmotifs, Durrell repeats them in a different context or setting, by different characters, or with different meanings. When variations on familiar episodes recur, as they frequently do in *Clea*, they are in different settings and between different characters. When settings or tableaus recur they include different characters or moods. Likewise relationships recur with variation. When the same two characters meet in similar circumstances, as Darley and Justine do in *Clea*, the relationships have quite different meanings. Furthermore different characters may play the roles played by other characters in an almost identical relationship.

Justine's exposition (Chapters 11—29), like any good literary exposition, introduces the major characters, suggests the major plot lines, and describes Darley's getting to know and first having sex with Justine. *Justine*'s exposition shows a city with characters who, although bored and decadent, seem quite knowable. *Balthazar*'s exposition, Part II, re-presents the characters and events of Justine through the eyes of Pursewarden, Pursewarden's Interlinear, and Balthazar. It contains troubling facts and interpretations which undermine Darley's vision of reality. Part II of *Clea* parallels the exposition of both Justine and Balthazar. Instead of Darley's returning to the old Alexandria and continuing as Justine's lover, Darley must refamiliarize himself with a city changed by time and war. He finds a new lover in Clea. And he must view himself in the light of the troubling characterization of himself presented in Pursewarden's notebook.

Developments: As Wolf explains, the development sections of sonata form have "no stereotyped plan." Some "begin with a restatement of the primary theme in the new key .... Others introduce new or related material at this point, frequently transitional. Conventional descriptions of development sections emphasize the intensive, concentrated character of their thematic treatment ... applying such techniques as melodic variation, fragmentation, expansion or compression, contrapuntal combination, textural or contextual change, re-harmonization, and re-orchestration of one or many themes of the exposition."[13]

The development which complicates *Justine* is presented in Part II through Balthazar's old, wise, and cynical eyes. Like the andante or largo and sometimes minor key of a musical movement's development, Part II presents the dark underside of Alexandria which tempers, complicates, and renders impossible the optimism and clarity of the exposition. Cohen dies; Melissa becomes terminally ill; and Clea is introduced. This developmental movement is quite fragmented: some episodes take as little as one page and the longest only 11 pages. This section is also compressed, having fewer than 50 pages, which makes it less than half as long as either other movement.

Part III of *Balthazar*, its development, produces further complication by showing both Balthazar's interpretation of Darley's manuscript (Justine) and Darley's attempt to understand and accept Balthazar's interlinear. This movement is also very fragmented and compressed... And there are significant variations as Darley confronts a variety of troubling facts— particularly that Justine had become his lover only because of marital and political motivations. In contrast with the development movement of Justine, in which Darley grew in self-confidence and optimism, here Darley must face very troubling questions about his own identity and about his relationship with Justine.

Finally, Part III of *Clea* is its development. Like the developments of *Justine* and *Balthazar*, this one is also fragmented. It takes less than 40 pages, but it nevertheless contains extremely important events. The war recedes; Capodistria writes letters describing incredible occult events; Balthazar tells the story of the sailor who died as the result of a "golden needle"; and Pombal's Fosca dies during a boating excursion on the Mediterranean and is buried; and Scobie prophecises that Narouz not only wants Clea to join him in death but will try to drag her down to the grave with him. There are various reverberations of both previous and subsequent events. Darley learns that Capodistria did not die in the duck shoot. Fosca's death by gunfire while boating not only echoes Darley's unfounded fears about the duck shoot, Capodistria's faked death in *Justine*, and Narouz's death by gunfire in *Balthazar*, but also harbinges Clea's impalement and drowning.

Recapitulations: Recapitulations "run the gamut from nearly exact restatement of the material of the exposition ... to thoroughgoing recomposition involving extensive compression or expansion." There are two kinds. One kind has a "primary theme [which] recurs in the subdominant rather than the tonic key." Another kind "is the partial recapitulation," which reestablishes "the tonic after the development section is entrusted to the secondary and closing themes alone; [in it] the primary theme does not reappear."[14]

In *Justine*, Part III, the recapitulation returns to the novel's primary subject, Justine herself, and has a simpler, more linear, and more unified plot than the earlier parts of the novel. In it, suspense mounts toward the novel's climax. Darley expects to be killed at the Mareotis duck shoot. World War II looms closer. And Justine leaves Alexandria, concluding the plot. In *Balthazar*'s recapitulation, Part IV, Darley spends much time with Clea (foreshadowing the last novel). Part IV and the novel itself reach their climax when Clea tells Darley that Narouz had confessed to killing Justine and of loving Clea. In *Clea* the last part of Part III functions as its recapitulation. It contains the climax not only of this novel but of the whole quartet—Clea's underwater impalement and near-drowning and the resolution, Darley's realization that he will leave Alexandria, never to return.

Codas: A coda is "a concluding section extraneous to the [sonata] form. ... and may consist of only a few perfunctory chords."[15] In *The Quartet* codas usually consist of letters and of descriptions of Darley's Aegean island. *Justine, Balthazar*, and *Clea* all have such codas. In *Justine* Part IV briefly describes Alexandria without Justine, Darley's island retreat, and his letter from Clea. In *Balthazar*, Chapter 14, the coda, contains two letters, one from Clea to Darley and one from Pursewarden to Clea, which she sends on to Darley. The coda of *Clea*, Part IV, also consists of two letters, a long letter from Darley to Clea and one from her to him which indicates that she will go to France, where she expects to meet and resume her love affair with him.

Just as the individual novels *Justine, Balthazar*, and *Clea* have an internal quartet form, *The Alexandria Quartet* itself maintains a quartet form, with each novel serving as a movement. Often the first movement does indeed serve as an exposition; it is in the controlling key (frequently a major key); it presents main themes; and it itself has a recapitulating binary form. *Justine* serves as exposition for the entire quartet, moves at a relatively rapid pace, establishes the primary key, evolves in a relatively straightforward manner, and brings the initial elements to at least a temporary resolution. Like the second movements of many musical quartets, *Balthazar* is slower and darker, offering a quite different and darker vision than the first movement. The narration is fragmented. And characters are recombined in various relationships, especially Darley and Justine, Justine and Nessim, Darley and Nessim, and Narouz and Clea. Like the third movement, *Mountolive* itself does not have a quartet form, but follows a simpler linear pattern. Finally *Clea* recapitulates the elements that have been generated through the first two novels and brings them to a satisfying resolution.

Not only does the overall structure of the novel adhere to quartet form, but there are also smaller devices common to many musical forms which are more frequently utilized by Durrell than by most writers. Repeated again and again are larger themes, smaller motifs, and very specific leitmotifs (settings, details, even sentences) which are reiterated contrapuntally in different contexts with many variations. Like the first violin, Darley is usually the central voice and the one who controls the presentation and entry of other voices, but other voices, such as Balthazar, may assume control. Conversations occur between many unlikely voices. There are duets, trios, and quartets in which pairs of conversations alternate or are juxtaposed. Sometimes the voices are in harmony; sometimes they are dissonant. At times the action is mono-metric and at other times it is multi-metric, with frequent changes of pace, or polyrhythmic, with different paces occurring simultaneously. What Paul Howard Epstein has said of Shostokovich's quartets is true of Durrell's *Quartet*, Sometimes the melody is traditional with dissonant harmonies. Sometimes the harmonies are traditional, and the melodies are dissonant. Sometimes there are common harmonies in "complex or startling progressions. ... [sometimes] passages of extreme harmonic dissonance [may move] in stately block patterns. Thus the music is held together even as it threatens to fly apart."[16]

Durrell's *Quartet* is indeed analogous to the musical quartet form—indeed to a very complex one. Eugene K. Wolf's conclusions about Beethoven's middle and late string quartets also describe *The Alexandria Quartet*. He describes an "extraordinary increase in dramatic intensity" and an "expanded pitch range and technical difficulty" of works which "are highly individual in conception" and have "large-scale forms." These works have a "pervasive interest in contrapuntal procedures" and an "enormous range of contrasts."[17]

By eschewing the traditional novel form in which the events of the story are presented chronologically (or even with traditional analepsis) and by utilizing instead the artificial structure of the sonata allegro form, Durrell has created a quartet of novels that are, as the best novels should be—innovative and truly "novel." The sonata allegro form provides a structure in which Durrell can readily utilize various modernist tactics, including a half dozen protagonists who are foregrounded at various parts of the quartet, episodes that are often merely unresolved fragments, and a score of narrators, many of whose reports are filtered through one or two other consciousnesses. Such a form and such tactics enable him to vividly demonstrate how very difficult it is to ascertain even the facts of certain events, much less any kind of truth.

Sherry Lutz Zivley

Notes

1. Eugene K. Wolf, "Sonata Form," *The New Harvard Dictionary of Music*, ed. Don Randall (Cambridge, Massachusetts: Harvard University Press, 1986), 764.

2. Lawrence Durrell and Henry Miller, *Lawrence Durrell and Henry Miller: A Private Correspondence*, ed. George Wickes (London: Faber and Faber, 1962–1963), 116.

3. Ian S. MacNiven, letter to Sherry Lutz Zivley, 23 January 1992.

4. Eugene Lyons and Harry T. Antrim, "An Interview with Lawrence Durrell," *Shenandoah* 22 (Winter, 1971), 54.

5. Durrell and Miller, 320.

6. Durrell and Miller, 327.

7. Durrell and Miller, 338.

8. Balthazar, 183.

9. Eugene K. Wolf, "Binary and Ternary Form," in *The New Harvard Dictionary of Music*, edited by Don Randall (Cambridge, Massachusetts: Harvard University Press, 1986), 96.

10. Wolf, "Sonata Form," 764.

11. Don Randall, "Introduction," *The New Harvard Dictionary of Music*, edited by Don Randall (Cambridge, Massachusetts: Harvard University Press, 1986), 402.

12. Wolf, "Sonata Form," 764.

13. Wolf, "Sonata Form," 764.

14. Wolf, "Sonata Form," 765.

15. Don Randall, "Coda," in *The New Harvard Dictionary of Music* (Cambridge, Massachusetts: Harvard University Press, 1986), 178.

16. Epstein, Paul Howard, Program Notes for the Emerson String Quartet performance, Wed., April 29, 1992, Stude Concert Hall, Alice Pratt Brown Hall, Rice University, Houston, Texas.

17. Wolf, "String Quartet" in *The New Hardvard Dictionary of Music* (Cambridge, Ma: Harvard U P), 809.

9

Music as a Locus of Social Conflict and Social Connection in Friedrich Torberg's *Süsskind von Trimberg*

In 1928, Mikhail M. Bakhtin and Pavel N. Medvedev wrote: "It is not the individual, subjective psychic states it elicits that are important in art, but rather the social connections, the interactions it brings about."[1] This observation is fully borne out in the aesthetic theories of such members of the Bakhtin Circle as Bakhtin, Medvedev, and Valentin N. Voloshinov. These theories have profoundly influenced contemporary understanding of such divergent disciplines as literary studies, philosophy, anthropology, linguistics, psychology, and social theory, and the role of music as a communicative medium.

The application of these theories to the realm of music can be of great value to musicologists and scholars with an interdisciplinary interest in music because they tend to explicate the importance of music from a different angle: instead of viewing music strictly as an object of hedonistic pleasure, Bakhtinian theories tend to illuminate music as an object of and vehicle for social intercourse. Music plays a simultaneous role as an aesthetic and social phenomenon. Music not only determines social interaction but is determined by it.

The theories of the Bakhtin Circle can therefore promote a sociological understanding of music. This can be demonstrated by using these theories to interpret Friedrich Torberg's biographical and historical novel of a thirteenth-century itinerant musician, *Süsskind von Trimberg* (1972).

It is the contention of this essay that music possesses semiotic value. Certainly it can be taken as a given that musical lyrics possess semiotic value just as much as lyric poetry. Furthermore, musical instrumentation and melody possess semiotic value through their efforts to convey emotions, feelings, and reactions that intensify the message of the lyrics. If the premise that music possesses semiotic value is accepted, then it also follows that music is a legitimate realm for ideological enquiry.

As Bakhtin and Medvedev point out: "The study of ideologies embraces all areas of man's ideological creativity."[2] Perhaps more than any other realm of human creativity, music possesses the ability to establish and promote relationships between individuals of varying social backgrounds. Because of the ability of differing personages to interpret music in different ways, it can be either a locus of social connectedness or a locus of social and ideological struggle. Music can transcend barriers created by differences in social class, ethnicity, and religion or it can accentuate such barriers.

Unfortunately the discipline of Semiotics has largely ignored its importance to music, because the ambiguity of musical signs has led many people to deny that they have semiotic value. However, music is an element that profoundly influences human consciousness and therefore must of necessity possess semiotic value. According to Voloshinov: "Consciousness itself can arise and become viable only in the material embodiment of signs."[3] The process by which music acquires semiotic value is closely linked to musical hermeneutics; the process whereby individuals infuse music with meaning. If a musical piece fails to elicit meaning from a listener, then it also fails to engage the listener's interest. But if it does in fact capture the listener's interest then it brings about a union between two individual consciousnesses.

The process of interpretation of a piece of music—the infusion of music with hermeneutical meaning—promotes the interaction between differing human consciousnesses even further. The musical piece as a locus of interpretation for both the performer and the individual members of the audience makes it a focal point of social interaction. Music mediates between differing individual consciousnesses. Music therefore can be seen to have ideological content—it is a system of ideological signs.

According to Voloshinov, what makes the ideological sign vital is its ability to possess differing meanings for differing individuals: its presence as a "refracting and distorting medium."[4] As Voloshinov explains: "The ruling class strives to impart a supraclass, eternal character to the ideological sign, to extinguish or drive inward the struggle between social value judgments which occurs in it, to make the sign uniaccentual."[5]

It also deserves mention that not only the musical piece itself is a locus of social interaction through connection, struggle, and conflict but also the conditions in which music is created, performed and promoted contribute further to its ideological and social function.

Such sociological concepts of music are wonderfully thematized in Torberg's historical novel, *Süsskind von Trimberg*. Torberg's novel was inspired by a genuine thirteenth-century personage, Süsskind von Trimberg, but his account is mostly imaginary.[6] In the novel, Süsskind begins his adulthood as a "Wandering Jew," because his family was killed in an anti-Semitic pogrom, which was not an uncommon event in thirteenth-century Europe. He is taken in by Konradin, the Duke of Trimberg, who turns him into a servant and otherwise oppresses him. Süsskind hopes that learning the art of songwriting will provide the tools to liberate him from Konradin's oppressive "friendship," and he seeks to apprentice himself to a popular Minnesinger.

Konradin learns about it and forbids Süsskind from pursuing a musical career:

> "It is not appropriate for you to write songs or epigramms. That is a noble art."
> "It seems that way to me, too, and therefore—"
> "A very noble, a knightly art. Do I need to tell you more directly than that? An art for knights and lords."
> "But it was indeed an itinerant singer, who ..." "Not for you, my little Jew. That was Lord Günther of Nördlingen, to be exact. And if someone like him travels through the countryside in order to sing at castles out of inclination or for money, he is still a lord as far as you are concerned. Do you understand me? You are usually not so stupid."[7]

Konradin wishes to preserve music and song as a locus for the values of the feudal nobility and does not wish to encourage members of socially disadvantaged classes—like the Jewish Süsskind—to infuse music with their values. He wishes to impart a universal, unalterable character to music and thereby prevent that it become a vehicle for changing society. He therefore joins with other feudal lords in only allowing members of the feudal nobility to write and perform music.

Konradin's tyranny provokes rebellious impulses in Süsskind:

> Süsskind remembered the exact place in his conversation with Konradin whereby his escape plan came to him. It had nothing to do with Konradin forbidding him to leave the castle—he would not have worried about that until the

coming fall and that was a long way off. But that somebody, feudal lord or not, rightly or not, forbade him from working with the sweetness of words and the loveliness of music—he could not tolerate that for a single day.[8]

For Süsskind, music is a vehicle for self-development and self-emancipation, as well as something that he does out of aesthetic enjoyment. At this early stage of the novel, music has already become a locus of social struggle and conflict through Konradin's decree that musical production shall be forbidden to Jews and through Süsskind's determination to become a musician despite the decree.

Süsskind wishes to use music as a means of expanding the role of Jews in his society and therefore chooses to become a musician despite Konradin's legal prohibition. He steals away from Konradin's castle at nighttime. He apprentices himself to a Minnesinger named Hartmann who engages Süsskind in a number of hostile conversations regarding his Jewishness. At one point, Hartmann admonishes Süsskind that his Jewishness makes it inappropriate for him to make music:

"And for that reason I should not write songs?" asked Süsskind.
"You should engage in moneylending, as is appropriate for a Jew."
"Is nothing else appropriate for a Jew?"
"No. Not at this time. Maybe earlier. But not now." "My father was a physician."
"An exception."
"Why can I not be an exception?"
"Because no nobleman is interested in making you into an exception. The previous Duke of Trimberg was interested in having a Jew as his personal physician. If the current duke were interested in having a Jew as a singer, you would be allowed to write songs. But according to what you told me, he is not interested in that, in fact he has clearly forbidden it. Therefore you are breaching two prohibitions by going on a concert tour. Am I not right?"
"Yes."
"Therefore you have two reasons not to let anybody notice that you are a Jew."[9]

Süsskind's debut as a musician forces him to take on a double identity: he is a Jew in his own private inner world who must pass as a Gentile in the outer world in order to continue making his music. He hopes that hiding his Jewishness and playing the parvenu will give him the means to ascend to social acceptability as a person and an artist in Christian feudal society. Musical production is dependent on deception in order to make itself heard. Süsskind's music exists both because of and despite social conflict. His

Jewishness is a source of continued tension between himself and his teacher Hartmann, because of Hartmann's uncritical acceptance of stereotypes that Jews are only fit to be moneylenders and his inability to accept and support the pioneering spirit of Süsskind, who wishes to open up the spheres of artistic production to the Jews.

At one point, Hartmann tries to convince Süsskind that the German language is not the province of Jews and that he therefore should not make songs in the German language:

> "I mean, why do you want to write songs?"
> "Because it is beautiful," answered Süsskind. It sounded like an apology.
> "I mean, why German songs? If you were a moneylender, as is appropriate for people like you, and if in addition to that, you wrote Hebrew songs for the enjoyment of yourself and other Jews, nobody would have anything against that. But that you want to write songs in our language—"
> "It is also my language!" Süsskind made himself nervous with the strong words he spoke to Lord Hartmann. "I have never spoken another language. I say my prayers in Hebrew, but I cannot speak Hebrew. Nor can I sing and rhyme in Hebrew. I can only do that in German."[10]

Hartmann wishes Süsskind to restrict himself to the stereotypical role of the Jew in his society: he does not wish for Süsskind to become a professional musician, but a moneylender, which was the traditional role for Jews in this society who had contact with Christians. Süsskind wishes to make music into a dialogical enterprise: an entity whereby a member of an oppressed minority can attempt to enter into dialogue with and influence the members of the ruling classes. Hartmann, on the other hand, wishes to preserve music as a monological entity whereby German nobles hear music only from other German nobles and Jews produce music only for other Jews.

Hartmann wishes even to exclude Jews from composing songs in the German language. He wishes to monologize not only German music, but also the German language itself by forbidding members of ethnic minorities from using it. Accordingly, he wishes to convey a universal, unalterable quality to musical signification and prevent its being used for subversive ends. Members of the feudal nobility, including Hartmann, wish to use music as an anchor for the feudal nobility and are therefore not eager to open it up to people from the lower strata of society.

The above passage is also important for presenting Torberg's criticism of the ideology of German ethnic homogeneity. Hartmann argues that the German language is the exclusive province of people of Germanic ethnicity, although people from ethnic minorities such as Jews and various Slavic groups had long since been living in German territories and had also mastered the German language. Torberg, an Austrian Jewish refugee who spent most of World War II in America, wishes to condemn the notion that German territories and the German language are only intended for people of Germanic ethnicity. He does so by portraying Süsskind as a man in conflict with Germanic society.

Süsskind faces opposition in his efforts to build a musical career not only from the German feudal nobility, but also from other Jews who fear that Süsskind's efforts to gain prominence in Gentile society will bring an anti-Semitic backlash upon all Jews living in the area:

> You are not doing us any good, Mordechai ben Jehuda, who calls himself Süsskind. You cannot prove anything to them. You can only deceive them. And they will not feel themselves convinced by you, but deceived and tricked. And they will only hate you all the more for it, you and us all. You are not doing us any good.[11]

Süsskind's musical endeavors bring him into conflict with his own co-religionists who wish to live in relative harmony with the outer German society. They therefore encourage all Jews to live according to the laws and decrees of the feudal nobility. Unlike Süsskind, they do not endeavor to dialogize the outer society because they do not wish to come into conflict with that society. They prefer instead to live a self-contained existence within the ghetto walls.

A musical rivalry eventually develops between Süsskind and Hartmann until Hartmann exposes Süsskind as a Jew. However, by this time Süsskind has already established himself as a musician of some popularity and certain noblemen continue to allow him to perform at their castles, legal prohibitions notwithstanding. It is clear at this point that Süsskind's efforts to use his music as a vehicle to dialogize his society are bearing fruit. A young nobleman, Burkhart, learns the art of songwriting from Süsskind. Music becomes a locus of social connectedness as the nobleman and the itinerant Jewish musician are drawn together by a love of music that transcends divisions brought about by class, ethnicity, and religion.

Süsskind tells Burkhart: "I wish that all people were like you. Then when a Jew sang songs they would perhaps concern themselves with listening to the song and not worry about the fact that they are listening to a Jew."[12] Although he is at the height of his musical career, Süsskind is still troubled by thoughts that his popularity as a musician is compromised by his identity as a Jew. Instead he wishes to be viewed as an artist whose abilities transcend ethno-religious identity.

Süsskind's growing fame and popularity lead Konradin to invite him back to his court with the explicit understanding that he can continue his career as a musician. Süsskind accepts but continues to rebel against the restrictions placed upon him as a Jew. At one point, Süsskind's song defending his Jewish coreligionists raises the ire of a prominent bishop. The bishop tells him:

> The comparison you make would not have been so bad. But you do not portray the usurers as the greedy wolves they are. You seek to defend the shameful usury that your co-religionists practice. You seek to justify it by claiming that they would otherwise starve and you claim that we are to blame for it. You find their predatory misdeeds trivial compared to ours. If I understand your song correctly, we are the bloodthirsty predators and you are the innocent lambs. In this song you have turned the truth on its head in an evil and deceitful manner. Do you consider us to be so stupid that we do not notice?[13]

Süsskind's attempt to use music as a means for protesting the negative social conditions under which his co-religionists suffer brings him into conflict with the Catholic Church and its hierarchy. They are unwilling to tolerate his efforts to democratize and dialogize music by making it the voice of the poor and oppressed and Süsskind comes to be regarded as a troublemaker. Consequently, Süsskind finds it increasingly difficult to bring his music to the castles and palaces where he had previously been greeted with enthusiasm.

Searching for venues in which can perform his music, Süsskind starts singing in inns, taverns, and public houses occupied by the lower strata of society:

> It was good. He sang it [the song about the nobility] as his last number and it is was good. With the two preceding songs they were already attentive and loudly applauding and nodding agreement with this or that section of the song and they made the nicely dressed singer with the strange pointed hat aware that his art was not lost on them, that they knew how to appreciate a good song. Even those in the lowly tavern liked a good song, not just those in the courts and palaces. Now, with this song about the nobility with which he concluded, he had the audience in the palm of his hand. Süsskind believed he

understood how they held their breath: this had never happened to him before; he had never before felt so close and unified to his audience; never before had one of his songs said so successfully that which the audience itself
would say and sing, if they could and would sing.[14]

In this scene, Süsskind's music becomes a locus of social interconnectedness, uniting Süsskind with the peasants in the tavern: binding them together in their misapprobation toward the nobility. The itinerant Jewish
musician and the peasants are brought together by a music which expresses
their mutual concerns, aptly illustrating the ways in which music can play
a social function by bringing people together who might otherwise have
had little to do with one another.

Süsskind had previously used music in an effort to became a parvenu
reaching social acceptability in the highest realms of feudal society. Once
he finds his efforts to become a parvenu permanently frustrated, he contents himself with being a socially conscious pariah, using his pariah stance
as a viewpoint from which to criticize the society that has marginalized
and excluded him. As the political and social philosopher Hannah Arendt
explained in her 1944 essay, "The Jew as Pariah":

> For the pariah, excluded from formal society and with no desire to be em-
> braced within it, turns naturally to that which entertains and delights the
> common people. Sharing their social ostracism, he also shares their joys and
> sorrows, their pleasures and tribulations.[15]

That very music which becomes a locus of social interconnectedness between Süsskind and the peasants also becomes a locus of social conflict
between Süsskind and the nobility which hears of Süsskind's popular songs
of social criticism and orders him to leave the city and never enter it again
under penalty of death.

Upon Süsskind's return to Trimberg, Duke Konradin forbids him from
engaging in any more musical endeavors. Süsskind once again leaves Konradin's court but has considerable difficulty finding venues in which to
perform his music. He dies in abject poverty.

Süsskind ultimately loses in his struggle against the nobility to make
his way as a musician and exert a major influence on the social discourse
omnipresent in music, although he does garner himself some temporary
victories on the way to the final showdown. Torberg's novel brilliantly
illuminates music in its sociological context. Music is a temporary vehicle
of social liberation for Süsskind, one which brings him into connection

with the nobility and brings him a certain amount of fame. For a time his fame brings him protection from the ill-treatment afforded Jews in his society but it also emboldens him to experiment with more pronounced social commentary in his music which in the end accentuates his pariah status by bringing him into an ever-growing conflict with the Church and with the feudal nobility. What once brought him connectedness with the ruling powers of society eventually propels him into a social struggle against them.

He then seeks to bring his music to the peasants who view it as a locus for social connectedness and a possible vehicle for their own liberation, a fact that does not go unnoticed by the ruling authorities who eventually succeed in silencing Süsskind. Ultimately Süsskind's dual attempts to assimilate into German society by the making of music that appeals to the feudal nobility and later by the making of music that appeals to the peasantry are doomed to failure.[16] Both the path of the parvenu and that of the socially conscious pariah are ultimately closed to him. This situation symbolizes the failure of the luminous author Torberg to be able to use his creative talents to assimilate into Austrian society before the rise of the Nazis as well as his personal traumas as he fled Prague for Hollywood. Although he was lionized as "one of ten outstanding German anti-Nazi writers" and received a contract as a script writer from Warner Brothers, exile was a bitter experience for Torberg. He felt isolated and cut off from his roots. He never mastered the English language well enough to make it a permanent vehicle for his artistic creativity and most of his American film scripts did not reach his prior level of excellence in his chosen metier as a novelist.[17] Assimilation into the popular culture of the Hollywood film industry—which proved a viable option for such prominent German exiles as Fritz Lang, Peter Lorre, and Marlene Dietrich among others— eluded Torberg because of his deep commitment to European high culture: eventually, he eagerly returned to Vienna in 1951.

Torberg had sought to dialogize Austrian society through the writing of novels presenting sympathetic portrayals of Austria's Jewish minority and he had already become a major writer by the time he was in his early twenties. As a result, he had to flee persecution when the Nazis came to power. As Arendt explains, Jewish emancipation in the Central European countries was conceived as a permit to ape the gentile, rather than admit Jews as purveyors of Jewish culture to the ranks of humanity.[18] Those Jews who retained a Jewish identity became pariahs, often criticizing the injustices of the society in which they lived and consequently bearing the burden of intolerable repression, a repression that eventually forced them to either flee Europe or to face certain death in the Nazi extermination camps (those Jews who successfully became parvenus were also not exempted from this tragic situation.) That the traumas unleashed by his ominous experiences in trying to escape the Nazis continued to haunt Torberg toward the end of his life in 1972 is more than evident.

Peter R. Erspamer

Notes

1. M.M. Bakhtin and P.N. Medvedev, *The Formal Method in Literary Scholarship: A Critical Introduction to Sociological Poetics*, (1928), translated by Albert J. Wehrle, Baltimore: Johns Hopkins University Press, 1978, 11

2. Bakhtin and Medvedev, *The Formal Method in Literary Scholarship*, 3.

3. V.N. Voloshinov, *Marxism and the Philosophy of Language*, (1929), translated by Ladislav Matejka and I.R. Titunik, Cambridge: Harvard University Press, 1986, 11.

4. Voloshinov, *Marxism and the Philosophy of Language*, 23.

5. Voloshinov, *Marxism and the Philosophy of Language*, 23.

6. See Brian Murdoch, "... Süßkind the Jew of Trimberg ...," in *The Yale Companion to Jewish Writing and Thought in German Culture*, edited by Sander L. Gilman and Jack Zipes, New Haven: Yale University Press, 1997, pp. 21–27.

7. Friedrich Torberg, *Süßkind von Trimberg*, Frankfurt am Main: S. Fischer, 1972, 63.

> "Es steht dir nicht an, Lieder oder Sprüche zu machen. Das ist eine edle Kunst." "So scheint's auch mir—und deshalb—" "Eine vieledle, eine adlige Kunst. Muß ich's dir denn noch gröber sagen? Eine Kunst für Ritter und Herren." "Aber es war doch ein fährender Sänger, der ..." "Nicht für dich, mein Jüdchen. Das war Herr Günther von Nördlingen, damit du's genau weißt. Und wenn einer wie er durchs Land fährt, um auf den Burgen zu singen—aus Laune oder um Lohn, dich kümmert's nicht—so bleibt er für dich noch immer ein Herr. Hast du verstanden? Du bist doch sonst nicht so blöde."

8. Torberg, *Süßkind von Trimberg*, 64.

> Süßkind erinnerte sich genau, an welcher Stelle seines Gesprächs mit Konradin der Fluchtplan ihm gekommen war. Es lag nicht an Konradins Verbot, die Burg zu verlassen—das wäre ihm erst im Herbst in die Quere

geraten, und bis dahin war's noch lange. Aber daß irgend jemand, Burgherr oder nicht, zu Recht oder nicht, die Süßigkeit des Worts und die Zärtlichkeit des Lieds ihm sollte verwehren dürfen—das hätte er keinen Tag lang ertragen.

9. Torberg, *Süßkind von Trimberg*, 90–91.

"Und deshalb darf ich keine Lieder machen?" fragt Süßkind. "Du sollst Geldgeschäfte machen, wie sich's für einen Juden schickt." "Sonst schickt sich nichts für einen Juden?" "Nein. Nicht mehr. Vielleicht früher einmal. Jetzt nicht mehr." "Mein Vater war Arzt." "Eine Ausnahme." "Warum kann ich keine Ausnahme sein?" "Weil es keinen Herrn gibt, dem daran gelegen wäre. Dem früheren Herrn auf der Trimberg war daran gelegen, einen Juden als Leibarzt zu haben. Läge dem jetztigen Herrn daran, einen Juden als Sänger zu haben, dann dürftest du Lieder machen. Aber soviel du mir erzählt hast, ist ihm nicht nur nichts daran glegen, sondern er hat's dir ausdrücklich untersagt. Also handelst du, indem du auf Sängerfahrt gehst, gleich zwei Verbote zuwider. Stimmt's?" "Ja." "Also hast du gleich zwei Gründe, niemanden merken zu lassen, daß du Jude bist."

10. Torberg, *Süßkind von Trimberg*, 91–92.

"Ich meine—warum willst du eigentlich Lieder machen?" "Weil es schön ist," antwortet Süßkind. Es klang wie eine Entschuldigung. "Ich meine: deutsche Lieder. Wenn du ein Geldverleiher wärst, wie sich's für deinesgleichen schickt, und wenn du nebenbei zu deinem und der anderen Hebrärer Vergnügen, dich an hebräischen Lieder versuchtest, hätte niemand etwas dagegen. Aber daß du höfische Lieder machen willst in unsrer Sprache—" "Es ist auch die meine!" Süßkind erschrickt über die Heftigkeit, mit der er Herrn Hartmann ins Wort gefallen ist. "Ich habe nie eine andre gesprochen. Meine Gebete sprech ich hebräisch, aber hebräisch reden kann ich nicht. Oder gar reimen und singen. Das kann ich nur auf deutsch."

11. Torberg, *Süßkind von Trimberg*, 127.

Du tust uns nichts Gutes, Mordechai ben Jehuda, der du dich Süßkind nennst. Du kannst ihnen nichts beweisen. Du kannst sie nur täuschen. Und sie werden sich von dir nicht überzeugt fühlen, sondern getäuscht und hintergangen. Und werden dich nur desto mehr hassen, dich und uns alle. Du tust uns nichts Gutes.

12. Torberg, *Süßkind von Trimberg*, 170.

"Ich wünschte, daß alle so wären wie du. Dann würden sie, wenn ein Jude Lieder macht, vielleicht das Lied heraushören und nicht den Juden."

13. Torberg, *Süßkind von Trimberg*, 242.

Das Gleichnis, das du da verwendest, wäre gar nicht schlecht. Aber du stellst ja die Wucherer nicht als die gierigen Wölfe dar, die sie sind. Du suchst den schändlichen Wucher, den deine Glaubensgenossen treiben, zu vertedigen. Du suchst ihn damit zu rechtfertigen, daß sie sonst hungern müßten, und gibst uns die Schuld daran. Du findest ihre räuberischen Missetaten geringfügig im Vergleich mit den unsreren. Wenn ich dein Lied richtig verstanden habe, sind wir die reißenden Raubtiere und ihr seid die Unschuldslämmer. Du hast in diesem Lied die Wahrheit auf böse, arglistige Weise entstellt und umgedreht. Hältst du uns für so dumm, das wir das nicht merken?

14. Torberg, *Süßkind von Trimberg*, 276.

Es war gut. Er sang's als letztes und es war gut. Schon bei den zwei anderen Liedern zuvor, zwei von den vielfach bewährten, hatten sie aufmerksam zugehört, hatten Beifall geklatscht und Verständnis genickt bei der und jener Stelle, hatten dem vornehm gekleideten Sänger mit dem sonderbar zugespitzten Hut so recht bekunden wollen, daß seine Kunst nicht an ihnen verloren wäre, daß sie ein gutes Lied zu schätzen wüßten, auch sie, nicht nur für die großen Herren auf den Höfen und Burgen, auch sie in der Schränke hier unten. Jetzt aber, bei diesem Lied vom Adel, daß er zum Abschluß sang, waren sie augenblicks in Bann geschlagen, schon von der ersten Zeile, Süßkind meinte es greifen zu können wie sie die Luft anhielten, wie sich's von ihm zu ihnen hinüberspannte und wieder zurück, Luft und Atem, Wort und Sinn, dergleichen war ihm noch nie geschehen, so nah und eins hatte er sich mit denen, die ihm zuhörten, noch nie gefühlt, so sehr traf noch keins seiner Lieder ins Tiefste dessen, was sie selbst, hätten sie nur sagen und singen können, gesagt und gesungen hätten.

15. Hannah Arendt, *The Jew as Pariah: Jewish Identity and Politics in the Modern Age*, edited by Ron H. Feldman, New York: Grove, 1978, 71.

16. See Frank Tichy, *Friedrich Torberg: Ein Leben in Widersprüchen*, Salzburg: Müller, 1995, 260.

17. David Axmann, "Freundschaft in dürftiger Zeit," in Friedrich Torberg, *Liebste Freundin und Alma: Briefwechsel mit Alma Mahler-Werfel*, Munich: Langen/ Müller, 1987, 5–6.

18. Arendt, 68.

10

A Defining Moment in Ezra Pound's *Cantos*: Musical Scores and Literary Texts

Of all the typographic and spatial elements of Ezra Pound's modern epic, *The Cantos*, perhaps the most visually striking is the musical score located in Canto LXXV.[1] Pound's text enjoys (and suffers) a reputation as a formidable and complex work. Indeed, if the subject matter of *The Cantos* may be laid aside for a moment—the role of strong leaders in the history of good government; the history of money and its production; the economic and executive conditions in which great art may flourish; and the career of the narrative persona through hell, purgatory, towards the unattained *paradiso terrestre*—the reader is left with an abundant alphabetic, ideogrammatic, hieroglyphic and visual apparatus to work through. That a score should appear in such a text may not seem altogether surprising. Yet its presence brings a singular challenge to the identity and function of Pound's poetic text, and raises pertinent questions as to its status within the work. Canto LXXV constitutes a lesson in aesthetics. It demonstrates the complex relations between artworks and between artistic media, and calls for a considered, singular meditation on the status of the literary text and its intersection with the musical score.

Canto LXXV presents one artwork (or a partial representation of an artwork) embedded within another: the violin line of Clément Janequin's *Le Chant des Oiseaux*, arranged by Gerhard Münch, follows the short poetic text (Münch, the German pianist and composer and friend of Pound, performed in the concert series Pound organized between 1933 and 1939 in Rapallo, Italy). Although the poetic material of the canto constitutes a mere seven lines and the page space is dominated by the score, the music is framed to be read within the poetic text. Further, it is a part of one canto in a series, *The Pisan Cantos*, in which it was first published before that text was absorbed, serially, into collected editions of *The Cantos*. The score has been read by critics (when read at all) as a kind of extended quotation, a thematic component of the poem's unfolding drama. Simply to read the music in this way ignores its peculiar status and risks downplaying the acute conditions of composition suffusing *The Pisan Cantos*. These conditions have been discussed at length by several textual and literary critics, but never with specific attention to this canto and its status. This situation is surprising, as musical scores make several prominent appearances in modernist texts: the scores of "The Ballad of Persse O'Reilly" in *Finnegans Wake*, and of the "Threne" in Samuel Beckett's *Watt* are two examples.[2] The presence of such a medium in a literary work already suggests the identity of that work is being placed under some kind of pressure.

Before a considered textual appraisal of the score's presence in Canto LXXV is possible, the identity and composition history of the canto and of the score require explanation. The poetic text was composed in extremely difficult circumstances, providing much insight into Pound's choice of a musical component. It will be shown that the identity of the text does not accord with available textual models or classic notions of authority. Equally, the score's identity—partly composed of its provenance and its location within a poetic text—forestalls the conventional philosophical division of music into the ideal work, the transient performance, and the sedimented, materialist score. Instead, the violin line in Canto LXXV shows the complex identities of both score and text to voice implicit critiques of uniformly idealist and materialist notions of music and of literature.

I.
The Provenance of Canto LXXV and its Score

The decision to include a musical score in his poem was perfectly in keeping with Pound's aesthetics and cultural interests. From the earliest stage his poetic career was complemented by a keen amateur interest in music. He knew personally various musicians and composers throughout his life: the American pianist Katherine Ruth Heyman, the English pianist Agnes Bedford, the Franco-German pianist and music historian Walter Morse Rummel, the English music antiquarian and scholar Arnold Dolmetsch,[3] the American pianist and composer George Antheil, the French tenor and music scholar Yves Tinayre, the Scottish collector and arranger of Hebridean folk songs Marjorie Kennedy-Frazer, the German pianist Gerhard

Münch, and most significantly, the American violinist and Pound's life-long companion, Olga Rudge.

Pound reviewed music from his earliest days in London and was music critic for *The New Age* between 1917 and 1921 under the pseudonym of "William Atheling."[4] With Rummel, he tried to put the poetry of the Troubadours to music in the spirit of *motz el son* (the lost union of words and music).[5] A further attempt followed, in collaboration with Agnes Bedford in 1920, comprising one Provençal song and five arrangements of Chaucer's poetry.[6] Moreover, Pound composed an opera, *Le Testament de Villon*, whilst living in Paris in 1921, a work that premièred in that city in 1926. Several smaller compositions, mainly for violin, were composed by Pound and performed by Olga Rudge and others during his time in Paris (1921–1924). Meanwhile Pound had published the monograph *The Treatise on Harmony* and the essay on Antheil together in 1924,[7] and a second unfinished opera, *Cavalcanti*, followed in Rapallo in 1932. In *Guide to Kulchur* he proposed a theory of *Great Bass*: a temporal concept linking the elements of artistic work into a whole, equally applicable to cadence in poetry as to the rhythm demanded by a combination of musical notes.[8]

Perhaps the most lasting effect of Pound's musical career is his contribution to the Vivaldi revival, through the "Tigullian music" concerts he organized with Olga Rudge between 1933 and 1939 in Rapallo (the town is situated in the Ligurian Gulf of Tigullio). Rudge traveled to Turin in 1936 to catalog the 309 Vivaldi manuscripts held in that city's National Library, and in the following year Pound ordered a set of microfilms from the collection of manuscripts held at the Sächsische Landesbibliothek in Dresden.[9] Their investigations did not actually initiate the Vivaldi revival, as has been claimed, but the ensuing performances of this material in Rapallo were among the first.[10] Pound passed on the Dresden microfilms to Count Guido Chigi Saracini (founder and patron of the Accademia Musicale Chigiana) who dedicated the entire program of the third *Settimana musicale* in Siena to Vivaldi's work in September 1939.[11] Rudge had been secretary of the Accademia Musicale Chigiana in Siena since 1938 and was to play a crucial role in its ongoing concerns for several years.[12]

One of the favorite pieces in the Rapallo concert series was the arrangement of Janequin's *Le Chant des Oiseaux*, known to have been played by Münch and Olga Rudge in the opening concert of 10 October 1933 (it was actually the opening piece) and in the last concert of the first series on 31 March 1934. Rudge also played the piece solo during the second Tigullian study session in the Rapallo Town Hall in April 1936. Jane-

quin's original composition dates from the early sixteenth century and it
was initially scored for choir. It was scored for lute by Francesco da Milano around the same time and hence its name-change to the *Canzone
degli Uccelli*. Eventually, Münch arranged the piece for violin and piano,
although it is not known whether this was done specifically for the Rapallo concerts. In any case, the violin line is reproduced photographically
from Münch's arrangement in Canto LXXV (his handwriting is visible in
the annotations) yet his score is itself twice removed from the original
composition.

Pound's admiration for the piece was to be reflected upon its musicians. Janequin's medievalism deserved praise for keeping alive aural precision: "I think Janequin inherited from the troubadours the fine clear
cut *representation* of natural sound, the exactitude of birds and flowers."[13]
Whilst the spirit of *motz el son* was transmitted from the thirteenth-century
canzone down to the sixteenth-century *chanson*, the balance between the
words and music had changed. No longer "made into one perfect fabric,"
Pound discerned that the "tune has learned from what the words, centuries earlier, had taught the music."[14] This general partitioning of words
and music led, according to Pound, to a decline in metrical ability and discipline amongst poets. Musicianship, on the other hand, could flourish:
"Francesco da Milano, wishing to express Janequin's concept without using
a chorus of twenty people, edited the *Canzone degli Uccelli* for the lute."
This arrangement afforded no aesthetic loss: "As early as 1475 Francesco
da Milano could present complicated voicings on the lute, comprising all
the dimensions of the chorus."[15]

Münch, the third composer in this line of transmission, performed the
task which was to become significant for Pound at Pisa. In the arrangement for violin he was able to cast back over music history to the early
source of the music's vitality: "By listening to the violin alone we reach
back to a period at least three centuries prior to Janequin, who was born
towards 1475 and was published in the sixteenth century."[16] In this way,
the music transcends the conditions of its composition and performance,
belonging instead to the cultural memory. "In one sense I don't care a
hoot about the authorship," Pound states, "The gist, the pith, the un-
breakable fact is there in the two pages of violin part."[17] For Pound, the
artist's obligation to art is to purify the work so that its essence is audible:

> One of the rights of the masterwork is the right of rebirth and recurrence.
> Janequin's Birds, out of Arnaut (possibly), out of immemorial and unknown,

takes a new life on Francesco da Milano's lute. The Rapallo music is more than justified when Münch's Janequin is followed by his reduction of Vivaldi's Sol minore Concerto.[18]

This idea of aesthetic purity was to become a rhetorical motif of Canto LXXV, and a justification for the placement of Münch's arrangement within *The Pisan Cantos*. The score's perceived essence was impervious to the immediacy of events that shaped the composition of its text.

The Pisan Cantos suite was composed during an especially difficult time in the author's life. Pound began the new series for his epic whilst living in Rapallo during the Second World War. The surviving drafts demonstrate that an Italian text was begun and then abandoned for an English text. The contents of these early drafts attempt a justification of the Fascist regime under Mussolini, by way of kindred models of leadership (as Pound saw it): in Confucian texts, and in the writings of Thomas Jefferson and John Adams. Since 1940, Pound had been broadcasting on the "American Hour" over Ente Italiano Audizione Radiofoniche (the radio station under the wing of the Ministry of Popular Culture in Rome).[19] The content of these speeches ranged from cultural, musical, and literary topics, to attacks on weak leadership in the American Presidency, and to Pound's perception of an international banking conspiracy led by Jewish interests. On the strength of these speeches, Pound was indicted for treason by a Grand Jury on 26 July 1943—the date, ironically, of the last broadcast under his name (several scripts were later sent to Rome and read, in August, under the pseudonym "Piero Mazda"[20]). He was taken into the custody of the United States Army in May of 1945, and was detained in the Detention Training Center at Pisa between 24 May and 16 November. After suffering three weeks in a cage reinforced with airstrip steel, open to the weather and continually floodlit during the night, Pound was moved to the medical compound. Here he composed the bulk of *The Pisan Cantos* drafts, accompanied only by his copy of Confucius, his Chinese dictionary, an Army issue Bible, and *The Pocket Book of Verse*, edited by Morris Speare, which he found on the seat of the DTC's communal latrine.

This brief sketch of the conditions in which *The Pisan Cantos* were composed sheds light on the presence of the music and its placement in the text. Pound was confined, unable to reach family or to notify them of his whereabouts. Finally on 18 September, permission was granted to receive and send mail via the "Base Censor" of the DTC. This was the conduit by which the score found its way to his publishers (James Laughlin at

New Directions in New York, and T.S. Eliot at Faber in London).[21] A typescript of Canto LXXV gives the seven lines of poetic material, and leaves a large blank space in place of the music, save for a personal note from the author to the publishers:

> (HERE FOLLOWS the music of Gerhart's Jannequin, as I think printed in Townsman, Canzone degli Ucelli.
> Probably have to be reduced in size as Townsman's page larger than usual page size.)[22]

The note refers to the first printing of Münch's arrangement in Ronald Duncan's journal *Townsman*. There the music follows an article by Pound in which he explains the provenance of the violin part and the general significance of Janequin's art.[23] The mixed register of the note gives some clue of the practical uncertainties facing the text, its author, and its publishers: the first sentence could conceivably serve as a reference for the reader's guidance; the second sentence could only serve as instructions for pre-publication eyes (interestingly, the photographic mode of the music's reproduction is already suggested in the phrasing "reduced in size").

The final stage of the canto's composition history was in locating the music to be printed in *The Pisan Cantos* by both Faber and New Directions. In a letter to James Laughlin, Dorothy Pound wrote:

> The pages are as I received them. I dont know whether the Censor bagged some. I am hunting for Gerhardt Münch's music. If I find I will enclose. A copy of it went to London.[24]

Robert Duncan had since sold *Townsman*, but Dorothy tracked down the music and sent it to Laughlin on December 28: "This goes in the Cantos: you will find the place mentioned in the M.S.S." Olga Rudge had already been able to find a copy of the music for T.S. Eliot.[25]

Once the text of Canto LXXV had been decided upon, it remained remarkably stable in its form. Ezra Pound, Dorothy Pound, James Laughlin, T.S. Eliot, and Ronald Duncan all knew what was meant by the instructions in the typescripts. In this way, Canto LXXV did not embody the complexities and contradictions of other cantos in the suite: in those, variant readings were introduced, text in the Greek alphabet was muddled, and Chinese characters were mis-transcribed and even omitted. Such a catalog of problems was to be expected considering Pound's acutely difficult circumstances in the Pisan DTC and his deteriorating condition afterwards when he was flown to Washington, D.C. to stand trial for treason. Canto LXXV is reproduced with few errors or variants—yet even this short poetic text is not free of blemishes: the incorrect "Stammbuch" appeared in the first Faber and New Directions collected editions of *The Cantos*, to be replaced later with the correct "Ständebuch."[26] Aside from this one error, the only variations occur with the publishers' font choices and with the language of translations and the obvious duplication of the text in bilingual editions.[27] Yet the music itself derives from the same photograph in all editions, and is the most stable element of the text. That the violin line is Münch's arrangement, and that his handwriting is visible within its borders, only makes the status of the music all the more curious in the context of *The Cantos*.

II.
Reading the Score: "not of one bird but of many"

It might be said that the spectacular presence of a musical score within a poetic text focuses attention upon its sheer visuality and may actually distract the reader from questions of attribution and provenance. The composition histories of Münch's arrangement of Janequin's *Le Chant des Oiseaux*, and of Canto LXXV in which it appears, reveal complex and problematic identity-structures that might otherwise pass unnoticed. Yet the sheer fact of its presence prompts the reader to ask: why this piece of music in particular? and why is it located at this point in *The Pisan Cantos*?

The significance of Münch's arrangement to Pound is clear in the light of the Rapallo concerts of 1933–1939. Still, a fuller answer to the first question—why this piece?—will rely somewhat on the answer to the second question—why is it exactly here? The previous canto, and the first of *The Pisan Cantos* series, Canto LXXIV, concludes with a meditation on the fate of the imprisoned *ego scriptor*.[28] Images of eternal patterns in nature and the design in things—the "rose in the steel dust" and "swansdown" (LXXIV/449)[29]—provide consolations to the poet's plight. The rise from the underworld concluding Canto LXXIV—"we who have passed over Lethe" (449)—crosses the river of forgetfulness and traces out a transcendental gesture through the medium of music. This music, emerging from memory, and recorded in the score, remains *in potentia*, and must be imagined by the reader.

Le Chant des Oiseaux echoes throughout *The Pisan Cantos*. Pound continually hears the birds calling around him: "with two larks in contrappunto/at sunset" (LXXIV/431); "three solemn half notes/their white downy chests black-rimmed/on the middle wire/periplum" (LXXXII/527); and, emblematically,

>   f   f
>   d
>   g
>   write the birds in their treble scale
>   (LXXXII/525)

Memory and sound combine to inscribe the score outside of Pound's tent. The birds write themselves on the wires as musical notation, and the reader is already reminded that "the Muses are the daughters of memory/Clio, Terpsichore" (LXXIV/445). The ephemerality of art (and that art traditionally closest to transcendence), is represented in a notation that is not inscribed for the narrating consciousness, but is instead the temporary formation of birds on electric wires.

The graphic seductions of the violin line are framed by the brief poetic text preceding it in Canto LXXV. The text bears out two crucial functions of music inflecting upon the entire *Pisan Cantos* sequence: the role of memory and its transformative powers (particularly during a time of physical estrangement); and the ability for the purest art to transcend the most trying of material circumstances. Music and memory thus combine powerfully in *The Pisan Cantos*. They sustain poetic consciousness and identity, quite literally in this canto:

>   Out of Phlegethon!
>   Out of Phlegethon,
>   Gerhart
>   art thou come forth out of Phlegethon?
>   with Buxtehude and Klages in your satchel, with the
>   Ständebuch of Sachs in yr/luggage
>   — not of one bird but of many (LXXV/450)

Pound, echoing Virgil, urges the crossing of another underworld river, Phlegethon, the river of fire. The insistent repetition or *palilogia* of these phrases motivates the shift from the Pisan DTC to the realm of music— just as Aeneas crosses Phlegethon to escape the city of Hades and discover the Elysian fields and the lyre of Orpheus.[30] This parallelism between the realms of art and memory and the rise from the classical underworld achieves a visceral urgency at this point in *The Cantos*. It is literally a life-saving function rather than simply an issue of saving cultural values and artistic integrity.

Despite the urgency of Pound's situation, he presents a brief catalogue of composers "for the record." "Gerhart" Münch appears alone in the third line, and is asked, in Pound's familiar archaic diction, and through *epanalepsis* (the terminal repetition of an initial word), to follow him out of the underworld. Münch is imagined carrying a satchel of composers' scores—Dietrich Buxtehude, the master of organ composition who profoundly influenced Bach and Hans Sachs, a prolific *Meistersinger* of the sixteenth century—as well as the work of anthropologist Ludwig Klages, "to whom Münch addressed a number of letters."[31] The major work of Klages is the five-volume *Der Geist als Widersacher der Seele* ("The intellect as adversary of the soul"). Thus Pound's musician, who arranges this score, brings his concerns for transcendence back to him in a satchel from the underworld.

The final line of the poetic text quotes a comment made by Olga Rudge upon playing the violin part of the Janequin: that the essence of the work remained intact, bringing the sounds "—not of one bird but of many."[32] Pound elsewhere explains the transmission of the *forma* (the concept of birdsong) from obscure roots in the Troubadour song of Arnaut Daniel and "god knows what 'hidden antiquity',"[33] through to its incarnations in Janequin, Francesco da Milano, and Münch:

> Clement Janequin wrote a chorus, with words for the singers of the different parts of the chorus. These words would have no literary or poetic value if you took the music away but when Francesco da Milano reduced it for the lute the birds were still in the music. And when Münch transcribed it for modern instruments the birds were still there. They ARE still in the violin parts.[34]

The birds of the DTC prompt a narrative of personal history combined with music, a narrative ultimately concerned with transcendental forms and the possibility of expressing such forms through art.

The music serves two rhetorical purposes for Pound. It provides an opportunity to show remorse for his errant ways—his support for the Fascist regime, and his enthusiastic criticism of the economic system he judged responsible for the cycle of warfare—and to redeem himself through the expression of beauty in his art. Pound is framed as a figure of stoical belief in the divine, glimpsed at in art and in nature. His is a portrait of a martyr-figure seeking consolation, if a rather pagan than patristic consolation. The tribulation by fire of the *ego scriptor* sets up the crossing over to the realm of art, where patterns of the divine are everywhere apparent. This crossing can be made, even under the difficult conditions of the Pisan

DTC, by the work of memory, itself the organ of artistic creation. And in keeping the birdsong alive through its complicated transmission, the *"forma," "concetto," "pith"* may be transmitted through its various iconic or material incarnations in the musical scores. The tension between transcendence and the very physical constraint of the poet is evident in the striking materiality of the musical score in his literary work. Its form and meaning contribute to the consolatory and repentant modes of *The Pisan Cantos*.

III.
The Status of the Text

The foregoing analysis has shown how the musical element of Canto LXXV can be read as a part of the canto's thematic texture. With some knowledge of the music's provenance and its role in the author's life, its inclusion becomes the more apposite; combined with some knowledge of the canto's composition conditions, its presence may even be considered somewhat poignant. Indeed, its presence in the published text at all is a fortuitous result of the precarious textual history of *The Pisan Cantos*, from initial manuscript and typescripts to publication in London and New York. Each of these aspects help frame a reading of the canto and the music within it, but they do not add up to a complete answer to the question: what kind of status is the reader—or for that matter, the author, or the editor—to ascribe to these interdependent elements of the poem? An answer is possible, but the way to it must be prepared by reflecting on the status of the literary text (and of *The Cantos* in particular) and on the status of the musical score. Canto LXXV is speaking to literary and aesthetic traditions as much as it speaks to its readers.

As Herschel Parker has observed, much literary theory and literary criticism proceeds on the tacit assumption of the text's cohesion as an integrated object of analysis: the "text itself" or "words on the page."[35] In recent years however, textual criticism has sought to construct a notion of the text that can accommodate fragments, variants, manuscript and typescript stages, and the contributing hands of several productive identities. In particular, the "social text" theories of such textual critics as James Thorpe, D.F. McKenzie, and Jerome J. McGann have sparked a great deal of debate concerning the status and function of texts, as well as the role of an authorial agent in the intentionality ascribed to the text. Their critique of copy-text theory (a theory where authority normally resides in the final manuscript prior to publication) has provided a space for the sociality of text production and reception.

For McGann (and this is crucial to *The Pisan Cantos*), textual authority and the production of literary value does not rest solely with the author:

> Authority is a social nexus, not a personal possession; and if the authority of specific literary works is initiated new for each work by some specific artist, its initiation takes place in a necessary and integral historical environment of great complexity. Most immediately—and this is what concerns us here—it takes place within the conventions and enabling limits that are accepted by the prevailing institutions of literary production—conventions and limits which exist for the purpose of generating and supporting literary production.[36]

The milieu in which the writer produces a text and in which it is transmitted and received is the foundational concern of the theory of the "social text." Such a milieu is a necessary condition for the existence of the text: "they do not even acquire an artistic form of being until their engagement with an audience has been determined." This is regardless of the kind of audience, whether it be a national or international readership, across time, "even if it should involve but a small coterie of amateurs" (43).

Such a requirement poses problems for a theory of the "social text" when confronted with the composition circumstances of *The Pisan Cantos*. This text was not written with any guarantee of its reception by a definite audience, and it lacked for some time a clear notion of audience at all. It is not satisfactory to propose that the text only came into literary existence when its manuscripts and typescripts were "out" circulating amongst amanuenses and editors or when the text was finally published. Its identity changed through the stages of its production, as did its form and attitude to the perceived audience. Pound's composition of *The Pisan Cantos* saw several incredulous onlookers at the DTC but no identifiably present or potential audience. But, in this case, the sociality of the page allows for an implied audience of potential readers to be present within the text's space, despite the precarious future of the text at the time of its composition.

A more flexible concept of audience can account for the status of the text during the early stages of its production. Composition in exile and a limited field of reception can still qualify, in principle, as special kinds of author-audience interplay. McGann comes to something of a similar conclusion: "As soon as an author utters or writes down his work, even for the first time, a mediation has to some degree come between or 'interfered with' the original, unmediated 'text'" (102). Although McGann flags the notion of an orally anterior text with quotation marks, and, indeed, because of this, mediation is seen to occur at each stage of text production. If this is the case, the presence of the Münch arrangement takes on a special function: being historically anterior, it mediates in the text's composition, and prompts the reader to question the status of the text that contains it.

McGann describes *The Cantos* as a kind of critical edition in its aims and subject matter: "A twentieth-century poem containing history will have to invent and display, somehow, at least the equivalent of footnotes, bibliography, and other scholarly apparatus."[37] For example, the use of Roman numerals "is a visual cue calling attention to the linguistic importance of the material form of every script" (136). Neither Arabic numerals nor English words, the number given to each canto thus draws attention to the importance of its intellectual and cultural sources and the kind of history that the poem itself collects and presents. The Roman form of serial enumeration summons the ghost of classical epic composition and is part of the text's rhetorical claim for cultural centrality.

Certainly, the text's identity and status calls editing and textual scholarship into question. Hugh Kenner once told James Laughlin: "The whole printing history of *The Cantos* is a bibliographer's nightmare."[38] Yet Richard Taylor observes that: "However private the discourse, the text is not so much a 'material thing' as it is an event or set of events in which certain communicative interchanges are experienced."[39] The problem of ascribing objecthood to such an artwork is only made the more explicit with the presence of musical notation, itself located in historic and private discourse, but also locating a faultline between the arts.

Ronald Bush has argued that the composition of *The Pisan Cantos* was advertised by Pound and perpetuated by critics as a distinct event— an account not complicit with the manuscript evidence. Pound had reported many years later that these cantos were composed at Pisa without any major revision taking place. That testimony has been used since as a polemical tool both for and against modernist verse: "I have in mind here value judgements about poetic immediacy that Pound subtly reinforced by suggesting he had composed on the spot poems that themselves had dramatized a spontaneous epiphany of terror, natural beauty, and compassion."[40] When it came time for Pound to compose the manuscript version of *The Pisan Cantos* in the medical compound of the DTC, he in fact translated the typed notes of earlier material (reproduced in the article by Bush) composed in Italian:

Pound's holograph manuscript comprises the first text of *The Pisan Cantos* proper, and at this point two things about it are worth noting. The first is that Pound's pencil manuscript, running to more than 300 pages, is a distinct version of the text, containing much that subsequent revisions do not. The second is that this version was in crucial ways conditioned by the earlier typescripts of the Italian Cantos 74 and 75 and their family of manuscripts. (188)

The dissonances of the published text for Bush—such as the role of natural life as a timeless lesson of nature, overshadowing passages which record the incursion of the "here and now"—produce a series of fault-lines from which to distinguish several processes of intention and authority. It seems clear that Pound turned from the world of nature and of the Grecian gods to memories of people dead, famous and obscure, and that this change motivates much of *The Pisan Cantos*. Bush places the burden of the text's achievement on this "premeditated exercise" of memory (196).

The complex task of assembling the typescript drafts into the published text of *The Pisan Cantos* ruled out classic notions of authority and authorship. In fact, the condition of exile—a deep exile complicated with the constraint of Pound's arrest—takes the text of *The Pisan Cantos* beyond the domain of "social text" theory. The process of composition is not marked by a sociality of artists and publishers but by an abstract notion of audience and the sociality of the page. Memory thus takes on a greater significance as it provides the means to situate the text culturally and aesthetically. These uncertainties and difficulties raise questions of identity and status. The quotation of a musical work captured by its notation but separate in essence from it, answers the call of memory for Pound. The work is not subject to questions of revision, and, for his purposes, is not conditioned by its mode of inscription or any variants which might arise. It is in this way an iconic object in the text, standing in for an aesthetic experience, and for Pound it describes that experience with considerable eloquence. Its representation in the text is referential in a further sense, as the typescript simply offers instructions to insert what cannot be replicated there in the DTC medical tent.

IV.
The Status of the Score

Canto LXXV can be read more fully with an awareness of its provenance, its composition conditions, and the semantic texture of its poetic and musical material. But the violin line is more than simply a quotation or an iconic reference to the ideal essence of music. The music can also be read on its own terms, and (since it still operates as an icon) as the subject of its own referential sign. Yet the symbolic weight music is made to bear in *The Pisan Cantos* makes even this prescription problematic. In this instance the status of the musical score challenges the orthodox reading of the musical work as an ideal entity and of the score as simply a material sedimentation or set of instructions.

Pound makes several musicological prescriptions for the score, work, and performance, and he articulates exactly the problems still current in philosophical and musicological discourse. Writing at the time of the Rapallo concerts, he asserts the idealist notion of music as a transient work: it is always to be repeated anew in performance and is never captured within the posterity of the score.

> The performing musician cuts his form in the air and in the time flow. He writes it as in less stable water ... After all, if I write a distich, the immediate public and all editors can go to hell and be damned. The bust outlasts the throne. The written line stands on paper or parchment or, if good enough, even in the oral tradition. But the sonata is played and must next time be replayed. The composer exists in a sejunct world. His composition does stand on the page. But the performer's "work" is transient. Only a slight residue remains to him as prestige.[41]

The score then evidently does not share the same status as the written or printed poetic text. The poet can rely on that permanence, and can, if good enough, fall back to the oral tradition if the printed text object is not realized or is otherwise put in jeopardy. The musician, on the other hand, can only inscribe a remnant or mnemonic of the work, which can properly exist in no performance and on no page.

The score is not mere residue however, as it marks out the precise time of music and the relations between notes.[42] The performance of music requires the score to be interpreted but with the strictest adherence to time. As Pound states: "There is an enormous leeway even in the best graph, BUT it is a leeway of intensity, not of duration."[43] To allow the performance to obscure the work is equally erroneous for Pound: "the theory that the audience really hears the performer not the composer, and that there can be no absolute rendering of the composer's design, ultimately destroys all composition, it undermines all values, all hierarchy of values" (197–198). The work, for Pound, is an intellectual structure that should not be made subordinate to the performance and the performing musicians.

Pound's attitude to the work, score, and performance is not straightforward. For example, the work's transcendence of any single performance allows it to fulfill its historic character: in this case, Münch's violin line fulfils the role of individual scoring in early modern music. Yet Pound identifies the vague borderlines of identity and function between score and work. His rhetoric suggests an idealist view of music, but he does not use overtly ontological terms. Rather, his theory of music resembles that of Roman Ingarden in allowing for an historical role in the status of the essentially abstract work. Following from the conditions under which Canto LXXV was composed, the score may also be read within an historicist context. In this way, the aesthetic lesson provided by Canto LXXV can attain a fuller appreciation; wherein the score may perform multiple roles by drawing attention to its status and to that of the poetic text in which it appears.

As one philosopher of music has argued, attempts to describe the musical work have tended to overlook the historical context in the struggle to identify ontological status.

> In recent philosophical literature, the concept of a musical work has been treated less in terms of its genealogy that in its role as an ontological category. Accordingly, it has been described in relation to two traditional ontological concerns: a concern to describe the mode of existence of different kinds of objects in terms of categories like universals, types, and classes and a concern to determine the essential properties or the identity conditions for these objects. The idea has been to describe the concept by describing the kind of object a musical score is.[44]

Such studies tend to divide the score and performance from the work by imposing such categorical dualisms as universal and particular, or type and token. This schema risks misrepresenting the status of the work and abstracts it from history. One idealist account seeks to avoid the psychologist view of music (where a new work is realized in each auditing) by proposing the work as an objective sound structure, an *abstract object*. It does not consist of sound, since sound is transient, nor of the score, since the work may be known without knowledge of the score. Rather the work is the *type* of which its score and various performances are *tokens*.[45] In this rationale each work is distinct and subject to a unique moment of creation since the "whole tradition of art assumes art is creative in the strict sense, that it is a godlike activity in which the artist brings into being what did not exist beforehand" (8). But both Canto LXXV and Münch's violin line are composed in a space of memory, quotation, and reference. Their

respective modes of originality do not rely on Romantic paradigms of creation *ex nihilo*. They could not be composed under such conditions.

A more nuanced account considers the work a *two-dimensional abstract particular*: it exists "in realizations (which are individuals) which are
discontinuous spatially and temporally with one another."[46] Here, the work
is not identical with any of its realizations, but only exists when and where
they exist. Being neither universal nor individual, music can exist in several
media from the familiar score and performance, to radio and recorded
forms (such as audio tape or compact disc). No medium may claim logical
priority. The authoritative realization of the work can take the form of a
performance, or else "the composer's manuscript or an early edition of the
score; but it could also be a recording of the composer's performance"
(62). This flexibility founders, however, by treating the internal relations
of a score as a quasi-linguistic grammar containing the work's meaning,
rather than a convention or instruction for its realization in sound (63).
In the case of Canto LXXV, the very fact that the reader cannot hear the
birds that Pound hears, or the music he wishes to be reproduced in his
text, plays on the distinction between the score and the performance.
Familiarity with the music (whether Janequin, Francesco da Milano, or
Münch) only renders the vestigial birdsong with a greater pathos.

Pound's pronouncements of aesthetic identity share important features with the work of Roman Ingarden. The musical work, for Ingarden,
is an *intentional object*. As such, it is not a temporal process but rather a
quasi-temporal structure, determined in the process of composition and
realized in each performance. The musical work "is mainly or wholly a
sounding work, while the notation of the score is simply a defined arrangement, usually of graphic signs."[47] Any recourse to psychologism is denied—
the work forms no part of mental experience, particularly that of its creator—but the work is endowed with a recorded history and a limited life-
span. Pound, in his most striking departure, sees the work as both a mental
fact and a part of history. The best musical work (all art is deeply ethical
for Pound) is a concept or form with exact proportions, and represents
the health of the civilization from which it derives.

For Ingarden, the work cannot be identified with any of its performances and "forms no element of them" (33). Equally, the work's identity
is not reducible to its score. If that were so, the manner of distributing the
ink on the page would be nothing more than a compact between composer, printer, and reader, and would lead to each instance of the score

containing its own musical work. Rather, the score is "an arrangement of *instructions* as to how to proceed in order to achieve a faithful performance of a given work" (39). As an intentional object, however, it has a material base (paper and ink) upon which signs supervene; and the signs themselves bear a "typical aspect" or form that carries the "intentionally ascribed meaning" of the sign (37). This deterministic notion of the score precludes the kind of textual criticism one might wish to carry out and seems to miss the crucial overlap between the most physical elements of a score and its signs, symbols, and "intentionally ascribed meanings."

Ingarden concedes the role of history in the work's identity, but history as a concept rather than a process: "The fact that [the work] came into being at a particular moment in time also rules out the notion that a musical work is an ideal object like, say, a number" (65). The process of composition, and its nuanced effect upon the work's identity, is submerged beneath the moment of creation. History does hold a place in Ingarden's schema, however. The division between work and performance allows for the continuance of a work into future epochs, where it may be interpreted differently in performance. This gives the work (strictly, its performances) a social identity that is known collectively through debate, opinion, and convention. It "becomes an element of the world surrounding that society, like other objects that surround us and are also intersubjective objects available to a whole society" (154). Finally, the score allows for the continued integrity of the work by revealing the invariant schema of the work whilst allowing for the multiple "profiles through which a work may manifest itself" (157–158).

These features accord well with Pound's musical notions: the transience of performance, the strict adherence to time as notated in the score, and the "right of rebirth and recurrence" belonging to the masterwork. Pound's pronouncements on the history and identity of the score are not fully consistent. The material form of the score constitutes an essential part of the work's history, yet, for Pound, the social aspects of the musical work are, in the end, subordinate to its essence or form. On the other hand, the violin line is not so much quoted as presented by him in Canto LXXV, even as it appears through the function of memory. The choice of Janequin's *Chant* is significant as an early example of programme music: intended not to be played alone, but in concert with choral elements. The violin line is not so much isolated as returned to its previous form of publication—musical works in the sixteenth century were transcribed into instrumental lines rather than collated into total scores. Pound's quotation of the line is a reference to Münch's reconstruction of musical history. Pound is drawing attention to the status of the *Chant* as a predecessor of the received (and largely Romantic) notion of the musical work and the score. He seeks a return to the "spirit of romance," the *motz el son* of Troubadour song, and its heritage in the madrigals of the Renaissance.

Musical aesthetics can accommodate the work's history and identity. Joseph Margolis proposes the work as *physically embodied* and *culturally emergent*. The first notion neatly avoids the problems of idealism or the plural-minds argument of psychologism (the work as a collective mental act): "*If* a work of art is 'embodied' in a physical object, then whatever convenience of reference and identity may be claimed for a physical object may be claimed for the work of art embodied in it in spite of the fact that to be embodied in an object is not to be identical with it."[48] The artwork's embodying object is in possession of properties independent of our perception. On the other hand, the notion of cultural emergence demands properties of the artwork other than those of its embodying object (although it may contain those as well). The extra-embodying properties are culturally significant, and give the artwork its distinctive, and Kantian, "purposiveness without purpose" (188, 189). Margolis's theory makes a more satisfying account of the constitution and transmission of artworks, but it encounters problems in seeking to fit the artwork within an ontological schema. The context of the work—its history, rhetoric, and the circumstances of its appearance—will override the application of logical categories, particularly in complex works.

Münch's violin line provides a complex test case for this theory. On first sight, the score would seem to be embedded within the poetic text, which serves as its object. Or is the physical book of *The Cantos* the proper object? If so, given the problematic composition and authority of the text, with its variants and instabilities, which edition of *The Cantos* will serve this function? And is the poetic text accorded the same ontological status as the score, or is it somehow more foundational in this case? The music in Canto LXXV can operate as a quotation or embedded referent to the full score (and its provenance and history), but it is clearly much more than this. By revealing the music's historical substance, it can be read on its own terms by the musically literate. Yet the music is read within the context and structure of the poem and thus does not exist solely on its own terms. Each context demands a new response to the question of identity: the music cannot claim the same identity as the canto, the series of cantos in which both appear, or the physical book "containing" all of these aesthetic objects. A hierarchy of dependence from the book to the text, then to the canto and finally to the music, can be inverted neatly when the production of the canto and the historical circumstances and technical means of the music's placement in it are considered. From this viewpoint Janequin's *Le Chant des Oiseaux* provides the ground upon which Canto LXXV is made possible.

The ontological shortfalls of the theories so far presented are due to the unsuitability of ontology itself as a descriptive tool for aesthetics. The historicist view of the musical work's identity seeks to redress the neglect of history and the cultural determinants of artistic production within "expressionist" views of art (where the artist seeks to produce a correlative to an inner state), and within "aestheticist" views (where the artist proceeds with a notion of aesthetic unity). Wolterstorff notes that such accounts rarely, if at all, mention audiences, patrons, the instruments available and the styles of playing them, and the current notions of artistic purpose and its evaluation: "In a word, nothing is said about the social realities of art, nor, indeed, about its cultural and material realities."[49] Ingarden warns against reading the score purely as a material artifact; but equally, it is a document sharing in the work's identity, not simply referring to it.

Many theories of music shift the burden of identity from performance to the work. This is due, in part, to the dominance of "non-functional" or pure music as the paradigm for all music (such theorists as Ingarden and Levinson even disclose their paradigm explicitly). But Wolterstorff suspects that the development of a detailed system of notation has led to the view of the score and the performance as ontologically transparent windows to the ideal work (127). When considered in its historical context, however, the score can also trace the composition and development of the work (as the violin line does so efficiently in Canto LXXV), and does not simply provide the structure of the work in notated form.[50] Thus the problems of ascribing status to the work may be considered productively: Treitler observes that music "offers itself as a guide—by way of the investigation of its ontology—into a distinct mode of cognition, communication and interaction that constitutes an essential element among the possibilities of human engagement" (483). Failure to account for the nature of music in philosophical aesthetics can make explicit the selection criteria of musical examples, usually pure musical compositions from the era of Bach to the late nineteenth century. Ultimately, Treitler's determination to read such difficulties as enabling for the history of music is instructive:

> Such differences about the conception of the musical work and its relations
> to scores and performances are markers of music history. They constitute
> one of the major dimensions in which music even *has* a history. (496)

Certainly a vast array of works—among them Treitler's favorite example,
Chopin's Mazurka opus 7#5, and Münch's violin line in Canto LXXV—
can be explicated more fully and precisely through historical difference
than through categorical rigidity.

The persistence of idealism in theories of the musical work may ultimately derive from the common stock of ideas informing philosophy and
music during the reign of pure music. The idea of the *Werktreue* stems
from E. T. A. Hoffmann's prescription that musical works not be considered from any extra-musical viewpoint, or in any context outside of their
own composition, performance, reception and analysis.[51] A precise score
allows for exactly repeatable performances (in theory) and thus realizes
the unique expression of the composer. This idea provides for the work's
ascendancy over the score and performance. Goehr's historical reading of
the idealist musical work reveals that the autonomy of the artwork was
similarly developed in Kantian aesthetics, and that music had, for the first
time, developed outside of the church, court, and scientific institution:
"Only with the rise of this new view of music did musicians, critics, and
the like begin to think predominantly of music in terms of works" (56).
Consequently, oppositions grew between composition and performance,
composition and transcription, and programme and pure music. These
tensions still held when Pound composed his text and inserted the music
in Canto LXXV. The foregoing analysis has demonstrated how deeply many
of these metaphysical assumptions still lie, and how the reader's appre-
hension of the canto must move through the same questions of identity.
The score continually issues the same challenge: to consider the ways in
which music and literature, individually and in combination, call their aesthetic identities to account.

V.
A Lesson in Aesthetics

Each of the sections above has demonstrated that the complex aesthetic
object, Canto LXXV, presents a challenge to assumptions of aesthetic identity. The unusual provenance of the poetic text, and the precarious authority guiding the score's inclusion meant that notions of originality and
textual authority (not to say textual status) were operating in sophisticated

and largely unanticipated ways. The image of the jailed poet composing from memory, and thus embodying a purer aesthetic of Romantic inspiration, is one that seems at odds with Pound's careful documentation of the score's complex history of transmission and arrangement and its subsequent reproduction.

The status of *The Pisan Cantos* is that of a fragile text composed in a condition of deep exile, without a meaningful notion of a direct audience. It provides a challenge to textual criticism, not least in the dispersal of authority amongst the many editorial hands. Canto LXXV renders this dispersal in lapidary aesthetic terms, by introducing musical notation over which the author has no claim beyond that of personal and cultural memory. But in Pound's aesthetics such a claim "outlives the throne."

Finally, an attempt to read the music on its own terms, or as more than a quotation of an aesthetic form external to the poem, raises complementary questions concerning the status of the score. The presence of Münch's arrangement in the canto challenges idealist notions of the musical work and discloses a complex composition and transmission history. Indeed, the provenance of the score, from Janequin and perhaps from Arnaut Daniel, precedes the era of pure music upon which idealist accounts of music derive their force.

The conjunction of the musical score and the poetic text in Canto LXXV does not entail a rivalry between the arts, but makes an eloquent request to the reader to value the identity and provenance of aesthetic production. The score in Canto LXXV is equally an element of music history as of personal and cultural memory. It is a crucial semantic element of the text and a part of its history and status. That status is in turn dependent upon the status of score and poetic text and their co-presence exactly at that point. The lesson in aesthetics is a lesson of productive art: to challenge the status of the artwork, and to invigorate new thinking about the function and possibility of art. Pound's song, under the threat of silence, is not of the birds or the violin, but sings of the urgent need for intelligent art.

Mark Byron*

* This essay quotes from unpublished material housed in the Beinecke Rare Book and Manuscript Library at Yale University. Copyright © Mary de Rachewiltz and Omar S. Pound. Used by permission of New Directions Publishing Corporation.

Notes

1. Ezra Pound, *The Cantos*, Fourth Collected ed. (London: Faber, 1987), 450–451. Further references to *The Cantos* will be from this edition, and will be incorporated into the text with canto and page number. Thus Canto LXXV, page 450 is LXXV/450.

2. Scores in modernist texts often function as humorous visual cues to traditional instances of scoring in miscellanies, psalters, and hymnals. They also draw on traditions of lyric interludes and libretti in prose texts, particularly the Elizabethan romance genre.

3. Pound was greatly influenced by Dolmetsch's book *The Interpretation of the Music of the XVIIth and XVIIIth Centuries* (London: n.p., 1915).

4. Pound's music criticism is collected in *Ezra Pound and Music*, ed. with commentary by R. Murray Schafer (London: Faber, 1978). Another indispensable source of information concerning Pound's musical interests, contacts, and analyses is Stephen J. Adams, "Ezra Pound and Music" (Ph.D. diss., University of Toronto, 1974).

5. The result of this collaboration was the publication of Walter Morse Rummel, *Heasternae Rosae, Serta II, Neuf Chansons de troubadours des XIIième et XIIIième Siècles pour voix avec accompagnement de piano* (London: Augener; Paris: Max Eschig; Boston: Boston Music Company, 1913).

6. Agnes Bedford, *Five Troubadour Songs*, Original Provençal words and English words adapted by Ezra Pound from Chaucer (London: Boosey and Co., 1920).

7. Ezra Pound, *Antheil and the Treatise on Harmony* (Paris: Three Mountains, 1924).

8. Ezra Pound, *Guide to Kulchur* (London: Faber, 1938), 73. The notion of "absolute rhythm" (a related notion) had been proposed as early as the introduction to the Cavalcanti poems. This is dated 15 November 1910, but was first published in Pound's *Sonnets and Ballate of Guido Cavalcanti* (London: Stephen Swift & Co., 1912). Schafer defines the two terms together: "*Absolute rhythm* governed the proportions of the elements of masterpieces; *Great Bass* links the elements into an indivisible whole" (479).

9. Schafer, 328. The Turin collection is the largest of Vivaldi manuscripts and Vivaldiana, whilst the Dresden collection is second in size only to that of Turin.

10. For further information, see *Vivaldiana*, Publication de Centre International de Documentation Antonio Vivaldi 1 (1969); Stephen J. Adams, "Pound, Olga Rudge, and the 'Risveglio Vivaldiano'," *Paideuma* 4.1 (1973): 111–118; and Schafer, 321–333.

11. Schafer, 449.

12. Rudge was to found, with the musicologist Sabastiano Luciani, the *Centro di Studi Vivaldiani* in Siena. Rudge contributed to *Antonio Vivaldi: note e documenti sulla vita e sulle opere* (Siena: Accademia Musicale Chigiana, 1939), which Luciani edited. Rudge later published some of the work deriving from the Dresden manuscripts in *Vivaldi: Quattro Concerti Autografi della Sächsische Landesbibliothek di Dresda* (Siena: Accademia Musicale Chigiana, 1949).

13. "Money Versus Music," *The Delphian Quarterly* (January 1936): 3, qtd. in Schafer, 379. See also Pound's "Ligurian View of a Venetian Festival," *Music and Letters* (January 1937): 40, qtd. in Schafer, 416.

14. "Mediæval Music and Yves Tinayres," *The Listener* (July 22, 1936): 188, qtd. in Schafer, 397.

15. "Tigullian Studies," *Il Mare* (April 25, 1936), trans. Maria Chiara Zanolli, qtd. in Schafer, 390, 392.

16. Schafer, 391.

17. "Janequin, Francesco da Milano," *Townsman* 1.1 (January 1938): 18.

18. Pound, *Guide to Kulchur*, 250–251.

19. Pound's initial broadcasts in late-1940 were scripted in Rapallo and sent to Rome for others to read, but in 1941 he was given permission to record his own talks. The speeches ran weekly or twice weekly for months at a time, between 21 January 1941 until 26 July 1943. After the fall of Mussolini and the subsequent establishment of the Repubblica di Salò, Pound once again broadcast. On 10 December 1943, he gave a speech himself and during 1944 he sent scripts to Milan to be read by authorized employees of Fascist Radio. See Humphrey Carpenter, *A Serious Character: The Life of Ezra Pound* (New York: Delta, 1988), 632–634.

20. Carpenter, 626.

21. Pound's wife Dorothy was only informed of his whereabouts on 24 August by Colonel Walter A. Hardie, provost marshal general of the Mediterranean Theater of Operations. The instructions for the exchange of mail were given by Lieutenant Colonel Ralph A. Tolve, the provost marshal. See Omar Pound and Robert Spoo, eds., *Ezra and Dorothy Pound: Letters in Captivity, 1945–1946* (New York: Oxford UP, 1999), 16.

22. This typescript derives from the Ezra Pound Collection in the Beinecke Rare Book and Manuscript Library at Yale University: YCAL (Yale Collection of American Literature) MSS 43, Box 76, Folder 3393. Other typescripts contain small variations in wording, but the same composition scheme adheres: the poetic matter is followed by a blank space or a signal to leave such a space for

the music. See YCAL MSS 43, Box 76, Folders 3394 and 3397; and Box 77, Folder 3404.

23. "Janequin," 18.

24. Dorothy Pound, letter to James Laughlin, 16 December 1945, James Laughlin Collection, Beinecke Rare Book and Manuscript Library, Yale University.

25. The letter from Dorothy Pound to James Laughlin is dated 28 December 1945, qtd. in Pound and Spoo, 229. The news of Eliot's receipt of the music is given in another letter, from Dorothy to Ezra Pound, dated 29 December 1945, also qtd. in Pound and Spoo, 229.

26. For a comprehensive list of printed variants and errors in New Directions editions, see Barbara Eastman, *Ezra Pound's 'Cantos': The Story of the Text 1948–1975*, intro. Hugh Kenner (Orono: National Poetry Foundation, 1979).

27. The Italian bilingual edition was produced by Pound's daughter, Mary de Rachewiltz. See Ezra Pound, *I Cantos*, ed. tradotta e curata da Mary de Rachewiltz, commento di Mary de Rachewiltz in collaborazione con Maria Luisa Ardizzone, 5th ed. (1972/1985; Milan: Arnoldo Mondadori Editore, 1996). A German bilingual edition of *The Pisan Cantos* is also available: see Ezra Pound, *Die Pisaner Gesänge*, übertragen von Eva Hesse (Zürich: Die Arche, 1956). *The Cantos* has also been translated in full into French and Spanish: Ezra Pound, *Les Cantos*, traduit par Jaques Darras (Paris: Flammarion, 1986); and Ezra Pound, *Cantares completos I–CXX*, introducción, anecdotario, cronología y versión directa de José Vásquez Amaral (Mexico City: Editorial Joaquín Mortiz, 1975).

28. This term—"I, the writer"—is used in the first of *The Pisan Cantos* (LXXIV/458). It is a diminution of the earlier phrase "Ego, scriptor cantilenae"—"I, writer of *The Cantos*" (LXII/350; LXIV/360). By the time of *The Pisan Cantos*, the *ego scriptor* uneasily inhabits both the world of the text and the world of the DTC. The use of the Latin phrase offers some small distance from the immediacy of the DTC. In counterpoint to this example, one critic offers an extensive account of Pound's use of Latin, as an elaborate means of constructing poetic personae and of avoiding immediate and explicit identification with the historical person of Pound; see Ron Thomas, *The Latin Masks of Ezra Pound* (1977; Epping: Bowker, 1983).

29. The first image is taken from Allen Upward, *The New Word* (New York: Mitchell Kennerley, 1910), 222; the second is a reference to Ben Jonson's poem "Her Triumph" in *A Celebration of Charis: in Ten Lyric Pieces* (1624).

30. See Carroll F. Terrell, *A Companion to 'The Cantos' of Ezra Pound* (1980; Berkeley, Los Angeles, and London: U of California P. 1993), 338–339.

31. Terrell, 389.

32. This comment was quoted by Pound in 1938: "The point is 'not one bird but a lot of birds' as our violinist said on first playing it." See "Janequin," 18.

33. *Guide to Kulchur*, 151–152.

34. *ABC of Reading* (London: Faber, 1961), 54.

35. Herschel Parker, *Flawed Texts and Verbal Icons: Literary Authority in American Fiction* (Evanston: Northwestern UP, 1984), x and 231.

36. Jerome J. McGann, *A Critique of Modern Textual Criticism* (1983; Charlottesville and London: U of Virginia P, 1992), 48.

37. *The Textual Condition* (Princeton: Princeton UP, 1991), 129.

38. Quoted in Hugh Witemeyer, review of *Ezra Pound's 'Cantos': The Story of the Text*, by Barbara Eastman, *Paideuma* 9.1 (1980): 215.

39. Richard Taylor, "The History and State of the Texts," in *A Poem Containing History: Textual Studies in 'The Cantos,'* ed. Lawrence S. Rainey (Ann Arbor: U of Michigan P, 1997), 240.

40. Ronald Bush, "'Quiet, Not Scornful'? The Composition of *The Pisan Cantos*," in Rainey, 169.

41. *Guide to Kulchur*, 170–171.

42. Pound's entire musicology is based on the precisions of time: his *Treatise on Harmony* asserts the "horizontal" nature of harmony stretching over notes "in duration"; Yves Tinayres commented on the score of Pound's opera *Le Testament de Villon* as being "longitudinal and linear" rather than conventionally melodic or harmonic (Charles Norman, *Ezra Pound* [London: Macmillan, 1960], 154); and the theories of "absolute rhythm" and *Great Bass* are founded upon the duration of notes rather than their pitch and harmony.

43. *Guide to Kulchur*, 198.

44. Lydia Goehr, "Being True to the Work," *Journal of Aesthetics and Art Criticism* 47.1 (1989): 62.

45. Jerrold Levinson, "What a Musical Work Is," *Journal of Philosophy* 77.1 (1980): 6–7.

46. William E. Webster, "A Theory of the Compositional Work of Music," *Journal of Aesthetics and Art Criticism* 33 (1974): 60.

47. Roman Ingarden, *The Work of Music and the Problem of Its Identity*, trans. Adam Czerniawski, ed. Jean G. Harrell (London: Macmillan, 1986), 2.

48. Joseph Margolis, "Works of Art as Physically Embodied and Culturally Emergent Entities," *British Journal of Aesthetics* 14 (1974), 188–189.

49. Nicholas Wolterstorff, "The Work of Making a Work of Music," in *What Is Music? An Introduction to the Philosophy of Music*, ed. Philip Alperson (University Park: Pennsylvania State University Press, 1994), 108.

50. Leo Treitler, "History and the Ontology of the Musical Work," *Journal of Aesthetics and Art Criticism* 51.3 (1993): 490.

51. Goehr, 55.

11
Harmonic Dissonance:
Steinbeck's Implementation and
Adaptation of Musical Techniques

F. Scott Fitzgerald once wrote to his daughter Scottie regarding her study of literature:

> Poetry is either something that lives like fire inside you—like music to the musician—or else it is nothing, an empty, formalized bore around which pedants can endlessly drone their notes and explanations. (*Life in Letters*, August 3, 1940, 460)

Fitzgerald goes on to explain the beauty of every syllable in Keats' "The Grecian Urn," explaining to Scottie that every syllable is "as inevitable as the notes in Beethoven's Ninth Symphony." The musical analogy is then reiterated as Fitzgerald discusses the poem's "chime" and "its exquisite inner mechanics." In Fitzgerald's opinion, Keats truly attains a unison of literary styles that reproduced reality on the printed page. He praises the poet for a "sense of workmanship" that provides a measuring stick for anyone "who wants to know truly about words, their most utter value for evocation, persuasion and charm" (460).

John Steinbeck also had an ear for music. In fact, references to it abound in his canon as well as his letters to friends and acquaintances. Therefore, it is not unlikely that as he perfected his craft, he too became entranced by the sound of words and by their power to impact and even re-create human feelings. Though not much critical attention has been paid to Steinbeck's interest in music, John Ditsky has offered one analysis that acknowledges the musicality in his canon. In his essay, "The Devil in Music: Unheard Themes in Steinbeck's Fiction," Ditsky quotes Gerard Manley Hopkins' libretto for Benjamin Britten's oratorio, "The Company of Heaven," and notes the famous poet's reference to the song of Lucifer, an incantation that Hopkins describes as "raising a counter-music, and a counter-temple and altar, a counterpoint of dissonance and not of harmony" (80). Ditsky then suggests that Steinbeck, like Hopkins' Lucifer, "sang his own song," a melody often tinged with dissonance; he also argues that much of Steinbeck's artistic output had to do with "his struggle with his black angel over many a long night and even over the eventually splitting of his ego into twinned possibilities" (83).

Thus, rather than working toward the facile harmonic resolution that Fitzgerald seems to value in Keats, Steinbeck, according to Ditsky, seems more interested in finding "stasis or the point of possible resolution." Musically, such an act might prove repugnant to the ear, but Ditsky reminds us that art has changed drastically since the turn of the century. Nowadays, there is a value and a beauty in conflicting tones, tones that initially seem wrong and unworthy of musical composition. Thus, although the musical elements in the Steinbeck canon are unorthodox, much remains to be done in the critical assessment of how they are employed in individual work. Ditsky only briefly mentions novels that might prove fruitful for such study. Surprisingly, however, he does not list Steinbeck's most musically oriented work, the novella, *The Pearl*, as a starting point nor does he acknowledge its potential as a repository where the author's musical theories are given full rein.

A closer look at Steinbeck's implementation of dissonance and the devil's interval in this novel will follow, but first a brief overview of the author's employment of musical elements in other works is in order, since it indicates that Steinbeck not only understood but valued the "sound" and the "musicality" of words.

First of all, it is clear that Steinbeck was uniquely aware of the power of rhythm and that he employed it effectively throughout his canon. Ditsky calls attention to the inter-chapter of *The Grapes of Wrath* that features car salesmen to illustrate this rhythmic sensitivity. Readers of this chapter almost feel as if they are listening to an auctioneer as the words bombard the car buyers at a pace that leaves them bewildered and vulnerable. Another illustration from *Grapes* that Ditsky does not mention but that also offers a positive illustration of Steinbeck's musicality is the square dance scene at the Weedpatch Camp. Most readers will agree that this passage can hardly be read without a sense of swirling or movement in a circular pattern, of feet tapping and instruments playing. Like William Carlos

Williams' "The Dance," the placement of words allows the listener to experience movement while sitting still.

Steinbeck's music in the square dance scene consists of a harmonica, a fiddle and a guitar:

> "the guitar beating like a heart, and the harmonica's sharp chords and the skirl and squeal of the fiddle. People have to move close. They can't help it. ... the squares close up and the dancing starts, feet on the bare ground, beating dull, strike with your heels. Hands 'round and swing. Hair falls down, and panting breaths. (*The Grapes of Wrath*, 363–364)

The following sentences continue to depict the passion that grows as the dance continues, eventually associating the dancers' building sexual emotions with religious fervor—praying and conversion—a seemingly unconnected and perhaps even dissonant event.

Peter Lisca, in his own identification of Steinbeck's varying musical styles, seems to agree that such dissonance is deliberate, as he discovers a first style he assesses as rich with a Biblical resonance and then identifies a deliberately opposite second style that seems to reflect the harsh staccato of the contemporary American scene (*Wide World*, 162–163).[1] It is this latter style, complete with onomatopoeic rhythms, which appears in Chapter 23 of *Grapes* (164). Steinbeck later returns to the square dance on page 378 as he prepares to describe an impending riot and fight, once again combining impassioned music with what appears to be opposite emotions that have no obvious connection. The text reads:

> And the girls were damp and flushed, and they danced with open mouths and serious reverent faces, and the boys flung back their long hair and pranced, pointed their toes and clicked their heels. In and out the square moved, crossing, backing, whirling, and the music shrilled.

Ultimately, the reader senses the fact that the building sexual tension may provoke possible violence. Although the fight is avoided, the musical interlude has stirred up the reader in two different ways and has set the stage emotionally for angry confrontation.

But it not only quick-paced prose that Steinbeck masters in *Grapes*. He is also able to entrance his readers with slow restless images, like those that begin the novel. Roy Simmonds notes that much of *The Grapes of Wrath* was composed to the accompaniment of gramophone recordings of Tchaikovsky and Stravinsky and that Steinbeck claimed that in writing the book he utilized "the forms and mathematics of music rather than prose"

(84). Consequently, the work became symphonic "in composition, in move-ment, in tone and in scope" as Steinbeck strove to put down words on paper that would impress themselves on the inner ear of the reader (*SLL*, 105). As readers experience the initial paragraphs of *Grapes*, a laconic mood develops. The patterns of repetition, the deliberate deadening of de-tails as the dying crops are described all help readers envision the shrivel-ing leaves, the slowly rising dust, and the barely moving individuals who watch helpless before a natural world that seems to wage a subtle war against the human population. Here, like Keats, Steinbeck's word choice transports readers into the scene. They become one with the characters, enmeshed in the fabric of Steinbeck's tapestry; the Dust Bowl is recreated aurally, and Steinbeck's accompanying visual depiction provides a even greater physical identification with the scene.

Other Steinbeck works that indicate the author's attraction to music include *Cannery Row* and *The Journal of a Novel*. In *Cannery Row*, the protagonist Doc is constantly listening to music in his laboratory at West-ern Biological Supply. Steinbeck writes that "a great phonograph stands against the wall with hundreds of records lined up beside it (126), and Doc's eclectic tastes are described not only in his music but in the art which adorns the walls. Titian and Leonardo (da Vinci) are balanced with Dali and Picasso. No doubt Doc's taste in music is similarly broad. In fact, Steinbeck's stress on paradoxical opposites in music is most evident in the melody Doc hears when he discovers the corpse of a young woman while searching for biological specimens in the great tide pool near La Jolla. As he observes the dead body, Doc is described by Steinbeck in the following passage:

> Music sounded in Doc's ears, a high thin piercingly sweet flute carrying a melody he could never remember, and, against this, a pounding surf-like wood-wind section. The flute went up to regions beyond the hearing range and even there it carried its unbelievable melody. Goose pimples came out on Doc's arms. He shivered and his eyes were wet the way they get in the focus of great beauty. ... He sat there hearing the music while the sea crept in again over the bouldery flat. His hand tapped out the rhythm, and the terrifying flute played in his brain. The eyes were gray and the mouth smiled a little or seemed to catch its breath in ecstasy. (196)

Again dissonance is suggested by the descriptive words. The flute is sweet sounding but terrifying; the event is shocking and tragic, yet appears to depict some sort of ecstatic beauty cloaked beneath the fearful signs of death and mortality.

Later in the novel as Doc listens to Monteverdi's Hor ch' el Ciel e la Terra (The Hour of the Sky and the Land), he associates its sadness with literature (Petrarch mourning for Laura) and with the reality of Mac's broken mouth, a injury incurred when Doc hits him in anger after the aborted birthday party turns violent. Not surprisingly, at the second party Doc chooses a different Monteverdi selection, "Ardor and Amor." This time the reaction to the musical interlude is far different as "the guests sit quietly and their eyes were inward. Dora breathed beauty." (259). Doc is paradoxically described as feeling a "golden pleasant sadness," and, as the music plays, he reads a selection translated from the Sanskrit and entitled "Black Marigolds" where the author describes in sensual detail his feelings for his lost love.

Finally, the book ends with a Gregorian chant, a simplistic unison vocal performance in which disembodied voices, described as incredibly pure and sweet, fill the laboratory with a single melodic line as opposed to the more complex chords found in Monteverdi. As Doc recites the Sanskrit verses, he revels in the sights, smells and sounds of the Row, and all mingle together into "the hot taste of life." (269). Loud sounds and whispers combine with visual and gustatory images to create a sense of wholeness, a balance that Doc revels in.

Yet another Steinbeck work that reveals the author's interest in utilizing musical qualities is the non-fictional *Journal of A Novel*. Published posthumously in 1969, the text contains Steinbeck's musings about composition and structure as he developed the plot of *East of Eden*. The journal entries, addressed a letters to his friend and editor Pascal Covici, often reveal Steinbeck's deliberately conscious attempts to mirror a musical structure in the work.

For example, in the February 12 entry, Steinbeck suggests he is trying to provide a musical balance in the text: "sooth[ing] and "exciting" at the same time, having "gaiety and movement" rather than just "dourness." Later in the text, Steinbeck announces how he will employ different tonalities and how his theme will emerge again and again as a way of echoing meaning and purpose. According to Steinbeck, the structural design of *East of Eden* revolves around counterpoint. First of all, there will be a change in pace as readers move from the aggressive action of the Trask chapters to contemplative deliberation in the chapters that record the lives of the Hamiltons (40). Later Steinbeck describes the balance he has attempted in tone, calling the Trask chapters as "dark and dour as a damp tunnel" while "the next Hamilton chapter is light and gay" (54). Steinbeck even confesses to changing time as he records events that happen to the Hamiltons. He moves events out of chronological order much as a musician might shift a time signature for a different movement of her composition. Moreover, Steinbeck also speaks of the selection of "harsh prose" to contrast with a more gentle poetic strain, and he frequently uses the term counterpoint as an indicator of the musical balances he is trying to maintain.

For example, in his March 27th entry, Steinbeck discusses subplots and how some listeners will find them "guileless and rather sweet" while they are hardly intended that way, consisting instead of "little blades of social criticism" (53). It is clear that as the Trasks and Hamiltons interact, Steinbeck intends us to hear dissonances rather than harmonics. While both families struggle with how to cope with the confusion and potential problems life brings, it is clear that Samuel Hamilton possesses an understanding of its complexities that clearly eludes Adam Trask.

The melodic themes appear and reappear in a fugue-like manner, suggesting methodical precision and deliberate planning. The motif is picked up in one voice or by one instrument and then is repeated in another timbre and vocal range so that what the reader has already heard in one plot line seems somewhat different, a subtle change that allows the author to revisit an idea without seeming to belabor it. Although some Steinbeck critics, notably Howard Levant, have suggested that structural flaws were a major reason for the failure of Steinbeck's later works to attain more renown, the entries in *Journal of a Novel* seem to suggest that just the opposite was true of Steinbeck's creative process. Steinbeck emphasizes that there was methodical planning and deliberate intent behind each musical movement and makes it clear that chapters and ideas were designed to reverberate, to echo, as it were, and give the readers an in-depth musical experience, one in which perceived dissonance would be seen as an integral part of a harmonic pattern and where resolution would only be suggested rather than achieved.

Steinbeck asserts that he joins the active and immediate with the passive and contemplative in *East of Eden* by creating a musical clash of words. As the June 26th entry states "the tempo of the book [changes] just as the tempo of the times changed. It will speed and rage then" (151). Moreover, since Steinbeck tells Covici that his musical plan was "set down long ago," readers can assume that it is hardly a random occurrence that musical techniques are employed in the novel. In fact, Steinbeck's most clear delineation in *Journal of A Novel* occurs in the June 27th entry where he says:

> There needs today to be the end of the kind of music that is Samuel Hamilton. It has to have that kind of recapitulation with full orchestra, and then I would like a little melody with one flute than starts as a memory and then extends into something quite new and wonderful as though the life which is finishing is going on into some wonderful future. (153)... Tomorrow I will take up this little flute melody, the continuous thing that bridges lives and ties the whole thing together, and I will end with a huge chord if I can do it. I know how I want it to sound and I know how I want you to feel when you have read it. ... And I will put my melody in the mail for you tomorrow. (155)

On page 166 of *Journal of a Novel*, Steinbeck announces his intent to employ refrain, yet another musical technique. "Refrain is one of the most valuable form methods," he says. "Refrain is the return to the known before one flies again upward. It is a consolation to the reader, a reassurance that the book has not left his understanding." Yet it is surely counterpoint that fascinates Steinbeck the most. He returns again and again to the contrast of opposites, the harmonic dissonance that seems to pervade all his work. This is especially true in the reprinted dedication to *East of Eden*, which concludes *Journal of a Novel*. Here he states:

> A book is like a man—clever and dull, brave and cowardly, beautiful and ugly. For every flowering thought there will be a page like a wet and mangy mongrel, and for every looping flight a tap on the wing and a reminder that wax cannot hold the feathers firm too near the top. ...
> I have written about one family and used stories about another family as well as counterpoint, as rest, as contrast in pace and color. (238)

It seems quite clear from the above citations that Steinbeck's use of music was not only widespread but intentional. Yet the work which most clearly reveals the author's understanding about the interrelationship between music and writing is neither *Grapes of Wrath* nor *Cannery Row*; nor is it *Journal of a Novel* or Steinbeck's other work of non-fiction, *The Log From The Sea of Cortez*. Instead it is the very brief literary fable that Steinbeck composed during the 1940's entitled The *Pearl*. Unfortunately, despite the novel's almost insistent recurrent emphasis on songs, little critical study regarding this dimension of Steinbeck's writing has been undertaken.

While the essential plot line of the novella was discovered by Steinbeck on a collecting voyage he took with his friend Ed Ricketts to the Gulf of California in 1940, (See *Log From The Sea of Cortez*, 105) the fictional result indicates that the author amplified and extended the original folktale from the brief retelling by natives who were familiar with the folk lore of La Paz. While aboard the Western Flyer, Steinbeck records the tale in a little over 1 1/2 pages, but later he transforms the rather slim plot into a much larger though still compact novella which first appeared in *The Women's Home Companion* in December 1945 under the title, *The Pearl of The World*, and was later published by Viking in 1947 (Simmonds, 137).

Though the novel begins with a visual panorama of the area around Kino's home in La Paz, it is not long before the emphasis shifts to auditory images as Kino listens for the songs, the music which identifies him with his people. By the end of the novel, references to songs or musical terminology appears on twenty-six of the novel's one hundred and eighteen pages. Clearly Steinbeck was acquainted with musical theory, especially Bach's *Art of the Fugue*, a work that he mentions specifically in "About Ed Ricketts," his celebratory essay about his close friend that serves as a preface for many editions of *The Log From The Sea of Cortez*. "He (Ed) once told me that he thought *The Art of the Fugue* by Bach might be the greatest music up to our time. Always "up to our time." He never considered anything finished or completed, but always continuing, one thing growing on and out of another" (xli). No doubt Ricketts and Steinbeck discussed Bach's technique as they tried to understand how his music worked and how to apply his musical concepts to other areas of study. Certainly, it seems as though Steinbeck tried to implement fugal elements in *The Pearl* as well as to display his appreciation of other techniques employed in classical music.

In *A Life in Letters*, for example, he writes to Annie Laurie Williams that all forms of music are "a part of us and we rise like trout to mayflies to them" (563). Indeed, musical textual references in *The Pearl* can be used to show that Steinbeck employed many of the elements that Bach advocated in *The Art of The Fugue*, the composition which was the culmination of his life's work and was finished shortly before his death in 1750. Bach's exquisite composition was designed to function as a textbook for future composers who wished to know the components of the form Bach had mastered, but it can also be argued that the work offered solid advice that could be used by other artists (notably poets and novelists) who wished to employ the techniques of Baroque music.

Given the details recorded previously about Steinbeck's musicality, it is not surprising that *The Pearl* emphasizes his delight in contrapuntal sounds, a delight which Bach himself shared. Steinbeck's dissonance often creates clashing notes as a result of voices playing off one another while a subject or melodic line is being repeated. In fact, such clashes, as we have seen, appealed to Steinbeck as being representative of life itself. Just as what appears to be wrong musically or uncomfortable to the ear often creates pleasure, so negative elements in life inexplicably often produce good. Similarly, the harmonic or "good" often create dull and uninteresting cadences and progressions, a reflection of the fact that positives in life may paradoxically result in the promotion of evil.

Such clashing realities may have been the thematic emphasis of Steinbeck's aborted novel entitled *Dissonant Symphony*, a work which he abandoned in 1931 and later destroyed. Had the manuscript of this unpublished work survived, this might have been the novel that most clearly defined the integral inter-relationship between sound and meaning in Steinbeck's work. In fact, Jackson Benson notes that purpose of this novel was to illustrate "the fact that sometimes the smallest event or circumstance can lead to profound changes in a person's course of action" (*True Adventures*, 201). Without this manuscript, however, *The Pearl* seems best fitted to add to an understanding of how Steinbeck employed Bach's techniques.

A second factor Bach advocates in order to create effective music is changing timbre—the auditory tone quality produced by a vocalist or an instrumentalist. As previously noted, Steinbeck was clearly aware of this musical element, recognizing that just as the audience's aural perception differs depending on whether the composer's main theme appears in the soprano or in the bass or whether it is executed in the orchestral setting by a flute or a bassoon or a trumpet so the reader is influenced by the variety of sounds and meanings presented by the author. Thus, wandering or partial repetition of the "subject" allows the tune/theme to be apprehended in a new way, tempered and modified by the instruments that produce it. Listeners/readers are aware that the melodic line/message is the same but somehow it is simultaneously different.

Similarly, when a writer selects a dominant motif for his work, he recognizes the need to reiterate that motif in a variety of different ways so that the reader will not be bored or overwhelmed by the insistent hammering of a moral or intellectual point. Thus while readers may be unaware of the complexities of a novel like *The Pearl* due to critical minimization of the novel's message, a close examination of Steinbeck's use of song will help to see the author's recurrent emphasis on moral ambiguity in the

novel, an element that he reinforces by reproducing this thematic emphasis in different timbres as he reiterates his concerns for humanity. For example, the human dilemma of selfishness is seen not only in the doctor
and in the pearl buyers but also appears in Kino's brother Juan Tomas
and in the protagonist himself. Following Bach's example, Steinbeck crafts
his words, his thematic melody, so that ideas repeat without calling attention to themselves. As a result, Steinbeck is able to imprint his message
on a reader's mind without appearing redundant or overly persistent.

A final musical technique advocated in *The Art of the Fugue* is a shift
in tempo. Steinbeck's sensitivity to this musical element is surely evident
in his discussions of *East of Eden* in *Journal of A Novel*, but his implementation of it in *The Pearl* is just as deliberate. In the Baroque period, many
of the musical tempos were based on the dance steps of the time: the sar-
abande, the minuet and the courant, and musical suites were commonly
organized by a variety of tempos with movements that were slow, moder-
ate and fast. This shift in pace was designed to hold listener's attention
and to provide a variety in pace that accompanied the shifting tonality.
Similarly, in *The Pearl*, Steinbeck's pace begins slowly with Kino's awakening from sleep in a peaceful surrounding, but it quickens as Coyotito's
life is threatened by the scorpion's sting. In later scenes, tension rises and
falls throughout as Kino's world alternates between peaceful and calm
stages and elements that are violent and destructive.

Steinbeck seems to understand, as Bach did, that the employment of
opposites (clashing melodic lines, variant timbre and tempos) is essential
to great music—in this case the music of prose fiction. Yet at times Steinbeck also breaks these normative rules and adds something new. This is
especially true of his refusal to return to a dominant chord in order to
complete his compositions. Instead of resolving contrapuntal notes and
returning to aural satisfaction with carefully controlled cadences that lead
to expected resolutions of sound, Steinbeck sometimes chooses to remain
with unexpected discord. This lack of melodic resolution brings us back to
John Ditsky's observation that Steinbeck frequently employed a forbidden
tri-tone in his fiction. Surely, the endings of *The Grapes and Wrath* and *Of
Mice and Men* demonstrate what Ditsky might label a less than satisfactory
open-closure. In fact, other works like *Pastures of Heaven, To a God Unknown* and *Winter of Our Discontent* also conclude with the reader caught
in an unsatisfactory limbo where she must struggle with an ending that
seems "wrong" or incomplete.

Though Ditsky does not fully describe what he calls the devil's music, its primary trait is harshness to the ear when played. Often known as an augmented fourth or a diminished fifth, the devil's interval is separated by four full steps, and the uncomfortable "noise" created by playing these two notes together caused it to be associated with the master of "wrong," Lucifer. Ditsky is correct in noting that a modern society would surely not object too much to such clashing melodic lines. For example, the riots that broke out after the first performance of Stravinsky's experimental "Rite of Spring" in 1913 would probably not occur in today's society because, as Steinbeck reminds in *Journal of Novel*, these dissonant lines mirror our present world with all its conflict and tenuous balances.

Though the Baroque qualities of dissonance, shifting timbre and tempos appear frequently, perhaps it is Steinbeck's deliberate attempt to reach open closure (what Ditsky calls "stasis on the possible point of resolution") that has caused critics to overlook a possible Bach or fugal influence in his canon. Since the fugue's harmonic endpoint, an element which would please the ear, is missing, Steinbeck's indebtedness to its techniques remains largely unexplored.

In addition, critical reaction to *The Pearl* has been so limited that evaluators have been hesitant to suggest a complexity in its musical structure. With its present status of simplistic parable and its relegation to a ninth grade curriculum and to limited or at-best basic intelligence, the novel is almost forbidden to possess nuances or depth of meaning. Instead its message must always be the moral caveat that greed for material possession is destructive or the corollary that manipulative upper classes (read patriarchal and colonial oppression) always exert domination over those whose poverty and ignorance leave them powerless and defenseless to fight against their so-called "fate."

But clearly *The Pearl* with its literary allusion to the Bible and to the Anglo-Saxon poem of the same name is much more than that.[2] Though its melodic lines, like those which sometimes appear in Bach preludes and then modify before they reappear in the connecting fugue, appear obvious, listeners are seldom aware of all the elements that comprise the genius of its creator. Hardly a black and white fable that some have labeled it nor a dismal failure at maintaining the simplicity of a folk tale while imbuing it with a moral lesson, this tale, as Steinbeck suggests, is one of frustration and dismay at maintaining the balances of life: the balance between the poor and the rich, between the religious and the atheist, between men

and women, and between Life and Death. The songs that people the text
reflect the harsh tri-tone, the devilish song that living in a fallen world requires. Notes clash wrongly as rich oppress and manipulate the poor, as
the church seeks monetary rewards rather than the well-being of its parish-
ioners, as the masculine beats and harasses the feminine, and, as the search
to improve Life, despite its good intent, leads only to Death, the fate of all
men.

Although one message of the novel might be to call attention to a shifting value system where "things" are more important than people, surely
the songs suggest a paradoxical duality in La Paz society where "progress"
is only attained through aggression and where the "Song of The Pearl
That Might Be" can not only offer escape from poverty and ignorance but
can also enmesh its owners in envy, greed and violence, voices that only
work to destroy an otherwise satisfactory existence.

Such contrasts are evident in the very first pages of the novel where
the narrator introduces his musical theme on page two by reminding listeners that Kino's people

> had once been great makers of songs so that everything they saw or thought
> or did became a song. The songs remained. Kino knew them, but no new
> songs were added. That does not mean there were no personal songs. In
> Kino's head there was a song now, clear and soft, and if he had been able to
> speak it, he would have called it the Song of the Family. (2)

Here Steinbeck accurately suggests that the melody of life continues with
no overt changes; there are merely variations that appear and disappear,
and essentially everyone's personal songs are merely rearrangements of
those sung by their ancestors. Steinbeck confirms this by having Kino's
wife, Juana, sing "an ancient song that had only three notes and yet endless variety of interval" (4). By identifying Juana's song as part of the family
song, the narrator seems to build an expectation that the sound that rises
will be comfortable and harmonic. Yet two sentences later it is described
as an "aching chord that caught the throat, saying this is safety, this is
warmth, this is the *Whole*" (4). Unexpectedly, the "family" sound resembles
a choking pain, and yet this pain ironically offers security. Dissonant opposites abound: the melody is aching but warm, part but whole, having
infinite variety but exquisite simplicity. Such musical duality certainly prefigures the complexity of life and living that the novel hopes to portray.

By page six, a new song surfaces, "The Song of Evil." Epitomized by
the scorpion, it is described as "the music of the enemy, of any foe of the

family, a savage, secret dangerous melody" (6). Embodying a physical threat to Coyotito, this countermelody becomes dominant for several pages. As it develops, "The Song of the Family "cries plaintively" (6) until Kino finds that soon "The Song of Evil roar[s] in his ears" (7). The positive song seems to disappear; yet, if we look closely at the text, it is apparent that the two songs mentioned are not separate entities. Instead the melodies merge, suggesting the inescapable fact that the human ear and mind often make disharmonic choices. The dominance of dissonant tones continues in the selfish actions of the town doctor and in Kino's anger at being treated as if he were a worthless animal rather than a fellow human being.

Chapter two begins with visual images before Steinbeck returns to his musical emphasis on page twenty-two. Here song is exalted and given almost mythical power. The narrator states:

> Kino's people had sung of everything that happened or existed. They had made songs to the fishes, to the sea in anger and to the sea in calm, to the light and the dark and the sun and the moon and the songs were all in Kino and in his people—every song that had ever been made, even the ones forgotten. (22)

Again dissonant polar opposites receive emphasis as the melody rises to encompass Kino's whole world: "The song was in Kino and the beat of the song was his pounding heart as it ate the oxygen from his held breath and the melody of the song was the gray green water and the little scuttling animals and the clouds of fish that flitted and were gone (23).

However, within this master song exists still another melody, "a secret little inner song, hardly perceptible, but always there, sweet and secret and clinging, almost hiding in the counter-melody and this was the 'Song of The Pearl That Might Be'" (23). As it is first introduced, this inner song seems innocuous, hardly capable of any negative effect on Kino, Juana and Coyotito. Instead, the narrator seems intent on emphasizing the positive when he notes that "whole phrases of it came clearly and softly into the song of the Undersea" (23).

However, some three pages later the wholesome melody has again transformed. Different timbrés and tonal qualities are emphasized. Kino's discovery of the great pearl is greeted not with a scream of exuberance but with an animalistic "howl" (26). Similarly, the music of the pearl that now "is" is described as "shrill"—hardly a complimentary word for a melodic line.

As Kino moves from being a satisfied human to a dissatisfied and frustrated animal and as Steinbeck associates his hardening nature with the scorpion (evil and destruction), readers can observe the author's growing craft in combining opposites. The music of the pearl seems to be more distressing and dissonant, and the more readers listen the more they identify with the pain it brings rather than with its pleasures. The melodic lines, seemingly quite opposite, again merge on page thirty-five where we read: "The music had gone out of Kino's head, but now, thinly, slowly, the melody of the morning, the music of evil, the enemy sounded, but it was weak and faint. And Kino looked at his neighbors to see who might have brought this song in" (35–36).

It is significant that Kino does not consider the possibility of his own complicity in the appearance of the song of evil but rather attributes its melody to an outside force. As with contrapuntal technique in music, the dissonant notes seem foreign (or from the outside) at times when actually they are an integral part of the whole. Such tensions continue on page thirty seven as the calm natural world where Kino previously found solace is transformed into threatening elements that elicit fear and dread. According to the narrator, "He [Kino] felt alone and unprotected and scraping crickets and shrilling tree frogs and croaking toads seemed to be carrying the melody of evil." The fact that good mingles with evil and vice versa remains a difficult concept to accept. Absolutes (harmonics) are preferable to the clashing tones of paradox. So Kino rubs the pearl and finds it warm and smooth against his skin; it must be a positive. Shortly thereafter the Song of the Family resurfaces "like the purring of a kitten" (37).

Yet the idea of paradox has been planted, and soon it becomes more difficult for Kino to ignore the dissonance and to deny that the repeating melody of life often contains harsh clashes that drown out the pleasant chords. By page forty-six, Kino actually finds himself anticipating such harsh sounds whereas previously they had been infrequent and unexpected. "He listened for any foreign sound of secrecy or creeping, and his eyes watched the darkness, for the music of evil was sounding in his head and he was fierce and afraid." The once small countermelody now seems to have become the central subject rather than a tangential and subordinate tune. The tranquility and security that were formerly a integral part of Kino's existence also seem to have faded into the background. Both the timbre and the tempo of the music have shifted, and Kino can no longer shut out or repress the realization that the evil tune is taking precedence, superceding and replacing safety with fear, satisfaction with greed, and love with hate. Steinbeck's opposites mentioned in *The Journal of a Novel* are surely in a titanic struggle here.[3]

Visual images return to reinforce melodic ones as the evil melody is appropriately associated with darkness. In fact, the physical darkness becomes a darkness of the soul as Kino becomes more and more determined to retain the pearl at all costs. Desperate for the absolutes that seemed constant in his previous naïve existence, he yearns for the return of the positive melodic lines and hopes that with the sale of the pearl "the evil will be gone and only the good remain" (50)

Surprisingly, as Ch. 3 ends and readers reach the middle of the book, this is exactly what happens. Steinbeck's artistry, in accord with his musical patterns, recapitulates, buoying the reader's hope for a potential happy ending and shifting the pace and tonal quality once again. In the light of a candle that dispels the surrounding darkness, the pearl shimmers and "cozen[s] his [Kino's] brain with its beauty. So lovely it was, so soft, and its own music came from it—the music of promise and delight, its guarantee of the future, of comfort, of security. Its warm presence promised a poultice against illness and a wall against insult. It closed the door on hunger" (51).

A brief calm follows, but it is soon broken by the tension that rises as Kino and Juana approach the pearl buyers. This time when Kino "hears in his ears the evil music" (66) it is accompanied by "the creeping of fate, the circling of wolves and the hovering of vultures," (65) and Kino feels "helpless to protect himself" (66). Again dissonance is present as the pearl buyers try to convince Kino that what he has found is not a priceless treasure but instead a frightful monstrosity, worth only a pittance rather than a great fortune.

As visual images accompany the aural ones, Steinbeck continues to restate his thematic melody, asserting moral ambiguity and the distressing fact that good and bad are inescapably intertwined. The moral tenets that Kino wishes were absolutes are clouded by his observation of clashing "facts" which turn out to be mere "hypotheses" that cannot be confirmed.

On page seventy-one, the narrator returns to the natural sounds that surround Kino, and readers will see a far different man than the individual whose vision of beauty opened the novel. As Steinbeck records the sensual observations of Kino, the text records this change: "A lethargy had settled on him and a little gray hopelessness. Every road seemed blocked against him. In his head he heard the dark music of the enemy" (71). But, just as the reader is ready to accept the conquering power of the dark music, Steinbeck returns us to yet another option as Juana attempts to restore the former balance between "The Song of Evil" and "The Song of the Family." Juana's voice is described as "brave against the threat of the dark music" as she "sings softly the melody of the safety and warmth and wholeness of the family" (72). For a moment at least, readers may entertain a hope that Juana's insight about the pearl will overcome Kino's stubbornness and that the tenuous balance between polar opposites will be restored.

But shortly thereafter, the two fight, and Kino beats his wife badly, angered at her desire to get rid of the pearl. Consequently, Juana's intuitive sense of danger is dismissed by the forceful Kino. But his confidence in his safety is very short-lived since Kino finds his smashed boat and discovers his burning house in the next few pages. "Now the darkness was closing in on his family; now the evil music filled the night, hung over the mangroves, skirled in the wave beat" (80). The pace quickens with these losses and with Kino's murder of the dark intruder who tries to steal the pearl. Moreover, the natural surroundings seem to mirror Kino's plight as Steinbeck uses verbs such as 'screamed', 'plunged', 'hung' and 'drove' to describe nature's distress. Similarly, Kino is pictured as "hard, cruel and bitter" as he identifies his fate more and more closely with the pearl, ultimately calling it "his soul." His determination to keep it, will, of course, lead to negative consequences that he cannot begin to anticipate.

Visual imagery again supplants musical references in the next twenty pages as Steinbeck varies the presentation of his thematic message. In a negative environment that juxtaposes mountains with seashore, the parched arid soil with land that is moisture-laden, and animals with humans, there is again a strange interaction of opposites, a contrapuntal mixing that arouses dismay in readers. Yet even in the midst of such surroundings, Kino relies on positive music for guidance. Steinbeck explains: "The quiet music of the pearl was triumphant in Kino's head and the quiet melody of the family underlay it, and they wove themselves into the soft padding of sandaled feet in the dusk" (91).

Yet Kino's hopes for a positive conclusion to his life-changing journey is soon revealed to be illusory. For, as early as page ninety-four, "the music of the pearl had become sinister in his ears and was interwoven with the music of evil." This strange combination is perhaps analogous to the yin/yang symbols of Taoism where the visual depiction reveals that opposites exist in the very center of the "other." As Kino flees from the trackers who seek to take away his "treasure," the musical sounds that previously were subordinate, now gain prominence as Steinbeck builds toward the conclusion of the novella and the harsh lessons Kino must learn. Recognizing that the trackers' goal is to kill his family rather than to force them to return to La Paz, Kino's feelings begin to shift. "Oh the music of evil sang loud in Kino's head now, it sang with the whine of the heat and with the dry ringing of snake rattles. It was not large and overwhelming now, but secret and poisonous, and the pounding of his heart gave it undertone and rhythm" (100).

The contradictions here are obvious—the music is "loud" but at the same time "secret" not "large and overwhelming" but still capable of creating a fearsome "pounding" of Kino's heart. In such paradoxical soundings, the Song of the Pearl and The Song of Evil acquire a mutual identity, and, as Kino plots the deaths of the three trackers, he rationalizes the evil he is about to undertake by ironically recalling the Song of the Family. Suddenly this pleasant warm melody is described as "fierce and as sharp and feline as the snarl of a female puma" (111). Again the sounds of nature echo Kino's negative observation, and, although Kino's own music seems to supplant "the music of the enemy, low and pulsing, nearly asleep," (111) there has been a modulation that makes the family music just as portentous as the former song of evil.

Soon the new-found fierceness of the family song leads Kino to a fatal conclusion, one which secures him one pearl and simultaneously causes the loss of another pearl, his only son, Coyotito. Thus while the songs merge, Kino is transformed from family man to madman, from sensitive father to brutal murderer. He is forced to acknowledge the duality that governs all of life, that inter-mixtures are far more evident than pure essentials. The destruction of Kino's enemies should provide a satisfying resolution to the fable, but Steinbeck refuses to give his readers such a facile ending.

Instead he complicates matters by having one of the trackers' random rifle shot strike Coyotito in the head, killing him instantly. Consequently, Kino does not go on to the capital and sell the pearl for its rightful purchase price. Instead he trudges back to La Paz, supposedly defeated, victimized by a fate which he has defied in order to seek his own pathway.

Thus, dissonance, that harsh and uncomfortable sound, returns to close the novel as Steinbeck refuses to provide the harmonic resolution his readers so desire. Rather, the book closes on an almost mystical silence that is only broken by the faint return of the Song of the Family. As Kino returns to La Paz with the corpse of his dead son, this original tune rises "as fierce as a [battle]cry" (116).

No doubt some readers are disappointed by Steinbeck's failure to return to a dominant chord, deciding instead to leave them in a questionable limbo of doubt. It is difficult for Kino to break through to an understanding, a knowledge that "evil" must be experienced in order to appreciate "good" and that what seems "good" may also have "evil" results. Kino's final perception of the Pearl's music is that it is "distorted and insane" (117). But Steinbeck seems to want his readers to sense more than such a reductionist message. The various tunes, like the complex employment of musical notes in Bach's fugues, make this novella a difficult puzzle to solve.

Steinbeck acknowledged this complexity when he said:

> If a writer likes to write he will find satisfaction in endless experiment with his medium. He will improvise techniques, arrangements of scenes, rhythms of words, and rhythms of thought. He will constantly investigate and try combinations new to him, sometimes utilizing an old method for a new idea and vice versa. Some of his experiments will inevitably be unsuccessful but he must try them anyway if his interest be alive. This experimentation is not criminal. Perhaps it is not even important but it is necessary if the writer be not moribund. ("Critics, Critics, Burning Bright," 20–21)

Separately, the parts of Steinbeck's musical experimentation in *The Pearl* seem clearly formed and easily integrated into a rather basic message which any adolescent could understand, but just as one completes a summary of the obvious meaning, the images become blurry, and other potential interpretations and possibilities appear. Surely *The Pearl's* multi-faceted construction is more appropriate to the appearance of a diamond since the smooth rounded perimeter of a pearl appears nowhere in the text. Rather the sharp brilliant edges and dissonant sounds leave readers disconcerted, unable to definitively assert the author's intent.

Just as the tranquil sounds of the Gregorian chant in *Cannery Row* are deceptive when compared musically to Monteverdi and just as *East of Eden* depends on the fugue like repetition of the Trask and Hamilton plot lines, so *The Pearl* offers a complexity that welcomes endless new interpretations. By establishing well-crafted musical overtones and undertones, Steinbeck is ultimately successful in creating a novel that stands the test of time. Hopefully, future criticism will recognize it as far more than just a fairly simple parable or fable with an obvious moral.

Though Steinbeck's preface states: "As with all retold tales that are in people's hearts, there are only good things and bad things and black and white things and good and evil things and no in-between anywhere," readers must wonder if his comments are not facetious or satiric, for this is hardly a book of absolutes. Steinbeck seems to acknowledge this fact by juxtaposing this sentence of absolutes with the following words, "perhaps everyone takes his own meaning from it and reads his own life into it." Rather than forcing us to hear only a simple monotone, the harmonic dissonance in Steinbeck's music allows us to do just that, discovering anew the complex in the simple.

Michael J. Meyer

Notes

1. In addition to Lisca's comments in *Wide World*, he also mentions Steinbeck's use of juxtaposition (a musical technique utilized in a fugue) in *Nature and Myth*, 94. In addition, John Timmerman's discussion of the Biblical analogues inherent in Steinbeck's use of the text of Julia Ward Howe's "The Battle Hymn of The Republic" is also relevant to the employment of fugal components in the novel. (See *John Steinbeck's Fiction: The Aesthetics of The Road Taken*, 105–106. Finally, Joseph Fontenrose also calls attention to the folk-dance pattern of Chapter Twenty-Three of *Grapes* and notes that it rhythm falls into or resembles the beat used in The Chicken Reel. (See *John Steinbeck*, 79)

2. Lisca suggests Steinbeck may have even been aware of the Gnostic document, "The Acts of Thomas" and utilized a passage from it usually known as "The Song of The Pearl" (*Wide World*, 223)

3. See also *The Log From the Sea of Cortez*, 97–98.

Works Cited

Benson, Jackson. *The True Adventures of John Steinbeck, Writer*. New York: Viking, 1984.

Ditsky, John. "The Devil in Music: Unheard Themes in Steinbeck's Fiction. *Steinbeck Quarterly*, XXV (Summer/Fall 1994: 3–4), 80–86.

Fitzgerald, F. Scott. *A Life in Letters*. ed. And annotated by Matthew Bruccoli. New York: Simon and Schuster, 1994.

Fontenrose, Joseph. *John Steinbeck*. New York: Barnes and Noble, 1963.

Lisca, Peter. *John Steinbeck: Nature and Myth*. New York: Thomas Y. Crowell, 1978.

Lisca, Peter. *The Wide World of John Steinbeck*. New Brunswick, N.J.: Rutgers, 1958.

Simmonds, Roy. *A Biographical and Critical Introduction to John Steinbeck*. Lewiston, N.Y.: Edwin Mellen Press, 2000.

Steinbeck, Elaine and Robert Wallsten, ed. *Steinbeck: A Life in Letters*. New York: Viking, 1975.

Steinbeck, John. *Cannery Row*. (1945) Penguin ed. New York: Penguin Books, 1949.

Steinbeck, John. "Critics, Critics, Burning Bright," reprinted in *Steinbeck and His Critics*. ed. E.W. Tedlock, Jr. and C.V. Wicker. Albuquerque: University of New Mexico Press, 1957.

Steinbeck, John. *The Grapes of Wrath*. (1939) New York: Bantam Books, 1969.

Steinbeck, John. *Journal of a Novel: The 'East of Eden' Letters*. (1969) New York: Bantam Books, 1970.

Steinbeck, John. *The Log From The Sea of Cortez*. (1951) New York: Penguin Books, 1976.

Steinbeck, John. *The Pearl*. (1947) New York: Penguin Books, 1976,

Timmerman, John. *John Steinbeck's Fiction: The Aesthetics of The Road Taken*. Norman: University of Oklahoma Press, 1986.

Williams, William Carlos. "The Dance" in *Selected Poems by William Carlos Williams*. Ed. Charles Tomlinson. New York: W.W. Norton, 1985.

12

Lady sings the Blues: Gayl Jones' *Corregidora*

PRELUDE

The creativity of African Americans found an outlet in music when few other means of artistic expression were available to them in America. During slavery, when the Africans brought forcibly to America were denied the right to speak in their own languages, engage in their own religious practices, or keep their own family and communal structures, music was even encouraged by advocates of white supremacy as a means of assuring the slaves' productivity and their internalization of social inferiority. However, slave holders underestimated or completely overlooked the socio-historical function of black music and its subversive role. Indeed, the first African American musical productions—work songs and spirituals, among others[1]—and the ones to follow, were rooted in the ethnic African musical traditions and then reshaped by the experiences of slavery, Reconstruction, and the two world wars. African American music emerges therefore as a historical product embodying a people's history and cultural tradition. As Angela Y. Davis explains, "through the vehicle of song, they [slaves and their descendants] were able to preserve their ethnic heritage, even as they were generations removed from their original homeland and perhaps even unaware that their songs bore witness to and affirmed their African cultural roots."[2] Rather than isolate them from their past, music provided African Americans with a cultural continuum that both linked them to their African roots and to each other, building a sense of community. Music became an instrument of resistance to oppression as it built a collective consciousness that yearned for freedom.

As a result, Black music rose, not only as African Americans' greatest artistic expression, but also, as the genuine *American* artistic expression. This fact was enunciated by the most influential African American intellectual of the first part of the twentieth century, W.E.B. DuBois, when he wrote that Black music stands as "the most beautiful expression of human experience born this side of the seas.... It remains as the singular spiritual heritage of the nation and the greatest gift of the negro people."[3] And, indeed, from the spiritual songs in slavery time, to ragtime music in the 1910s, jazz and blues in the 1920s, swing music in the 1930s, bebop, rhythm & blues in the 1940s, rock & roll since the 1950s and the most recent rap music and its derivation, gangsta rap, African American music has been embraced and adopted by Americans as representative of their own and the country's experiences.[4] Houston A. Baker's observation about the origins of the blues, for example, dwells on the representative character of African American music. Thus, "[t]he signal expressive achievement of the blues," Baker claims, "lay in their translation of technological innovativeness, unsettling demographic fluidity, and boundless frontier energy into expression which attracted avid interest from the American masses."[5] This is so to the extent that African American music has become *the* American music, leading some to polemically conclude, together with Zora Neale Hurston, that "There is no more Negro music in the US. It has been fused and merged and become the national expression.... [T]he fact remains that what has evolved here is something American."[6]

The fact is, furthermore, that not only American music, but also American culture *and* identity are vastly indebted to African American musical creativity. But if Black music occupies an honor position in American culture, the consensus about its impact on the remaining African American Arts cannot be overlooked. Thus, Toni Morrison explains that "Music provides a key to the whole medley of Afro-American artistic practices,"[7] while, in the same vein, Angela Y. Davis acknowledges that music "has been our central aesthetic expression, influencing all the remaining arts."[8] In literature, Black music stands both as a model of aesthetic perfection to be emulated and as a symbol of African American national identity. Therefore, as African American writers try to capture in the printed text that elusive intrinsic characteristic that makes African American music recognizable as Black all over the world, they struggle to achieve in literature the excellency reached in music. As a result, many have sought to infuse their works with the strategies found in Black music, in an attempt that "[w]hat has already happened with the music in the States, the literature will do one day, and when that happens it's all over."[9]

Hence, African American music has not only become a thematic element in works such as James Weldon Johnson's *The Autobiography of an*

Ex-colored Man (1912), where ragtime and the protagonist's musical ambition occupy central stage, but it has also been the inspiration for formal innovations in literature. This is the case with Jean Toomer and Langston Hughes, for instance, or with Ralph Ellison and Gayl Jones, whose works *Invisible Man* (1952) and *Corregidora* (1975), respectively, share their complex patterns and ethos with the blues.

An examination of Gayl Jones' *Corregidora* reveals how this black author undertakes the difficult task of adapting the genre of the novel to the blues form and ethos in order to convey the hidden history of African American women from slavery times to the present. Simultaneously, the blues turns into the protagonist's main tool in her quest for individual and communal identity.

BLUES MUSIC

At the beginning of the twentieth century a new kind of music spreads through the United States from the South, although New Orleans is soon identified as its epicenter. Self-taught musicians who played in taverns and street corners in the 1890s captured in their songs the disappointment and pain caused by the unfulfilled promises made to Blacks about freedom and social mobility after the Civil War. Instead of the longed-for equality, African Americans saw their new and cherished freedom limited by racist written and unwritten laws which result in an increasing exploitation and marginalization. The blues recreates that feeling of struggle against adversity even as it expresses a determination to endure and overcome hardships. Unlike other previous African American songs, namely the work songs and spirituals, this music is not religious but secular, with its main focus on intimate personal relationships. And due to the obvious profane folk roots of the blues, it could not be considered a model of black expression at a time when black intellectuals such as W.E.B. DuBois and James Weldon Johnson, were striving to elevate black art, making it palatable to middle-class white Americans. As a consequence, the spiritual song was deemed the best example of African American musical achievement and the embodiment of the dignity of a people who aspired to live harmoniously integrated in the larger white society, whereas the blues was only representative of the marginal elements within black society. The blues, nevertheless, reached a national audience thanks to the record industry, which saw a vast market for "race records" with the great migration of African Americans from the rural South to the cities of the North. In the mid-1920s, the blues craze reached its peak, as Bessie Smith, known as "the Empress of the Blues," recorded her best songs. She was one of an array of black women singers who dominated the blues, together with Ida Cox, or with Ma Rainey, "the Mother of the Blues."[10]

The language of the blues is the black vernacular of ordinary speech focusing on love and sex. As Gayl Jones herself observes in her study of oral tradition in African American literature, *Liberating Voices* (1991), "The language of blues is generally concrete, graphic, imagistic, immediate."[11] The blues creates an imagery of a very earthy quality,[12] as the metaphors and symbols employed have sexual or physical referents.[13] But one must also look for a hidden meaning behind the sexual language of the blues. As Angela Davis illustrates with the case of Ma Rainey's blues, the language of sexual love "metaphorically reveals and expresses a range of economic, social, and psychological difficulties."[14]

The blues' expressive power is derived from the African American oral tradition and enhanced by the simplicity of means it employs. Structurally woven through repetition with variation,[15] the blues song is interpreted by a soloist who establishes a call-and-response relationship with the audience or with the accompanying instrument or instruments, instead of being interpreted by a group of singers or a choir. In addition, the blues uses other vernacular elements characteristic of African American folklore, such as testifying, "blue notes," improvisation and compelling rhythms, all of which are put to the service of the plaintive tone of the song.

The blues usually focuses on heterosexual conflict and its consequences of desire and loneliness. In the case of female blues singers, these are mostly caused by a man's desertion. Besides communicating a personal and individual experience, the interpersonal relationships that are the themes of the blues symbolize the singer's and the community's "search for a life that would be free of the countless brutal realities encountered in postwar America."[16] By communicating and sharing African Americans' individual suffering, the blues forges a communal consciousness based on the listeners' realization that they share the singer's experiences in one way or another. The utterance of one's troubles, together with the empathetic feeling and the possibility presented by the blues of prevailing over unassailable problems causes a kind of catharsis on both singer and audience, and life may become bearable again. Resistance and survival are therefore at the core of the blues, too, as it is clearly put across in some of Billie Holiday's best-known blues: "I've been down so long, down don't worry me" (in *Stormy Blues*), or "I know I won't die" (in *Lady Sings the Blues*).

Thus, the blues is evocative of a series of experiences, rather than of a single one. As Houston Baker notes, "the blues song erupts, creating a veritable playful festival of meaning. Rather than a rigidly personalized form, the blues offer a phylogenetic recapitulation—a nonlinear, freely associative, non-sequential meditation—of species of experience. What emerges is not a filled subject, but an anonymous (nameless) voice issuing from the black (w)hole."[17] Individual and community are hence merged in the blues at the same time as they embody the past and the present of African Americans' experience.

However, the blues does not only reflect the mood of a particular painful experience as lived by an individual, but it becomes the musical representation of a mood that permeates the lives of African Americans characterizing their spirit as a community. It is possible then to identify a blues *ethos*, which is described by Ralph Ellison as

> an impulse to keep the painful details and episodes of brutal existence alive in one's aching consciousness, to finger its jagged grain, and to transcend it, not by the consolation of philosophy but by squeezing from it a near-tragic, near-comic lyricism.[18]

Although the blues ethos dwells on pain and sorrow, it transmits endurance and final triumph, the note of irony or humor "audaciously challenging fate to mete out further blows."[19] "[T]heir attraction," explains Ellison, "lies in this, that they at once express both the agony of life and the possibility of conquering it through sheer toughness of spirit. They fall short of tragedy only in that they provide no solution, offer no scapegoat but the self."[20]

CORREGIDORA AS LITERARY BLUES

The blues in *Corregidora* works at several interconnected levels. Blues as a theme is at the core of the novel, which focuses on Ursa, a female blues singer whose life is patterned according to the blues ethos, determined by the three generations of foremothers who ground her own story in the remote past of slavery. The actual blues, with immediate roots in the present time of the narration, is sung by Ursa, the protagonist, for whom the creation and performance of blues songs is both an outlet to her feelings and the means to make a living. In addition, *Corregidora* becomes a deft—

though limited—adaptation of the blues mode, conveyed not only through its theme and ethos, but also through the language and structure of the work.

Blues at the crossroads

According to W.C. Handy, the "Father of the Blues," the blues originated at a railroad juncture.[21] The metaphor of railroad crossings standing for junctures in human beings' lives at the moment of vacillation is also at the basis of *Corregidora*, a novel that develops through a multiplicity of crossings, both in the protagonist's life and in the other characters' courses. The novel and Ursa's blues seem to be inspired by the most important juncture in Ursa's life—the spring night four months after her wedding when Mutt, drunk and jealous, threw her down the stairs at *Happy's Café* causing the loss of their baby and of her womb as well as her separation from Mutt, the man she will keep on loving despite herself. However, this single moment is displaced by a multitude of junctures, not only in Ursa's life but in the lives of a past and present African American community. Thus, the blues sung by Ursa and embodied by the novel are a synthesis or, in Houston Baker's words, "an amalgam that seems always to have been in motion in America—always becoming, shaping, transforming, displacing the peculiar experiences of Africans in the New World."[22]

After her hysterectomy, Ursa finds herself in the most important juncture of her life. Having lost confidence and trust in her man, she feels forlorn, and having been deprived of her reproductive power, she feels crippled, both physically and psychologically. To complicate things even more, Ursa has to confront her involuntary betrayal of her foremothers' memories at the same time as she must face her own defeminization and the loss of her personal identity, both negative experiences which will lead her to new crises or junctures in her life. Her blues is then triggered by a single event, which determines her own contradictory position with respect to her past and to her future.

When Ursa finds out that she will be unable to have children, her sexuality is drawn into question as well as her feminine identity. She becomes a contradiction in herself, a woman with no womb. Her blues emerge as the most natural way to accommodate this ontological contradiction, since contradiction and ambiguity are the constitutive elements of the blues. The heterosexual conflict that led to Ursa's uterus extirpation is aggravated with the accident and, in time, it will be accepted by her as part of her life since the complete resolution of the problem is not a feasible

possibility. Besides, the heterosexual conflict that marks her life, impreg-
nating it with the major theme of blues songs, raises the issue of lesbianism,
complicating even further the contradictory nature of Ursa's feelings. What
is she? Is she still a woman? Can she still be attractive? Can she feel sexual
pleasure? What will her position be with respect to men from now on?
The crisis unleashed by her hysterectomy impels Ursa toward an inner
quest for a non-reproductive sexuality, as well as it pushes her to marry
Tadpole in an effort to reaffirm her femininity. This precipitates the next
blues juncture in her life. Ursa believes that a man, in this case a husband,
would clarify her position to the world and, even more important, to herself. But, as Cat Lawson warns her, she is taking that step out of fear that
she may stop being desirable to men, and not because she and Tad are fit
for each other. Their marriage failure can be foreseen at this early point
of the novel and takes place as a consequence of Ursa's inability to feel
sexual pleasure with Tad. There is a glimpse of a solution for this problem
in the form of clitoral pleasure,[23] but as pleasure turns into pain this possibility is abandoned. Although Ursa tries to accommodate the absence of
sexual pleasure in her life, Tad cannot. He fights the emasculation he
feels at not being able to arouse Ursa's orgasm by having sex with another
woman. The marriage rupture is precipitated when Ursa finds out and
Tad lets her know his feelings: "You can't even *come* with me. You don't
even know what to do with a *real* man."[24]

It comes as no surprise that Ursa's crisis raises the question of lesbianism, which is just hinted at in the novel but not solved. This is in keeping with a novel that follows the blues parameters, rejecting easy solutions
even to resolve its heterosexual conflicts. As Ursa struggles to recover her
power and to negotiate her former feminine identity after the operation,
she rejects the possibility of homosexual support since lesbianism appears
as a disempowering option or state.[25]

The crossroads Ursa finds herself at after her hysterectomy concerns
not only her future but her past too, as she must come to terms with what
she considers a betrayal of her foremothers' memories and tradition. Faced
with the distortion of history and the forgery of truth represented by Corregidora's burning of documents after the abolition of slavery, the Corregidora women engrave in their minds the pain that had already been
imprinted in their flesh and use oral narrative to make sure that their own
version of history will reach the future generations. Thus, although, like the
story told by Toni Morrison in *Beloved*, the story of Ursa's foremothers
"was not a story to pass on," the Corregidora women "were suppose [sic]

to pass it down like that from generation to generation so we'd never forget."[26] Their memories, dwelling on pain and survival, constitute their blues, their spiritual scars: *"we got to keep what we need to bear witness. That scar that's left to bear witness. We got to keep it as visible as our blood."*[27] Now Ursa, who was taught by her foremothers "to want. To make generations"[28] so that their lives are not obliterated from history, will break the generational chain because she is unable to procreate and to transmit her foremothers' version of history. To them, procreation was something innate to women. This notion is implied by Ursa's mother in a monologue patterned after the blues device of repetition, explaining how she felt about her pregnancy:

> I went to bed real early that night. But still it was like something had got into me. Like my body or something knew what it wanted even if I didn't want no man. Cause I knew I wasn't looking for none. But it was like it knew I wanted you. It was like my whole body knew it wanted you, and knew it would have you, and knew you'd be a girl. But something got into me after that night, though, Ursa. It was like my whole body knew. Just knew what it wanted, and I kept going back there.[29]

Now, after her operation, Ursa wonders "and where's the next generation."[30] Even as Ursa ponders on her failure to transmit her foremothers' legacy as a result of her inability to procreate, the blues offers itself as the means to pass on her foremothers' ethos and their epic lives through a process of appropriation and transformation. What Ursa must undertake is the transformation of the narrative of desire, from her foremothers' narrative based on reproduction to a new articulation of desire that is not centered on the biological womb but on the blues as matrix.

Paradoxically, Ursa's lack of actual womb is the genesis for her blues and the source of her creativity. The void left by her womb is filled by the blues, and the blues, in turn, become her matrix, her womb, the space where her past and her present are accommodated, her outlet to make her pain known and the means to understand herself and the world around her. Ursa's blues act then as "a point of ceaseless input and output, a web of intersecting, crisscrossing impulses always in productive transit," which is Baker's definition of both a matrix and the blues.[31]

Ursa's songs

The blues songs that the protagonist, Ursa Corregidora, makes up and sings during her performances at *Happy's Cafeé* and later at *The Spider* constitute the most explicit example of blues in the novel. These songs respond fully to the concept of the blues. They talk of her individual experiences of desire and loneliness, of love and hate, the *can't -live-with-him, can't -live-without-him* blues, or what Claudia Tate terms as "the dialectics of love—a synthesis of pleasure and pain."[32] Ursa's blues at this level also exemplify Ralph Ellison's definition of the blues as "an autobiographical chronicle of personal catastrophe expressed lyrically."[33]

In the tradition of the blues, the lyrics of Ursa's songs metaphorically refer to her desire, to her sexual encounters, or to sexual demands. "Sharing and communicating need was a central feature of the blues,"—Davis explains—"and the process of developing an awareness of the collective nature of the experience of need was very much related to the ability of the African-American people to survive when all odds were against them."[34] Two examples of Ursa's canalizing of her desire through the blues are the songs she chooses to sing when she first meets Mutt, one about a train tunnel "closing tight around the train", the other about a bird woman "who took this man on a long journey, but never returned him." Or the song entitled "Open the Door, Richard," which Ursa stops singing after Mutt asks her "'When are you going to let Richard in?'."[35]

Ursa's monologues, dreams, and stream-of-consciousness narration complete her mental blues' universe. The rich vernacular loaded with sexual symbology characteristic of the blues is present, for example, in her imagined encounter with Mutt, where she senses his desire for her, but will not give away because she cannot forgive him:

> "Ursa, have you lost the blues?"
> "Naw, the blues is something you can't loose."
> "Gimme a feel. Just a little feel... Just give me a little feel. You lonely, ain't you?"
> "I been there awready."
> "Then you know what I need. Put me in the alley, Urs."
> "Something wrong with me down there."
> "I Still want to get in your alley, baby."
> "Naw, Mutt."
> "What you looking for, anyway, woman?"
> "What we stopped being to each other."
> "I never knew what we was."...[36]

But Ursa's blues are not only defined by the lyrics of her songs. The texture of her voice proves as important, because it transmits authenticity and contributes to the successful communication of her pain, her blues. This is first noted by Cat, the first person to realize the transformation that has taken place in Ursa's voice after the removal of her womb: "it sounds like you been through something. Before it was beautiful too, but you sound like you been through more now."[37] And Max Monroe, the owner of *The Spider*, is only too well aware of Ursa's voice: "'You got a hard kind of voice... You know, like callused hands. Strong and hard but gentle underneath. Strong but gentle too. The kind of voice that can hurt you. I can't explain it. Hurt you and make you still want to listen."[38] Max's reaction to Ursa's blues is caused by the power of the blues to articulate feelings and moods that remain otherwise hidden, unuttered, either by the singer or by the sympathizing audience. So, Ursa acknowledged once that she sings the blues every time she wants to cry,[39] and alludes explicitly to the articulating power of the blues when she claims: "It helps me to explain what I can't explain."[40] Similarly, Max, as representative of Ursa's audience, finds his own troubles, hopes, and dreams somehow expressed in Ursa's voice.

Besides, Ursa establishes with her audience the call-and-response interaction characteristic of the blues. A case in point is the exchange between Mutt, Ursa's first husband, and herself during her performances. A dramatic representation of the call-and-response interplay at work in Ursa's performance takes place the night she is singing and Mutt appears ready to humiliate her in front of her audience by putting her body for sale: "I was singing one of Ella Fitzgerald's songs, and as soon as I saw him I kind of gradually increased the volume, hoping people wouldn't notice."[41] Mutt's presence modifies ostensibly Ursa's interpretation of the blues song, and her performance becomes at once a direct confrontation with her husband, "calling his bluff."[42] When the battle is over and Mutt leaves without daring to carry out his threat, Ursa ends the song loud and then proceeds to sing a very soft one. Some twenty years later the same interaction between Ursa and her audience is still at play. She knows how to handle it, as she demonstrates with the drunk man who shouts obscene proposals to her on her way to the stage: "I started singing a song, hoping that would make him quiet. It did. I put him where he wanted to get. I sang a low down blues."[43] And when Mutt appears after twenty two years, Ursa's blues go full circle: "I knew I was singing to him. I think he knew too. But I knew I hadn't forgiven him. Even when I felt excited about seeing him, I knew I hadn't forgiven him too. I think he knew that as well."[44]

Ursa's blues ethos as determinant of the novel's structure and theme

As it has been stated above, the blues emerged as "a new song" which expressed the new troubles faced by the freed slaves through the metaphors of personal private relationships. Deeply rooted in history, therefore, it created a communal consciousness by communicating individual suffering. Like the blues, Ursa's life and the blues she sings are clearly the product of her personal experiences, as well as of the long history of exploitation, resistance and hope that characterizes the African American experience. So, her life is as determined by her private sexual and love experiences as by the events that transformed her foremothers' lives and which are indelibly engraved in her memory.

Those memories, which are not her own, constitute a substantial part of her self, and are fundamental in her quest for and construction of identity. They transmit a world view, a life's stance, or a philosophical perspective that is the result of African Americans' historical experience, or what may be identified as the blues *ethos*. The role of the past in the configuration of Ursa's present and future is such that her process of identity formation could be perfectly summarized in Zora Neale Hurston's words at the beginning of her autobiography: "I have memories within that came out of the material that went to make me."[45] Her blues stand then as a hybrid product, the synthesis and articulation of the feelings caused both by the events she lives through and by those lived by her foremothers. Ursa's blues, like her memories, encompass therefore her present as well as her most remote past, and are just as influenced by her relationship with Mutt as by her foremothers' sexual exploitation by the slave owner Corregidora.

The way Ursa's foremothers' memories affect her blues is suggestive of hidden meanings that are implied rather than stated outright. As Ursa explains in an interior monologue addressed at her mother, she tries to explain her foremothers' ordeals and contradictions through the blues: "if you understood me, Mama, you'd see I was trying to explain it, in blues, without words, the explanation somewhere behind the words."[46] Her blues embody a history of black female exploitation and resentment, not in the lyrics, as Ursa herself points out, but "*in the tune, in the whole way I drew out a song. In the way my breath moved, in my whole voice.*"[47] Ursa, the blues singer, thus becomes the griot, the carrier of her foremothers' history, of black women's ordeal in America, as will become apparent below. Her voice becomes the communal voice, a voice fraught with a history of abuse and resistance, of pain and survival, a voice that embodies the blues *ethos*.

The novel starts in Ursa's first-person voice looking back in time to 1947, when she and Mutt are married, and soon the narrator's reminiscences are mixed up with dialogue. The autobiographical account of Ursa's present, her interior monologue, is then interrupted by her ancestors' voices in the form of stream of consciousness, and typographically distinguished from Ursa's present by the use of italics. A simultaneous account of Ursa's present life and of her memories discloses Great Gram telling her her own story as a slave whore, transmitting her anger and hatred to her great-granddaughter. The memories and lives of Ursa's grandmother and mother are equally rendered. A call-and-response narrative is then established involving past and present events in a mirroring interaction. The blues, therefore, functions as a structural device from the very beginning of the novel, breaking the linear direction of the plot and substituting it with repetition and variation. Madhu Dubey[48] finds the black musical device of the "cut"—"an abrupt, seemingly unmotivated break with a series already in progress, and a willed return to a previous series"[49]—at work here. Hence, every time the narration starts a linear direction forward, like in the case of Ursa and Tadpole's relationship, the plot is suspended, cut back to Ursa's foremothers' past, producing the effect of temporal impasse.

Thus, the period of time covered by the novel does not only comprise the years of Ursa's present autobiographical narration (from 1948 to 1969) but stretches back to slavery times, and moves through geography as well as through time, passing from Portugal to Brazil, to the United States, from rural life in Kentucky to Ursa's urban blues. The novel becomes "A new world song"—with all the ambiguity that the phrase contains, alluding both to the hope ingrained in the "American Dream" and to the harsh reality of slavery and sexual exploitation in the New World—that touches Ursa's life "*and* theirs."[50] By intertwining Ursa's and her foremothers' lives, Gayl Jones succeeds in her intent of making "some kind of relationship between history and autobiography."[51] The autobiographical account turns then into a diasporical narration that encompasses not just Ursa's life but also African Americans' lives through history. Slavery is thus placed at the center of Ursa's narrative or blues, identifying it as both a personal and a communal story.

In accordance with other African American writers, —Margaret Walker and Toni Morrison among them—Gayl Jones claims the importance of historical memory. Like Toni Morrison's *Beloved, Corregidora* deals with the desire to forget the terrors of slavery and the impossibility of forgetting. Furthermore, the novel emphasizes the consequences of the past in the present and the present as determined and informed by the past. The

African American past is an intrinsic part of Ursa's identity, and it is rendered in all its rawness. The novel acts in this sense as a corrective of the common attitude towards history in America, "a land where the past is always erased," according to Toni Morrison, who further explains: "The past is absent or romanticized. This culture doesn't encourage dwelling on, let alone coming to terms with, the truth about the past."[52] On the contrary, and following the blues ethos which dwells on the painful details of existence keeping them alive in one's consciousness, —to paraphrase Ralph Ellison as quoted above—Ursa Corregidora values the past as much as the present, to the extent of seeming obsessed by it. The past, which is ever-present in her life, is the fabric her blues are made from.

By bringing slavery to the forefront and making history an indivisible part of Ursa's identity, the past, very far from being romanticized, becomes a crude presence. Only by accommodating the past into her own persona, will Ursa Corregidora be able to overcome her crisis and come to terms with her own life. In one of her imagined dialogues with Mutt, she establishes the keeping of her memories as a precondition to going back to him: "*If I do [come], I'll come with all my memories. I won't forget anything.*"[53] At the same time as Ursa must assimilate her own personal past with Mutt, she must also negotiate her position with respect to her foremothers' past.

Because Ursa's life can only make sense when considered together with her foremothers' lives, their memories aligned with her own, she resents not knowing her mother's past. Her mother would repeat Great Gram and Grandmama's memories, but never tell her own: "*How could she bear witness to what she'd never lived, and refuse me what she had lived?*"[54] In her quest for self-understanding, Ursa "could not be satisfied until I had seen Mama, talked to her, until I had discovered her private memory."[55] When Ursa finally inquires about her mother's past, the mother's own memories become melded with Great Gram's in a way that lead Ursa to think that it wasn't her who was talking, but Great Gram:

> It was as if she had *more* than learned it off by heart, though. It was as if their memory, the memory of all the Corregidora women, was her memory too, as strong with her as her own private memory, or almost as strong.[56]

Once she knows her mother's memories of "The lived life, not the spoken one"[57] she is in a position to understand her own life, which presents itself as a repetition of her foremothers' experiences. However, Ursa's accommodation of the past implies transformation. She needs, for example, to interpret the silences in her ancestors' narratives so that she can turn the dialectic of hate and desire characteristic of her foremothers into one of desire and love. Although she needs to establish a relationship between herself and her foremothers, she rejects the idea of being just like them when she vehemently exclaims: "*But look at me, I am not Corregidora's daughter. Look at me, I am not Corregidora's daughter.*"[58] So, Ursa's life is not a simple repetition of her foremothers' lives but a repetition *with* difference, or as she herself puts it, "a song they've sung themselves but with different lyrics."[59] Ursa becomes then the blues musician who, in Ralph Ellison's words, "must learn the best of the past, and add it to his [her] personal vision."[60]

As it has been pointed out above, the repetition-with-variation pattern may create the illusion of a temporal impasse or of the circularity of time. This view is supported by multiple examples in which Mutt is equated with Corregidora, whereas Ursa is likened to slave women with the result that the present looks like a reenactment of the past. For instance, Mutt teaches Ursa to use obscene language, the same as Corregidora did with Ursa's great grandmother.[61] Mutt's words calling Ursa his "piece a shit"[62] echo Corregidora's when he called Great Gram "his little gold piece." Similarly, the moment Mutt decides to sell Ursa's body as in an auction— "'You think I won't. I'ma be down there tonight, and as soon as you get up on that stage, I'ma sell me a piece a ass'"[63]—mirrors Corregidora's use of Great Gram as a prostitute. Even Ursa's empowerment at the end of the novel, revealed to her in the act of fellatio, transports her and the reader to the past, as she becomes aware that she and Great Gram share the same source of sexual power. As Dubey brilliantly explains, the movement of the plot is "a process of accumulation and variation on her foremothers' stories... The device of the cut achieves a sense of structural and temporal continuity, and allows a formal containment of the potentially discontinuous terms, past and present."[64]

The circularity of time is similarly observed in the ending of the novel, where Mutt's and Ursa's desires remain as incompatible as at the beginning. Their blues at this point are still characterized by ambiguity and contradictory feelings representative of the extremes of love and hate, rejection and desire. Ursa has been able to accommodate the contradictions of her present and her past, rather than reconcile them. So, her eventual reunion with Mutt does not represent a solution to her inner conflict. As she acknowledges, "I knew I hadn't forgiven him,"[65] "I knew that I still hated him. Not as bad as then, not with the first feeling, but an after feeling, an aftertaste, or like an odor still in a room when you come back to it, and it's your own."[66] In the scene where Mutt asks her to come back to him, readers can sense Ursa's contradictory feelings and the power of her desire for him. She had recognized it twenty years before in one of her imagined dialogues: "*I'm still thick with you. I can't get you out.*"[67] So, when Mutt asks her to come back, she wants to say no, but she is paralyzed and muted by her inner struggle of hatred and desire and the possibility of making up and finally being able to love and be loved. Looking in his eyes, she realizes that the dialectical relationship between the two of them will continue: "I felt that now he wouldn't demand the same things. He'd demand different kinds of things. But there'd still be demands."[68]

The intrusion of the past at the precise moment when Mutt appears turns Ursa's mother into a mirror in which she can see herself. Like her, Ursa has been unable to reconstruct her love life because "only one man could remake that world."[69] But, unlike her mother, Ursa now contemplates the possibility of remaking her own world with the only man who can do so, and says yes, even when she wants to say no. Her troubles may be a repetition of her mother's life, but she will do her best to improve upon it taking into account the conclusions drawn from the past. Once again, repetition with difference is the blues strategy used at this juncture in Ursa's life.

In keeping with the blues themes, Ursa's final encounter with Mutt is a sexual one. However, the notion of a happy ending is complicated by the exclusion of reproduction, as well as by the negation of Ursa's sexual pleasure. Indeed, Ursa and Mutt's sexual reconciliation is centered on the act of fellatio, and therefore on Mutt's capability to experience sexual pleasure. But by becoming the object of sexual pleasure, he also becomes vulnerable. In "a split second of hate and love"[70] Ursa discovers her own power "to make him hate her so bad he wont [sic] to kill her one minute and keep thinking about her and can't get her out of his mind the next."[71]

The paradoxical, even contradictory feelings which assault Ursa at this point liken her to her foremothers when she realizes that this potential violence, the power to give pleasure and pain, the power to castrate or even kill, is also the key to Great Gram's power. Ursa and her past melt in her sexual encounter with Mutt: "It was like I didn't know how much was me and Mutt and how much was Great Gram and Corregidora—like Mama when she started talking like Great Gram."[72] Ursa envisions her experience as an echo or a repetition of her foremothers':

> But was what Corregidora had done to *her*, to *them*, any worse than what
> Mutt had done to me, than what we had done to each other, than what Mama
> had done to Daddy, or what he had done to her in return, making her walk
> down the street looking like a whore?[73]

Even as Ursa denounces the wrong done to the female members of her
family—including herself—by their male partners, she becomes aware of
her own and her foremothers' part in inflicting pain on their men, extend-
ing the female blues to their male partners.

In their last dialogue, Ursa and Mutt reproduce the repetition-with-
variation structure of the blues. As if sensing what is crossing Ursa's mind,
Mutt starts:

> "I don't want a kind of woman that hurt you," he said.
> "Then you don't want me."
> "I don't want a kind of woman that hurt you."
> "Then you don't want me."
> "I don't want a kind of woman that hurt you."
> "Then you don't want me."
> He shook me till I fell against him crying. "I don't want a kind of man that'll
> hurt me neither," I said.
> He held me tight.[74]

Ambiguity is present even at this final stage of the novel in Mutt's use of
the second person pronoun—"you"—which is logically understood as im-
personal, referring to himself or to all men. However, it could also be understood in its usual sense as referring to Ursa. In that case, Mutt would be
telling her not to torture or punish herself. He could be implying a demand to forget the past and start anew, thus fulfilling what Ursa had foreseen in one of her dreams a long while ago. As in her dream, Ursa refuses
to change and leave her past behind. In the final dialogue, Ursa, who had
finally emerged as the self-reliant and independent blues singer, recognizes her own power to hurt and to make herself wanted as well as her
vulnerability to be hurt by Mutt. The final embrace signifies the need for
each other, though not the resolution of their problems as a couple.

Resistance of the novel to the adoption of the blues mode

As the novel unravels, the text adopts some of the features of the blues
such as its theme and ethos and the black vernacular that characterizes
both the narrative voice and the characters. Its structure is also determined by the repetition and variation proper of blues songs, as well as by
the call-and-response interplay between Ursa and the rest of the charac-

ters and between the past and her present. However, the adaptation of
the novel to the blues mode becomes problematic when some aspects of
the use of the call-and-response technique and of the use of language are
taken into consideration. As a result of the dialogic relationship established between a written form—the novel—and an oral one—the blues—,
Corregidora stands as a major exponent of "a mixed genre that subjects
both the blues and the fictional modes to a process of mutual enhance-
ment and modification."[75]

In contrast to the simple and direct language of the blues as it is man-
ifested in Ursa's songs and dialogues, Ursa's narrative may turn obscure,
even opaque sometimes. A case in point appears in one of Ursa's reveries
set out by her memories of a conversation with her mother about the evil
of the blues: "*Songs are devils. It's your own destruction you're singing. The
voice is a devil*'."[76] But Ursa goes on, reaffirming herself in her will to sing
her grandmother's life, tainting her own voice with her grandmother's:
"*But still I'll sing as you talked it, your voice humming…*" Ultimately, Ursa's
language becomes cryptic, just evocative of bitterness, pain, and a desire
to procreate, to transmit those feelings and to point to the culprits of all
that sorrow, unmasking their hypocrisy:

> *Then let me give witness the only way I can. I'll make a fetus out of grounds of
> coffee to rub inside my eyes. When it's time to give witness, I'll make a fetus out
> of grounds of coffee. I'll stain their hands.*[77]

Another instance connects again Ursa's sorrow to her foremother's past
as her music becomes the tool to unveil the tyrants and punish them:

> *I am Ursa Corregidora. I have tears for eyes. I was made to touch my past at an
> early age. I found it on my mother's tiddies. In her milk. Let no one pollute my
> music. I will dig out their temples. I will pluck out their eyes.*[78]

The imagery used turns most cryptic in some of her dreams. A case in
point takes place the time when one of Ursa's imaginary descendants re-
enacts the past of her foremothers: "*Who are you? I am the daughter of the
daughter of the daughter of Ursa of currents, steel wool, and electric wire for
hair.*"[79] Another instance is Ursa's dreamed conversation with Mutt, where
she resents her lack of a womb in the following words: "*Sperm to bruise
me. Wash it away. Vinegar and water. Barbed wire where a womb should be.
Curdled milk.*"[80]

In the same way as language turns away from the simplicity and di-
rectness of the blues, the call-and response exchange that takes place be-

tween the solo blues singer and his/her audience fails to come alive in some of "the interior monologues where the storyteller becomes her own hearer."[81]

One of the most outstanding examples of Jones' technique in the use of a stream-of-consciousness discourse that subtly shifts its addressee, takes place after Ursa breaks away with Tadpole, her second husband. Her tone and mood change from sympathy to impotence, to anger, to vengeance, to fear, to understanding, to perplexity, and eventually back to anger— even hatred—when she remembers the source of all her present troubles— Mutt abandoning her by throwing her down the stairs. The narrative voice in italics first addresses Cat, *"Because I knew why he* [Mutt] *kept me waiting, Cat, that's why I knew what you felt, why I wouldn't tell you that I knew."* Then Ursa launches a question to herself *"What am I thinking?"* and tries to answer it at the same time as she goes on to address Tadpole, then herself and, immediately afterwards, she turns back to Cat:

> *'Anyway, you knew what was wrong before you snatched after my ass. No, what's inside my head because those other women they could do it. Afraid of what I. No, I didn't push it, Cat.'*[82]

Ursa's interior monologue proceeds in the same vein, throwing questions that concern Mutt alone, *"Why won't you turn back toward me."*[83] Then she ends the monologue with an imagined dialogue between Mutt and herself.

Ursa's addressees determine her narrative the same as an audience may determine the blues singer's interpretation, but attention must be drawn to the fact that the exchange between Ursa and her interlocutors is only in her mind. It is not actually taking place. We might wonder about the extent to which Ursa's discourse is determined by the other characters, or rather whether she is the one determining their words and attitudes, since those characters are physically absent and cannot make decisions about their own performances or opinions. Their words and behavior are but a projection of Ursa's perception of them. Instead of a real call-and-response interaction, what we find in Ursa's imagined dialogic conversations is "a disquieting sense of silence and exclusion."[84]

The call-and-response relationship between the text and its reader does not exist either, since the reader of this novel is just that, the reader of Ursa's narrative, and the passive *voyeur* of her fantasies and her memories. The narrative voice does not address the reader, whose position is frequently "usurped," in Dubey's words, by the characters Ursa does address. It is here where the novel most clearly fails to adapt the blues mode, since the reading activity is intrinsically different from the act of live listening. The interaction between the solitary reader and the narrator does not take place. The reader neither disrupts nor influences Ursa's narration or the course of the novel.

POSTLUDE

Corregidora stands as a novel that attempts to convey the inexpressible black feminine identity by means of the use of the blues as a thematic and structural device. Thanks to the appropriation of the cyclical structure of the blues with its repetition-with-difference pattern, Ursa Corregidora emerges as a new black woman who eventually attains the capacity to acknowledge both her power and her vulnerability by means of her reclamation and acceptance of the past. The use of the blues' form and language in the novel also grounds Ursa's individual story in a communal background, as it leads to the inscription of African American oral practices in the written text.

Yet, the novel falls short of appropriating the blues' mode in all its extent. Although the call-and-response characteristic of African American oral performances is deftly replicated in the dialectic relationship between Ursa's present and her foremothers' past, as well as in the interaction between her listeners and herself when she sings the blues, the novel fails to establish a call-and-response relationship between the reader and the characters or the author. Even the call-and-response typical of Ursa's interior monologues and dreams is only an illusion. It is also in these monologues where language turns away from the simplicity of the blues, becoming cryptic and enigmatic.

Nonetheless, the novel stands as a remarkable attempt at using the blues as the structuring and thematic resource. Like a good blues song, *Corregidora* is capable of arousing the reader's empathetic feelings as he or she starts understanding Ursa's position as a castrated black woman who must suddenly negotiate her identity taking into account her present circumstances and the inheritance of the past. Her troubles, together with her foremothers' and those of the rest of the characters who surround her, form a multi-vocal blues song of pain and endurance, of desire and survival, which is rendered in all its ambivalence and complexity. Even the ending does not provide a closure but rather another juncture in Ursa's life, a crossroads that pushes her forward in her self-knowledge as she attempts a new life and relationship with Mutt. In her personal adaptation of the blues, Jones challenges the genre of the novel, which emerges as a hybrid product, the result of the métissage of western literary tradition and the traditional oral performance of the blues.

Ana Mª Fraile-Marcos

Notes

1. In his work "The Roots of Jazz," Ernest Borneman has enumerated eight different kinds of songs that reveal the community's cultural patterns: songs of courtship, songs of challenge, and songs of scorn, associated with young men who wished to influence young women, mothers' educational and calming songs, songs associated with the boys' rite of passage from boyhood to manhood, work songs, and team songs.

2. In Davis, 5.

3. In DuBois, *The Souls of Black Folk*, 265.

4. The impact of African American music is not only clearly perceived in the United States, but all over the globe. Suffice it to think of youngsters anywhere in the world, from America to Europe to Japan, dressed in the rapper's style, imitating his body movements, cadence of speech, rhythms and overall attitude.

5. In Baker, *Blues*, 11.

6. Zora Neale Hurston to Burroughs Mitchell, October, 1947. Quoted by Hazel Carby in her Foreword to Hurston's *Seraph on the Suwanee*, X.

7. In Gilroy, 181.

8. Davis, 4.

9. Toni Morrison in Gilroy, 182.

10. For a brief but well documented history of the blues, see Graeme M. Boone's "Blues" in William L Andrews, 84–87.

11. 196.

12. Southern, 333.

13. Williams, 131.

14. 14.

15. Langston Hughes defined the blues as "one long line repeated, and a third line to rhyme with the first two. Sometimes the second line in repetition is

slightly changed and sometimes, but very seldom, it is omitted." Quoted in Lorenzo Thomas, 87.

16. Davis, 12.

17. Baker, 5.

18. In "Richard Wright's Blues" compiled in *The Collected Essays of Ralph Ellison*, 129. Hereafter listed as Ellison.

19. Southern, 333.

20. Ellison, 143. Other writers and critics who have sought to describe or define the blues ethos are Richard Wright, Albert Murray, Craig Werner, Amiri Baraka, Stephen Henderson, Sterling Stuckey, Houston Baker, Gayl Jones, and Henry Louis Gates, Jr.

21. Bontemps, 78.

22. Baker, 5.

23. *Corregidora*, 75.

24. *Corregidora*, 88.

25. The lesbian models in the novel are Cat and Jeffy, although lesbianism may be identified centuries before in the figure of Corregidora's Portuguese wife who, unattended by her husband, looked for pleasure at the hands of Great Gram. Lesbianism touches Ursa more directly when May Alice, her best friend in adolescence, finds out that she is pregnant and laments that Ursa is not Harold, her boyfriend, "and then nothing would have happened" (141). Cat turned to lesbianism trying to escape the humiliation she had to put up with both outside and inside her home: "'You don't know what it's like to feel foolish all day in a white woman's kitchen and then have to come home and feel foolish in the bed at night with your man" (64). Ursa refuses to show Cat her empathy precisely because she shares the same experience of rejection and humiliation forced on her by Mutt. By the end of the novel, we bear witness to Cat's final punishment and defeminization symbolized by the loss of her hair, which was painfully pulled out by a machine while she was at work. "That kind of thing"—says Jeffy—"makes you don't feel like a woman" (177). Like Ursa, Cat struggles to put herself together after her accident, but the loneliness and rejection enforced by society on lesbians characterize Cat's blues. Cat is very conscious of it from the beginning of the novel, when she states "They never let you live it down" (66). As to Jeffy "she was like that" (39). Her lesbianism seems to be as essential to her as her roughness and sassiness. The pneumonia she overcomes at the end of the novel seems to be the foreseen punishment for her sexuality. The question of Jeffy's pneumonia rises when Ursa discovers Jeff's lesbian impulses and, infuriated by the girl feeling on her breasts, the following dialogue between Cat and herself follows: "'Well. She can catch pneumonia of the asshole for all I care.'/'Don't worry, she catch

it'" (40). Similarly, the other two characters connected in one way or another with lesbianism, Corregidora's Portuguese wife and Mary Alice, are also punished when they become ostracized from society. The former is locked up in a loft for life, whereas the latter has to move to another town with her mother. These lesbian characters stand as disempowered figures who cannot offer Ursa a suitable model.

26. *Corregidora*, 9.

27. *Corregidora*, 72.

28. *Corregidora*, 22.

29. *Corregidora*, 114.

30. *Corregidora*, 9.

31. Baker, 3.

32. In Tate, 95.

33. Ellison, 129.

34. Tate, 15.

35. *Corregidora*, 152.

36. *Corregidora*, 97–98.

37. *Corregidora*, 44.

38. *Corregidora*, 96.

39. *Corregidora*, 46.

40. *Corregidora*, 56.

41. *Corregidora*, 160.

42. *Corregidora*, 160.

43. *Corregidora*, 168.

44. *Corregidora*, 182.

45. *Dust Tracks*, 3.

46. *Corregidora*, 66.

47. *Corregidora*, 103.

48. 82–83.

49. Snead, 67.

50. Ursa's desire to sing "A new world song" fraught with ambiguous meaning, echoes W.E.B. DuBois' description of African Americans' "new song" after the coming of freedom for the slaves in the South: "There was joy in the South. ... A great song arose, the loveliest thing born this side of the seas. It

was a new song... It was a new song and its deep and plaintive beauty, its great cadences and wild appeal wailed, throbbed and thundered on the world's ears with a message seldom voiced by man. It swelled and blossomed like incense, improvised and born anew out of an age long past, and weaving into its texture the old and new melodies in word and thought" (*Black Reconstruction in America*, 124).

51. Tate, 95.

52. 179.

53. *Corregidora*, 104.

54. *Corregidora*, 103.

55. *Corregidora*, 104.

56. *Corregidora*, 129.

57. *Corregidora*, 108.

58. *Corregidora*, 103.

59. *Corregidora*, 182.

60. In "Living with Music" compiled in *The Collected Essays of Ralph Ellison*, 229.

61. *Corregidora*, 153.

62. *Corregidora*, 165.

63. *Corregidora*, 159.

64. *Corregidora*, 83.

65. *Corregidora*, 182.

66. *Corregidora*, 183.

67. *Corregidora*, 76.

68. *Corregidora*, 183.

69. *Corregidora*, 182.

70. *Corregidora*, 184.

71. *Corregidora*, 184.

72. *Corregidora*, 184.

73. *Corregidora*, 184.

74. *Corregidora*, 185.

75. Dubey, 88.

76. *Corregidora*, 53.

77. *Corregidora*, 54.

78. *Corregidora*, 77.

79. *Corregidora*, 67.

80. *Corregidora*, 76.

81. Gayl Jones in Tate, 91.

82. *Corregidora*, 89.

83. *Corregidora*, 90.

84. Dubey, 87.

Works Cited

Andrews, William L., et al., eds. *Oxford Companion to African American Literature*. N.Y.: Oxford UP, 1997.

Baker, Houston A., Jr. *Blues, Ideology, and Afro-American Literature: A Vernacular Theory*. Chicago: U of Chicago P, 1984.

Bontemps, Arna. *Father of the Blues*. N.Y.: Macmillan Co. 1941.

Borneman, Ernest. "The Roots of Jazz." *Jazz*. Ed. Nat Hentoff & A.J. McCarthy. N.Y.: Da Capo Press, 1975.

Davis, Angela Y. "Black Women and Music: A Historical Legacy of Struggle." *Wild Women in the Whirl-wind: Afra-American Culture and the Contemporary Literary Renaissance*. Eds., Joanne M. Braxton and A.N. McLaughlin. New Brunswick, N.J.: Rutgers UP, 1990. 3–21.

Dubey, Madhu. "'A New World Song': The Blues Form of *Corregidora*." *Black Women Novelists & the Nationalist Aesthetic*. Bloomington: Indiana UP, 1994. 72–88.

Du Bois, W.E.B. *Black Reconstruction in America*. N.Y.: Meridian Books, 1964.

———. *The Souls of Black Folk*. N.Y.: New American Library, 1969.

Ellison, Ralph. *The Collected Essays of Ralph Ellison*. Ed. John F. Callahan. N.Y.: The Modern Library, Random House, 1995.

Gilroy, Paul. "Living Memory: A Meeting with Toni Morrison." *Small Acts: Thoughts on the Politics of Black Cultures*. London: Serpent's Tail, 1993. 175–182.

Hurston, Zora Neale. *Dust Tracks on a Road*. Ed. Robert E. Hemenway. Urbana: U of Illinois P, 1984 (1942).

———. *Seraph on the Suwanee*. Ed. Hazel Carby. New York: Harper and Row, Publishers, 1991.

Jones, Gayl. *Corregidora*. Boston: Beacon Press, 1975.

————. *Liberating Voices: Oral Tradition in African American Literature*. Cambridge, MA: Harvard UP, 1991.

Snead, James. "Repetition as a Figure of Black Culture." *Black Literature and Literary Theory*. Ed. Henry Louis Gates, Jr. N.Y.: Methuen, 1984.

Southern, Eileen. *The Music of Black Americans: A History*. N.Y.: W.W. Norton & Co., 1983.

Tate, Claudia, ed. *Black Women Writers at Work*. New York: The Continuum Publishing Corporation, 1983.

Thomas, Lorenzo. "Blues Aesthetic" *Oxford Companion to African American Literature*. Eds. William L. Andrews, et al. N.Y.: Oxford UP, 1997. 87–9.

About The Authors

Michael J. Meyer, editor, is Adjunct Professor of English at DePaul and Northeastern Illinois Universities in Chicago. He is the new Steinbeck bibliographer, and his essays on Steinbeck have appeared in numerous books and journals. His most recent Steinbeck scholarship is *Cain Sign: The Betrayal of Brotherhood in the Work of John Steinbeck* (Mellen 2000). Meyer has also edited three other books for Rodopi Press's series entitled *Perspectives in Modern Literature* including *Literature and Ethnic Discrimination, Literature and Homosexuality* and *Literature and the Grotesque*. He is presently working as co-editor of the new *Steinbeck Encyclopaedia* (Greenwood, forthcoming).

Joseph Acquisto's main intellectual interests include 19th and early 20th century poetry, poetics, and esthetics, interdisciplinary studies in music and literature, and reinterpretations of the Robinson Crusoe myth. He is currently a doctoral candidate in the Department of French at Yale University. His dissertation is entitled "(Mis)Reading Music: The Crisis of Rewriting in French Symbolism."

Composer, performer and teacher, **Sarah Baker** has been writing and recording American music for over twenty years. She has recorded four CDs, including a compilation of Delta blues, entitled "Maybe Someday" and an album of original songs called "Sarah Baker," which has received popular and critical acclaim internationally. In addition to the intersections of music and literature, Ms. Baker's research interests include American music and cultural studies, electronic music composition and performance, and Hindustani classical singing. Currently, she lectures in Music and English at Sonoma State University, and is a Ph.D. candidate in Interdisciplinary Creative Arts at The Union Institute.

Cecilia Björkén-Nyberg is Lecturer in English Literature at Halmstad University, Sweden. She specializes in Edwardian literature and has written about Nietzschean patterns in D.H. Lawrence's early fiction. In her current research she focuses on the social and political function of music as conveyed in novels from early 20th century England.

Reine Dugas Bouton received a PhD. in Modern British and American Literature from the University of Southern Mississippi. She is an Assistant Professor of Developmental English at Southeastern Louisiana University. Her research interests include southern literature, Eudora Welty, twentieth-century American literature, and composition studies. Another article on Eudora Welty is expected out in the *Arkansas Review* at the end of this year.

Mark Byron has recently completed a doctoral dissertation in the Faculty of English at the University of Cambridge, entitled: "Exilic Modernism and Textual Ontogeny: Ezra Pound's *Pisan Cantos* and Samuel Beckett's *Watt*." He has article publications on Renaissance drama and on the concept of technology in the writing of Heidegger and Beckett, and has contributions in the forthcoming *Ezra Pound Encyclopaedia*.

Mary F. Catanzaro is currently an independent scholar in Milwaukee who has contributed articles on Beckett in series collections such as *The World of Samuel Beckett* (Johns Hopkins, 1991), *Beckett in the 1990s* (Amsterdam, 1993), and *Literature and the Grotesque* (Amsterdam, 1995) as well as in *Modern Drama, The Journal of Aging and Identity, The Journal of Dramatic and Literary Criticism*, and *Notes on Modern Irish Literature*, among others. Her concerns with Beckett have been his developing concept of the couple and his affinity for the musically textured narrative, particularly the speaking voice.

Peter R. Erspamer Peter R. Erspamer is Adjunct Professor of History and English at Mount Senario College in West Allis, Wisconsin. He is the author of *The Elusiveness of Tolerance: The "Jewish Question" from Lessing to the Napoleonic Wars* (University of North Carolina Press, 1997), which received the Choice Outstanding Academic Book Award.

Thomas Fahy received his Ph.D. from the University of North Carolina at Chapel Hill. He is co-editor of the forthcoming collection *Peering behind the Curtain: Disability, Disease, and the Extraordinary Body in Contemporary Theater* (Routledge 2001) and has published several articles on the role of music in literature and film.

Marion Fay is an Instructor of English at the College of Alameda in Alameda, California where she has developed techniques for using music to teach composition and literature. As Coordinator of Cultural Events, she produces concerts at the college involving music and text. In addition, she reviews books for the Express, published in Berkeley. Recent scholarly publications include "Music in the Classroom: An Alternative Approach to Teaching Literature," in *Teaching English in the Two-Year College*, 24: 4, May 2001, and "Anais Nin's Narrative Dilemma: The Artist as Social Conscience," in *Anais Nin's Narratives*, ed. Anne T. Salvatore, University of Florida Press, September 2001. A clarinetist, Ms. Fay is an active chamber musician and orchestral player.

Ana María Fraile-Marcos teaches American Literature and English at the University of Salamanca, Spain. She has written a number of articles on canon formation, ethnicity, and gender for different journals and has contributed to the Rodopi Perspectives of Modern Literature series with chapters about the works of Zora Neale Hurston, Alice Walker, and the present one about Gayl Jones. She is the editor of bilingual (English/Spanish) editions on the works of Jacob A. Riis, *Como vive la otra mitad* (2001), Langston Hughes, *Oscuridad en España* (1998), and Zora Neale Hurston, *Mi gente! Mi gente!* (1994). Her other interests are immigration literatures in the United States at the turn of the 19th and 20th centuries, and postcolonial literatures.

Sherry Lutz Zivley is an Associate Professor at the University of Houston, where she teaches contemporary fiction, women's literature, the poetry of Milton, and structures of poetry. Her most recent writings have been on the phenomenology of space in fiction and on the poetry of John Milton.

Abstracts of Arguments

Ch. 1: "Music, Desire, and Death in *The Magic Mountain*"

This essay investigates the role music plays within Thomas Mann's larger discourses of time, subjectivity, and politics. Beginning with an evaluation of the position of Mann's character Settembrini, who claims that music is to be avoided because it is "politically suspect," the paper goes on to examine protagonist Hans Castorp as he is initiated simultaneously into the powers of music and sexual desire. Seduced at first by folk melodies and then by recordings of grand opera, Hans goes to his death humming a Schubert song, which may be seen as the integration of the folk tradition and serious music. Mann's choice of Schubert as the composer of the soundtrack to *The Magic Mountain* raises questions of German nationalism. In its final section, this paper examines Mann's writings on music and literature from the time of the composition of *The Magic Mountain*, where issues of cosmopolitanism vs. nationalism and ineffability vs. articulateness are played out against the backdrop of the music of Schubert and Wagner. In the context of World War I, Mann's writings explore boundaries between the musical and literary arts and question their abilities to represent discourses of literal and metaphorical, personal and political illness.

Ch. 2: "Making Her Work Her Life: Music In Willa Cather's Fiction"

Although not a musician herself, Willa Cather imbued her life and work with music. At least 21 of her short stories and all 12 of her novels involve musicians and/or music, either directly or indirectly. Personal, philosophical, and literary considerations underlie these musical references. This essay focuses on Cather's use of music in her fiction to advance a quasi-philosophical belief, namely, that artistic achievement demands single-minded dedication. The choice to so dedicate oneself, she makes clear, inevitably involves emotional sacrifice and conflict; and those who do reach artistic fulfillment risk estrangement from others. Cather's fiction explores these claims as they affect men and women, but gives especially detailed attention to their meaning in the lives of women who study and perform music. For them, the necessary sacrifice often entails rejection of emotionally-binding personal relationships. "Making Her Work Her Life" traces the development of Cather's aesthetic convictions from childhood experiences to their expression, first, in newspaper commentaries and later in five short stories and two novels, *Lucy Gayheart* (1935) and *The Song of the Lark* (1915). Opera singer Thea Kronberg, the protagonist in the latter work, best exemplifies Cather's prescription for personal sacrifice in the pursuit of artistic achievement.

Ch. 3: "The Enslaving Power of Folksong in *Cane*"

The African-American men of Jean Toomer's *Cane* feel estranged from their cultural and spiritual heritage. After leaving Georgia for the educational and financial opportunities of the North, they become nostalgic and begin seeing black southern culture, particularly the folksongs of women, as embodying an identity they want to regain. This essay argues that black men, in their search for a tangible connection to the past, transform the songs and bodies of women into symbols for the South and its history. In doing so, they trap women into restrictive roles, reconstituting a type of slavery. For Toomer, the resulting conflict between men and women fracture the community of Sempter, preventing both meaningful heterosexual relationships and this community's successful integration into middle class America.

Ch. 4: "'Pings' and 'Murmurs': The Music of Defamiliarization and Emotional Response in Beckett's *Ping*"

Although Beckett's *Ping* (1967) is characterized by a language that musicologists would call the "statistical arrangement of events," this short work is actually one of the author's more emotional pieces. Statistics in music appeared first in the serialist compositions of the 1950's in Cage and Stockhausen. This article argues that *Ping* borrows the serialist notions of the manipulation of sound and space and their multiple realizations as a new concept of textual performance. Borrowing from Stockhausen, Beckett utilizes physical space, chance and intuition to generate new perspectives on the nature of identity. Characterized by the melodic and contrapuntal elements of conflict and opposition often found in serialism, the unnamed subject in *Ping* experiences defamiliarization and depersonalization.

Ch. 5: "I Gotcha! Signifying and Music in Eudora Welty's 'Powerhouse'"

Henry Louis Gates Jr.'s *The Signifying Monkey*, serves as the theoretical construct for this essay illustrating how and why Powerhouse signifies as he leads his white and black audiences—and readers—with his improvisational music and stories. The character of Powerhouse seems larger than life as he wields words and music with flamboyant style. He calls on his African heritage to signify and provoke indirection by tricking his audiences, altering songs, and weaving astonishing stories.

Like signifyin(g), jazz centers around orality and exemplifies music that black musicians claim as their own distinctive sound, their discourse, and a representation of their heritage. The musician's ability to "stretch" rather than merely "articulate" the form suggests an inclination to revise, to take the known and make it new, unexpected, and nontraditional. Powerhouse emerges as a strong, conquering character because he—"teacher," "musician"—shows that overcoming oppression must be a constant, tenacious endeavor.

Ch. 6: "'Listening, listening': Music and Gender in *Howards End, Sinister Street* and *Pilgrimage*"

In a time when the British Empire was disintegrating, music, and particularly Beethoven's music, was felt by the Establishment to uphold traditional values keeping threatening, new forces such as demands from women and the masses for political justice at bay. Composing music was considered a male concern whereas for a long time performance had been the task for middle- and upper class women in the private sphere of the home. Thus, women had been reproducing the male canon without really questioning its legitimacy.

This essay focuses on the act of listening. It argues that in a strongly patriarchal society like the Edwardian, listening was tainted by male values, making it virtually impossible for women to derive other meanings from it. By studying the function of music in three Edwardian novels, a process is traced towards a new and challenging way of listening. Compton Mackenzie's *Sinister Street* defines the conventions of male listening by describing the response of a male character to Beethoven's Fifth Symphony. This response is challenged to some extent in E.M. Forster's *Howards*

End, where a female protagonist has difficulties identifying with the heroic keynote usually read into the Fifth Symphony. However, the most complete breakthrough in female listening is to be found in Dorothy Richardson's *Pointed Roofs* in which the heroine deliberately disrupts traditional performing habits and the expectations of the sonata aesthetic arriving at a way of listening that escapes the confinement of the patriarchal cage.

Ch. 7: "Ernest Gaines and *A Lesson Before Dying*: The Literary Spiritual"

Framed within the context of the spiritual, "Were You There," the narrative of Ernest Gaines's *A Lesson Before Dying* evokes undertones of the crucifixion while sounding the story of a young black man, Jefferson, unjustly accused of robbery and murder in a small southern town. Gaines signifies on the lyrics of "Were You There," pairs it with a second crucifixion spiritual, "He Never Said a Mumblin' Word," and critiques the societal constructs of midtwentieth century life. Conventions associated with the traditional spiritual, such as the structural techniques of repetition, call/response and antiphony, provide an elegant counterpoint to the little radio in Jefferson's cell, and weave the oral into the written word. Through these textual strategies, Gaines remythologizes the crucifixion and composes a literary spiritual.

Ch. 8: "A Quartet That Is a Quartet: Lawrence Durrell's *Alexandria Quartet*"

Durrell utilizes the quartet-sonata allegro-form to structure his *The Alexandria Quartet*. Movement I, *Justine*, is a rational European portrait of a declining Egyptian city. *Balthazar*, a slower movement in a minor key, presents an Alexandria that is oriental and unknowable. *Mountolive*, the third movement, has a single, linear plot. Durrell calls *Mountolive* "the third movement (rondo) of a symphonic poem." *Clea*, the fourth movement incorporates the themes and repeats the motifs of *Justine* and *Balthazar* and provides new perspectives on the quartet's characters and events. Except for *Mountolive*, each of these novels is itself structured on a sonata allegro form.

Ch. 9. "Music as a Locus of Social Conflict and Social Connection in Friedrich Torberg's *Süsskind von Trimberg*"

The theories of the Bakhtin Circle illuminate music as a vehicle of social intercourse rather than merely a means of hedonistic enjoyment. Special insights into relations between Jews and Gentiles and between feudal nobility, church, and peasants arise when such theories are used to interpret Friedrich Torberg's novel of 1972, *Süsskind von Trimberg*.

Ch. 10: "A Defining Moment in Ezra Pound's *Cantos*: Musical Scores and Literary Texts"

When one artwork is embedded within another, how is the effect to be understood? The violin line of Janequin's "Le Chant des Oiseaux," arranged by Gerhard Münch, is framed within "Canto LXXV" of Ezra Pound's *Cantos*. Critics have usually treated its presence as a thematic component of the poem's unfolding drama. Yet the canto foregrounds questions of status basic to both textual criticism and musicology: of the physical and typographical constitution of the literary work, on one hand; and of the precise relations between score, performance, and musical work, on the other. Thus the score is able to be read in several ways: as an embedded referent or quotation; as a score (or a part thereof) to be read on its own terms; as an element of music history; and for the poetic persona, as an element of cultural and personal memory. A part of a poetic text, and sharing its space, the score is a lesson in aesthetics. It demonstrates the relations between artworks and artistic media to be more complex than either idealist or materialist terms allow. The imbricated histories of the canto and its score challenge the reader to rethink the ways music and literature are perceived, separately and together.

Ch. 11. "Harmonic Dissonance: Steinbeck's Implementation and Adaptation of Musical Techniques"

By exploring Steinbeck's interest in classical music and Bach's *Art of The Fugue*, this essay argues that the author deliberately applied the techniques of repetition, harmonic dissonance and contrapuntal sounds in several novels, specifically examining *The Grapes of Wrath* and *The Pearl* as works that demonstrate Steinbeck's meticulous employment of musical elements. The non-fictional *Log From The Sea of Cortez* is also cited as evidence of the author's intent to present musical subtexts in his work. Close analysis of the musical references in *The Pearl* center on "The Song of The Pearl That Might Be," "The Song of the Family," and "The Song of Evil" as concrete evidence that Steinbeck presents human duality in the context of music.

Ch. 12: "Lady Sings the Blues: Gayl Jones' *Corregidora*

This essay draws attention to the exploration of black feminine identity carried out by Gayle Jones, using the blues as a thematic and structural device. The blues ethos emanating from the novel, based primarily on the events that constitute the plot, is enhanced by the language and the appropriation of certain structural characteristics of the blues music, such as the cyclical structure of the blues with its repetition-with-difference pattern, and the call-and-response pattern that is emblematic of African American oral performances. Yet, the novel falls short of appropriating the blues' mode in all its extent. Although the call-and-response is deftly replicated in the dialectic relationship between Ursa's present and her foremothers' past, as well as in the interaction between her listeners and herself when she sings the blues, the novel fails to establish a call-and-response relationship between the reader and the characters or the author. Even the call-and-response typical of Ursa's interior monologues and dreams is only an illusion. It is also in these monologues where language turns away from the simplicity of the blues, becoming cryptic and enigmatic. Nonetheless, the novel stands as a remarkable attempt at using the blues as the structuring and thematic resource. In her personal adaptation of the blues, Jones challenges the genre of the novel, which emerges as a hybrid product, the result of the métissage of western literary tradition and the traditional oral performance of the blues.